Praise for *Reputation Rules*

"I first met Professor Daniel Diermeier when I attended the CEO Perspectives Program at Kellogg. I found Daniel's class on reputational risk thought provoking and took from it many actionable items. *Reputation Rules* takes this to the next level by helping you to a better understanding or 'sixth sense' for both reputational risks and opportunities. The actionable items to build reputation management capability can lead to enhanced value creation. I highly recommend the book."

—SAMUEL ALLEN, Chairman and Chief
Executive Officer, Deere & Company

"CEOs and boards understand the criticality of a firm's reputation to its overall success—and are often blindsided by external events that damage this vital asset. Daniel has the unique ability to look over the horizon in ways that apply science to the art of reputation management. With the help of his insights, we can anticipate and analyze new ways to strengthen and protect the reputation of the enterprise."

—CHERYL FRANCIS, Co-Chairman, Corporate Leadership
Center; Member of the Board of Directors, Aon, HNI, and
Morningstar; Member of the Board of Trustees, Cornell University

"A corporation's reputation is among its most valuable assets yet it is the most fragile asset to protect. When your reputation takes a hit, it is nearly impossible to repair a damaged image. Recent events prove, time and again, that few corporations possess effective reputation management skills to operate in today's real-time social environment. In many cases, it is not the crisis itself which impacts the corporate reputation but rather it is how its executives mishandle the resulting communications. *Reputation Rules* provides an executive with a framework for a real-time assessment and programmatic responses when facing a reputational risk event. If you wish to avoid the negative scrutiny by a suspicious public, I recommend you read this book and keep it close to your desk."

—KEVIN HOSTETLER, Vice President–
Group Executive, IDEX Corporation

"Reputational risk management is a key issue for corporate boards and executives. It takes consistent attention over a long period of time to build a great reputation, but a single incident can destroy it in a second. Companies need to build reputation management skills. This book shows them how."

—SHEILA PENROSE, Chairman of the Board, Jones Lang LaSalle; Co-Chairman, Corporate Leadership Center; Member of the Board of Directors, McDonald's Corporation

"Daniel Diermeier has continuously caught the attention of the business world with insightful and compelling facts that should once again challenge our thinking and actions. In today's fast-changing business environment values and reputation are the foundation and Daniel presents sound reasoning and experience as to why they are so important."

—JEFF STRATTON, Executive Vice President and Chief Restaurant Officer, McDonald's Corporation

"Daniel Diermeier provides an actionable view of reputation management. *Reputation Rules* is a book that any executive in any industry can use to immediately get results!"

—TERESA TAYLOR, Chief Operating Officer, Qwest Communications

"*Reputation Rules* is required reading for any executive! Professor Diermeier is the leading authority on corporate reputation management, and his latest work captures the essential elements of this critical management role. His case studies and insights provide the corporate road map for business leaders to manage this crucial function in today's multicultural global economy."

—ROBERT C. KNUEPFER, JR., Partner, Baker & McKenzie LLP

"*Reputation Rules* breaks new ground in what has until now been an elusive challenge for companies and consultants alike. An exquisite compendium of navigational tools and vivid storytelling, Diermeier has clearly authored an opus for the ages on building and protecting reputation. This is a game-changing book to be sure."

—HARLAN A. LOEB, Executive Vice President, Director of U.S. Crisis and Issues Management, Edelman

"Daniel Diermeier provides important insights for managing reputation and turning challenges into opportunities. The frameworks are grounded in research, and the vignettes are powerful. The lessons will stick and become an essential component of a manager's repertoire."

—DAVID BARON, David S. and Ann M. Barlow Professor of Political Economy and Strategy, Emeritus, Stanford Graduate School of Business

"Reputation matters. Diermeier convincingly argues that managing a firm's reputation is distinctly different from managing its brand or public relations strategy. In the process, he outlines a clear strategy and concrete tools for actively managing reputation. At its core, it's all about the process of managing trust in an increasingly complex and uncertain business environment."

—SALLY BLOUNT, Dean, Kellogg School of Management, Northwestern University

"Safeguarding a company's reputation is one of the top concerns for CEOs and board members. But corporations struggle to get it right. Daniel Diermeier's book will be an invaluable tool for companies to build this critical capability."

—DON JACOBS, Dean Emeritus, Kellogg School of Management, Northwestern University; Member of the Board of Directors, Terex; Member of the Board of Trustees, ProLogis

"More than ever, reputation has become the major currency for global corporations. In *Reputation Rules*, Daniel Diermeier brilliantly tackles the new rules for managing this currency, beginning with the new environment in which businesses now operate—including the risk factors that make the topic so timely and imperative. He also demonstrates a way forward based on a strategic mindset that reflects his own role as a key bridge between academic theory and business practice."

—DIPAK JAIN, Dean, INSEAD; Member of the Board of Directors, Deere & Company, Northern Trust, and Reliance Industries

"Daniel Diermeier is truly a brilliant professor! I had the opportunity to witness him teach a class on the topic of 'reputation management' on several occasions and found his materials to be enlightening, informative, and, most important, applicable to the real business world. I have quoted him numerous times in the board meetings that I attend for several Fortune 500 companies and entrepreneurial firms. My exposure to his teachings has strengthened my governance contributions!"

—STEVEN S. ROGERS, Director of the Larry and Carol
Levy Institute for Entrepreneurial Practice; Member of
the Board of Directors, SC Johnson and SuperValu

"Reputation is emerging as one of the most critical, yet most fragile and least effectively managed, organizational assets. In this indispensable book, Diermeier provides a comprehensive survey, anchored in research and illustrated by current examples, of some of the most innovative frameworks and tools in this area. A must-read for any CEO or board member!"

—EITAN ZEMEL, W. Edwards Deming Professor of
Quality and Productivity, Vice Dean for Global Initiatives,
Stern School of Business, New York University

STRATEGIES FOR
BUILDING YOUR COMPANY'S
MOST VALUABLE ASSET

REPUTATION RULES

DANIEL DIERMEIER, Ph.D.

NEW YORK   CHICAGO   SAN FRANCISCO
LISBON   LONDON   MADRID   MEXICO CITY   MILAN
NEW DELHI   SAN JUAN   SEOUL   SINGAPORE
SYDNEY   TORONTO

The **McGraw·Hill** *Companies*

2 3 4 5 6 7 8 9 10   DOC/DOC   1 9 8 7 6 5 4 3 2

ISBN   978-0-07-176374-5
MHID   0-07-176374-0

e-ISBN 978-0-07-176394-3
e-MHID   0-07-176394-5

Library of Congress Cataloging-in-Publication Data

Diermeier, Daniel.
     Reputation rules : strategies for building your company's most valuable asset /
by Daniel Diermeier—1st ed.
          p.   cm.
     Includes bibliographical references and index.
     ISBN 978-0-07-176374-5 (alk. paper)
     1. Corporations—Finance.   2. Risk management.   I. Title.

   HG4026.D54   2011
   659.2—dc22   2010052537

The interior design is by Mauna Eichner and Lee Fukui.

McGraw-Hill books are available at special quantity discounts to use as premiums and sales promotions or for use in corporate training programs. To contact a representative, please e-mail us at bulksales@mcgraw-hill.com.

This book is printed on acid-free paper.

CONTENTS

FOREWORD

Every year, *Fortune* magazine publishes a list of the most admired companies. In 2010, the top 10 included Apple, Google, Berkshire Hathaway, Johnson & Johnson, Amazon.com, Procter & Gamble, Toyota Motor, Goldman Sachs, Wal-Mart, and Coca-Cola. None of these "star" companies surprises us.

Managers who are invited to vote look at the following criteria in casting their votes: innovation, long-term investment, management quality, people management, financial soundness, product and service quality, social responsibility, global competitiveness, and use of corporate assets. There are no surprises here either.

What we do know is that getting on this Most Admired Companies list is worth its weight in gold. Being listed gives the company's customers and partners confidence that it can be trusted to do well and give a good return. That trust allows these companies to earn a premium for their work.

There are many reasons why more companies are becoming intensely interested in reputation management. They certainly have been interested in managing their brands, supporting a whole cadre of brand managers. More recently, some companies have appointed a high-level manager to be responsible for strengthening and protecting the company's reputation. After all, it takes years to build a good reputation, and bad news can destroy it in a matter of seconds.

Companies typically leave their reputation to be managed by the CEO and the company's public relations department. Most of the PR department's work is defending and protecting the company's reputation rather than building it. But companies are coming to realize that everything that they or their people say, do, or don't do can have an impact on that company's reputation. In today's new social media age, impacts go beyond what the company and its people say or do. Everything good or bad about a company can be picked up in social media and disseminated throughout the world. Worse than that, anyone can go on the Internet and send out misinformation or disinformation if they want to hurt a company's reputation. No wonder companies are eager to learn how to build, manage, and protect their reputations.

In my field of marketing, brand reputation is everything. We focus primarily on how customers see our brand. But company reputation goes beyond customers. It includes investors, employees, channel partners, and society at large. Building a stellar reputation is becoming more essential and at the same time more difficult. Businesses operate in a world that is driven by rapid technological advances, the emergence of a truly global marketplace, and an increasing need of companies and people to find meaning and purpose, not just material fulfillment.

Companies today are facing ever more demanding expectations from their own stakeholders and from the public. They are being asked to take more responsibility for their impact on the environment and on the communities in which they operate. Until recently, companies only had to cover their economic costs and make a profit. Now they must pay attention to the uncovered social costs that their operations might generate, such as air and water pollution, child labor, job discrimination, and other "bads." Companies are increasingly subject to nongovernmental organizations (NGOs) and other watchdog groups that are ready to broadcast any negative fallout from company activities.

Companies that succeed in this environment are those that develop a clear purpose backed by a strong set of values that are built into the DNA of their employees wherever they are located in the world. Those who work for such companies as IBM, GE, and a host of other admired companies know not only their brand but their stand with respect to their social responsibilities. These companies achieve a consistency of their brand identity, integrity, and image that is sensed by their customers, employees, partners, and investors.

Daniel Diermeier's book *Reputation Rules* tackles these issues head-on. CEOs and board members are increasingly recognizing that a company's reputation is among its most valuable assets. Yet we hear of one major corporate crisis after another. Such respected companies as

Toyota, BP, and even Johnson & Johnson have suffered crises in recent times. Diermeier's diagnosis is that most companies lack effective reputation management capabilities to operate in this ever more challenging business environment.

Diermeier shows why existing reputation management approaches fall short and how to develop effective strategies and processes. One of his key insights is that reputation management needs to be closely integrated with the company's position in the marketplace; it cannot be delegated to experts, but constitutes a needed and vital leadership skill and organizational capability.

Developing effective reputation management capabilities requires the right mindset, driven by values and supported by processes. Diermeier draws on extensive research and illustrates these insights with rich case studies from a variety of industries. He shows how to integrate reputation management deeply into the culture and structure of companies. I expect *Reputation Rules* to set the standard for years to come.

—Philip Kotler
S.C. Johnson & Son Distinguished Professor
of International Marketing
Kellogg School of Management
Northwestern University

Immer Wieder

for Ariela

TWO ITEMS ON THE CEO'S AGENDA

When it comes to innovation, I'll raise a question with you:
What is the most important financial innovation in
the past 20 or 30 years for the average person?
I think it's the automatic teller machine.

—**Paul Volcker,** former head of the
Federal Reserve[1]

One bright summer day a few years ago, I had breakfast with Dipak Jain, then dean of the Kellogg School of Management. During the conversation, Dean Jain asked me to become the academic director of the new CEO Perspective Program. I had just returned from a lovely vacation, and I agreed. The program is now going strong in its seventh year and has taught me many invaluable lessons, one of which became the seed for this book.

A defining component of the program is the sessions taught by the CEOs of some of the world's leading companies. Perhaps the most striking characteristic of these sessions is the enormous variety that can be seen among these individuals—differences in personal style, management approach, corporate culture, strategy, and company challenges. Despite these differences, however, there are also striking commonalities. Ask CEOs what items are at the top of their agenda, and you'll find that the top two issues are common across companies and industries, and that they rarely change. The other issues vary tremendously across time and industries; "innovation" is currently a core concern, whereas "survival" was very popular in 2008 and 2009. However, the two leading items on the CEO's agenda are constant. Item number one is "people." The other issue was a surprise—at least to me: "reputation." Some CEOs even stated that it was their company's reputation that most distinguished it in the marketplace—its most important asset.

Surveys of CEOs and corporate boards report a similar list of priorities.[2] For boards, "reputation" is as important as "people" issues such as CEO selection and compensation, succession planning, and oversight. Indeed, many board members view the board as the ultimate guardian of the company's reputation. Of course, for board members (as for CEOs), the company's reputation and their personal reputation are intimately linked, further elevating the issue's importance.

Recent events confirm this perspective. Almost every day, another company faces a battle for its reputation, and the costs of losing that battle can be severe. During its recent crisis triggered by the sudden acceleration issue, Toyota's stock price dropped by as much as 24 percent, wiping out about $33 billion in shareholder value, close to the total market value of Time Warner. In its battle with the U.S. government in the aftermath of the 2008–2009 financial crisis, Goldman Sachs lost $24 billion of its market capitalization, a 26 percent drop in share price that exceeded the entire value of American Express.[3] Finally, there is the BP oil spill disaster in the Gulf of Mexico, which at one point cut the stock price in half and destroyed about $90 billion in shareholder value, more than the market value of Procter & Gamble.[4]

Of course, some of these effects are transitory; companies can and do recover from reputational harm. Also, a company's stock price is affected by more than just the company's reputation. Indeed, establishing the exact cost associated with reputational damage is a difficult challenge requiring careful analysis. That said, these are massive events in the life of a company, comparable to a big acquisition gone wrong or the collapse of an entire market segment. Perhaps CEOs and their boards are right to be concerned.

One may think that this is all a coincidence, a temporal disruption of the normal business environment. *Reputation Rules* will demonstrate that there will be no return to a "normal" business environment; instead, the intense scrutiny that companies have been facing over the last decade is the new normal. The underlying forces that elevate reputational concerns are not transitory, but instead will increase in importance and will shape global business environments for years to come. It is true that reputational concerns take center stage in the context of a crisis, but crises are merely the tip of the iceberg of significant changes in the global environment of business.

From this perspective, one fact becomes painfully obvious: most companies have shockingly underdeveloped capabilities to manage their reputations effectively. This becomes evident when one directly compares "reputation" with the other leading item on the CEO's agenda, "people." Not only do companies have entire corporate functions (human resource management, "chief people officer") devoted to this issue, but managers have a host of tools and concepts at their disposal—from compensation strategies to evaluation and development approaches to the management of culture and change. Most important, CEOs have learned that they need to own the people process.

What about reputation? For the most part, you would find an

> When it comes to reputation, many companies face a mismatch between assets and capabilities. Reputation is widely considered a core asset, and its protection is near the top of the CEO's agenda. Yet most companies have woefully inadequate reputation management strategies and processes. The result is one reputational crisis after another.

underfunded initiative in the communications department matched by nervous questions from the board—in other words, a striking lack of awareness, skills, and capabilities.

Underdeveloped capabilities in an environment of growing reputational risks will inevitably lead to an increase in reputational crises. Perhaps it all started with Enron and the accounting scandals at the beginning of the decade, but this era of reputational crises has not stopped since. Business, it seems, has entered the age of crisis, with the demolition of the global financial industry as its most recent pinnacle. Venerable companies and institutions continue to find themselves in the headlines, usually not in a flattering context. Entire industries have seen their reputational capital eroded at a shockingly rapid pace, such as the global banking and financial services industry, ratings agencies, the U.S. auto industry, the U.S. health insurance industry, and the global pharmaceutical industry.

Consider some data from a sequence of polls conducted by Harris Interactive. In the survey, respondents were asked the following question: "Which of these industries do you think are generally honest and trustworthy—so that you normally believe a statement by a company in that industry?"

The results are given in Table P.1.[5]

Notice the overall erosion of trust across industries, with the particularly striking collapse in the banking sector.

Losing the battle for public perception has dire consequences. Erosion of customer trust is only the most obvious example. Regulators and politicians may feel public pressure to take decisive action, changing market environments and the rules of competition. The history of the tobacco industry is perhaps the best-known example, but many others exist. Consider the effect of Sarbanes-Oxley on accounting practices and corporate governance, the fate of genetically modified food in Europe, changes in global labor standards after Nike's child labor scandals, health-care reform, and the proposed levies on financial institutions. Clever lobbying and legal strategies can stem the tide for a time, but companies have been put on the defensive and find themselves fighting a rearguard battle that occupies substantial management time and effort.

Table P.1 **Industries I Can Trust**

Industries	2003 %	2006 %	2009 %
Hospitals	34	28	28
Electric and gas utilities	n/a	14	16
Packaged food companies	23	14	16
Online retailers	n/a	11	16
Banks	35	31	12
Airlines	20	16	10
Life insurance companies	11	11	10
Pharmaceutical & drug companies	13	7	9
Car manufacturers	14	9	8
Health insurance companies	7	7	7
Managed care companies such as HMOs	4	4	5
Oil companies	4	3	5
Tobacco companies	3	2	3

n/a = industry not asked about that year   *Source: Harris Interactive (2009)*

Four main factors are responsible for the increase in reputational risk.

The first is straightforward; media coverage has increased dramatically, as has its global reach. On the one hand, we have the birth of the Internet as a communicative and connecting medium and the rise of user-generated content, from blogs to Twitter and YouTube. On the other hand, we now live in an ever-faster-moving news cycle, driven by intense competition between 24-hour news channels, wire services, and online news providers.

This increased media scrutiny has many dramatic consequences for companies. First, they have less and less control over their messages. A YouTube video shot from the cell phone of an unhappy customer or disgruntled employee, a negative tweet, or a Facebook campaign can dramatically damage a brand, and once it is on the Web, it will stay there forever. The rise of the Web has dramatically shifted the balance of power from companies to customers and other stakeholders. When this is combined with the global reach of the media, it is virtually impossible for a company to hide. Transparency is increasingly in demand.[6]

The second factor is the unintended consequence of globalization, the "dark side of living in a flat world."[7] The globalization of activist organizations has matched the global reach of companies. Today, a nongovernmental organization (NGO) that tries to make an impact on human rights will not protest in front of a foreign consulate or the UN headquarters; instead, it will target a multinational company with global operations.

> The dramatic rise in reputational risk is no accident or passing fad. It is driven by sustained forces, from 24-hour media coverage to higher expectations of acceptable business conduct in a globally operating economy.

Shell experienced this over its oil extraction operations in Nigeria and the connection to the Nigerian government's execution of human rights leaders. Nike had similar experiences involving its global labor standards.[8] My collaborator, David Baron, and I have used the term *private politics* for these phenomena.[9] Regulation, for example, is usually understood as the result of government action, exercised and implemented by legislatures, agencies, and the courts. Public institutions, however, are no longer the sole source of constraints on commerce. Instead, political activists and NGOs have increasingly succeeded in forcing *private* regulation: the "voluntary" adoption of rules and standards that constrain certain forms of company conduct without the involvement of public agents. In many cases, the mechanism driving change is the creation of reputational crises for companies that, when effective, leave the companies with no choice but to change their business practices.

The third factor is not usually considered in the context of reputation management, yet it is a critical multiplier and enabler of the previous two factors, considerably amplifying their effects. Various observers have noticed some marked generational differences between older and newer population segments. Frequently discussed as a "Generation Y" phenomenon, commentators have pointed out an increase in concerns about the moral dimensions of businesses, especially among young people.[10]

Evidence for these trends can be found in the explosive growth of areas such as corporate social responsibility, sustainability, and socially responsible investing. Some critics have dismissed these trends as passing fads that lack impact, but this assessment may be premature. In addition to typical business issues such as quality and product safety, reputational concerns are increasingly arising out of moral or ethical concerns. Child labor, dolphin-safe tuna, and fair trade coffee are just some of the best-known examples. NGOs and the media coverage that follows them will be particularly attuned to these issues, but in order for such issues to have a real impact, at some point somebody has to care, and has to demonstrate it by changing behavior. A customer may decide to buy a different product, an employee may leave, or an investor may divest her holdings. A gradual shift in value orientations provides the needed motivation.

The first three factors were changes in the environment of business, while the last one is a complementary shift in business strategy: the rise of business models based on trust. Over the last decade, marketing scholars have pointed out the importance of creating customer-focused organizations. Practically speaking, this means a shift from selling products and services toward selling experiences or selling a solution. In the consumer segment, these trends are well understood, as in Starbucks's focus on the customer experience. We find similar developments among industrial companies. For example, Caterpillar makes repair parts for broken equipment available to customers anywhere in the world within 48 hours, a critical differentiator from its low-cost competitors. To develop unique experiences and solutions, companies need to understand their customers even better, and they need to get closer to those customers' unarticulated—perhaps even unconscious—desires and needs. Building these relationships and maintaining them requires trust, and trust has both rational and emotional components.[11]

This surely provides new opportunities for value creation, but only if a company maintains the relationship of trust. In other words, if brands are promises, then even the mere perception of a broken promise will elicit strong negative emotions of mistrust and betrayal. In many cases, a company can fix the problem directly. A Starbucks customer who is unhappy with the preparation of his café latte may be appeased by being given a new one, plus a free cookie as a little apology.

What about a customer who is concerned about the labor conditions of workers on coffee plantations? Combined with sufficiently evocative images from the media, such concerns can quickly undermine a pleasant experience for even the most loyal customer. Building the brand is not enough; it must also be defended.[12] The more business models are based on reputation, the higher the stakes.

Recent surveys provide further evidence for these trends. In the 2010 trust survey by the public relations firm Edelman, transparency and trust surpassed product quality in determining corporate reputation. Financial performance was at the bottom of the list.[13]

To summarize, recent developments have dramatically increased the need for effective reputation management. On the one hand, companies are increasingly basing their business models on trust. On the other hand, the threats that may undermine that trust have grown rapidly, driven by new media technologies, globally operating advocacy organizations, and the relative growth of population segments that care about the moral dimension of business. CEOs and boards have begun to appreciate the importance of this challenge, but feel unsure about the capabilities and strategies needed to respond to it.

The gap between needs and capabilities is untenable. *Reputation Rules* will help companies close this gap. As with any capability, doing so requires the proper mindset and processes, and the values and culture to support them.

ACKNOWLEDGMENTS

This book is based on a decade of research, lecturing, and consulting in the area of reputation management. I have had the pleasure of teaching and interacting with the brightest students and seminar participants one could hope for. Much of this work is a direct consequence of their inquisitive questions and stimulating discussions, both in and outside of the classroom.

The Kellogg School of Management and my home department, Managerial Economics and Decision Sciences (MEDS), provided a wonderfully supportive environment in which to explore new directions. Many thanks especially to David Austen-Smith and Tim Feddersen, who have been supportive colleagues and trusted friends over many years. Kellogg's former deans Don Jacobs and Dipak Jain believed in this approach when it was just an idea and gave me the freedom and support to develop it. Thank you to Kellogg dean Sally Blount who embraced the project and to Kellogg's Marketing and Communications team, especially Meg Washburn, who helped spread the word. Financial support from Kellogg's Office of the Dean and the Ford Motor Company Center for Global Citizenship is gratefully acknowledged. In addition, I am grateful for the financial and intellectual support from the Canadian Institute for Advanced Research (CIFAR); CIFAR's CEO, Chaviva Hosek; and especially my terrific colleagues at the Institutions, Organization, and Growth research group led by Elhanan Helpman. One could not ask for a more stimulating (and challenging!) group of scholars.

Over the last years, Tori Briscoll, Adam Galinsky, Justin Heinze, Jennifer Jordan, George Newman, Malavika Srinivasan, David Tannenbaum, Mathieu Trepanier, Bei Yu, and especially Eric Uhlmann have been terrific research collaborators, sharing the goal of giving this area the rigorous foundation it deserves.

I am grateful to my great group of researchers and research assistants, Brian and Katie Chen, Diane Culhane, Dennis Hsu, Alexandra Markowski, Evan Meagher, Hilary Richardson, Charlotte Snyder, Lisa Stein, and especially Philip Butta. Charlotte and Evan read the entire manuscript and provided invaluable comments and suggestions for improving it. In addition to providing superb research support, Ali Niederkorn did a wonderful job managing the final stages of the project. As she has done for many years, my assistant, Denita Linnertz, kept everything organized and running smoothly, showing tremendous grace under pressure.

Eitan Zemel, Ekkart Kaske, Dylan Minor, Georgy Egorov, and Galina Egorova read the entire manuscript and provided many helpful comments and suggestions. And a very special thank you to David Baron, who taught me how to think about business and politics. True to character, David read the entire first draft on short notice and, as always, provided great insights and support.

The case studies on Arthur Andersen and Wal-Mart are based on cases co-written with Rob Crawford; the one on the Mercedes A-Class was collaborative work with Astrid Marechal. The case studies on Monsanto and Calgene benefited from the research assistance of Ward Detweiler, Barbara Pawlikowski, and Justin Heinze. Justin also provided superb research assistance for the Southwest Airlines case study and many of the other case examples.

Many thanks to my editor at McGraw-Hill, Gary Krebs, who believed in this project when it was little more than an idea, and to Andrew Malkin, who introduced me to Gary and provided much-needed encouragement in the early stages of the project. My gratitude also goes to Ron Martirano, my project editor; Jane Palmieri, my production editor; and to Julia Baxter and Ann Pryor, my marketing team at McGraw-Hill.

And finally, my biggest gratitude goes to my wonderful family: my wife and partner, Ariela Lazar, who is a constant source of loving support, my conscience, and my toughest critic; and our boys, Matan and Oran, who remind me daily of what really matters.

With public sentiment, nothing can fail;
without it, nothing can succeed.
Consequently, he who molds public sentiment,
goes deeper than he who enacts statutes
or pronounces decisions.

—Abraham Lincoln, First Debate
with Stephen Douglas
(Ottawa, Illinois, August 21, 1858)

INTRODUCTION

BEYOND THE OBVIOUS

The ideas which are here expressed so laboriously
are extremely simple and should be obvious.
The difficulty lies, not in the new ideas, but in escaping
from the old ones, which ramify, for those brought up as
most of us have been, into every corner of our minds.

—John Maynard Keynes[1]

The misconceptions about reputation management begin with having the wrong mindset, as most companies view reputation as a corporate function, not a core capability. This attitude is based on the following beliefs:

1. A good reputation follows naturally from having good business practices and doing right by one's customers, employees, and suppliers.
2. If there is a problem, it can be safely delegated to Public Relations, Legal, or outside advisors.
3. Reputation management requires little else but common sense and the willingness to do the right thing.

Each one of these beliefs is flawed. First, the need to manage the organization's reputation *actively* is critical for any organization. Moreover, the importance of doing so is likely to increase, not decrease, in the near future. Of course, good business practices are important, even necessary, but they are not sufficient for successful reputation management.

Second, the responsibility for reputation management lies with business leaders, who cannot and should not simply delegate it to specialists such as lawyers or public relations experts. Although such experts can play a valuable role in the reputation management process, they should not own it. In most companies, if a reputation management process exists at all, it is typically located within the corporate communications department. If the company's reputation is truly one of its most precious assets, why delegate it to a department that all too often has insufficient funding and lacks influence over business decisions? Yet, most companies do precisely that.

The operating word here is *delegate*. Communication will play an important role in any reputation management process, but such a process needs to be tightly integrated with the business. Reputation management should be the responsibility of the business leaders, led by the CEO as the steward of the corporate reputation. An analogy with the "people" dimension can help make this point more clear. CEOs and general managers have learned over the last decade that they need to own the "people" process, taking their cues from some of the most influential business books of the last decade, such as *Good to Great* and *Execution*.[2] Human Resources departments play a crucial role in the day-to-day management of people by enabling, implementing, and facilitating much of this process, but the business leader must own the process itself.

Challenges to a company's reputation typically arise out of a specific business context and thus require management and execution as an integral part of business decisions. As we will see, this is critically important for the prevention of reputational crises, which can arise as a result of any business decision, whether it involves product design, marketing strategy, the pricing model, the compensation process, or even market entry or M&A activities. In many cases, the most effective way to manage reputational risk is to improve the capabilities of business leaders by

> Reputation management should never be delegated to specialists. Business leaders need to serve as reputation stewards. Reputation management needs to be integrated into a company's strategy, organization, and culture.

helping them develop a sixth sense for reputational risks and opportunities (supported by well-designed processes) rather than adding another corporate layer.

Third, reputation management is difficult. It requires a high level of strategic sophistication and mental agility that sometimes runs counter to day-to-day business decisions. A company's reputation is shaped not just by its direct business partners, customers, and suppliers, but also by external constituencies. Frequently, constituencies that have lain dormant for many years can suddenly spring into action, particularly in the case of reputational crises. They include not only the media, but also advocacy groups, influencers, regulators, and politicians.

A company's reputation consists of what others are saying about the company, and not just its business partners and customers. It is essentially public. Successful reputation management therefore requires the ability to assume external actors' perspectives and viewpoints.[3] Many of these actors (although certainly not all of them) are motivated by moral or ideological concerns that the company or its managers do not share, and indeed may be openly hostile to the company's business practices. This often leads to a defensive, reactive posture on the part of business leaders, which may engender overly emotional reactions based on anger or self-pity.

A strategic approach requires the emotional fortitude to treat reputational difficulties as understandable and even predictable challenges that one should expect in today's business environment. As a result, companies should handle reputational crises like any other major business challenge: based on principled leadership and supported by sophisticated processes and capabilities that are integrated with the company's business strategy and culture.

Reputation Rules develops the concepts and frameworks needed to help companies master these challenges. More specifically, we will introduce a toolbox for managers containing frameworks, strategies, and processes. Effective reputation management will always be challenging and, like any business skill, will require innovation and adaptation. However, appropriate conceptual frameworks can dramatically reduce the complexity of reputational challenges, help spot problems early, and assist in the development of effective strategies that are deeply integrated with the rest of the business.

> A good reputation is not simply a consequence of doing the right thing or serving customers and stakeholders well. Reputation management needs to be handled like the major business challenge that it is: based on principled leadership and supported by sophisticated processes and capabilities that are integrated with the company's business strategy and culture.

Our first chapter discusses reputational crises, events that require managers to pay attention to the company's reputation. We show that the existing views of reputation management are insufficient to deal with the current challenges generated by global operations, complex value chains, and 24-hour media scrutiny. We show why reputation management cannot be delegated to functional experts, and we develop a useful tool to deal with urgent reputational crises: the Trust Radar. We use the recent case of lead contamination in toys as our main example, but we also discuss many other examples from various industries, including the recent crises involving BP, Goldman Sachs, Johnson & Johnson, and Toyota.

Reputations can be rebuilt, but doing so requires smart strategies and a sustained approach. In our second chapter, using the Mercedes Moose crisis, we show how Mercedes first mishandled a reputational crisis, but then recovered. The key factor in Mercedes's success was a keen understanding of the role of the media in shaping corporate reputations. We develop the concept of Reputational Terrain to help leaders navigate today's media landscape and apply the tool to various business challenges ranging from hedge funds to medical devices.

Reputational challenges can arise from anywhere. Chapter 3 discusses the strategic use of reputational challenges for political and social purposes, as used by NGOs, advocates, and politicians. Clever activists have learned how to use the media to force companies to change their business practices. Examples include Shell's confrontation with Greenpeace and many others. We also discuss strategies used by public officials, such as those employed by the former attorney general of New York, Eliot Spitzer. Dealing with advocates requires high levels of strategic sophistication. Activists know how to select targets strategically, act globally, and attack companies' value chains effectively. Companies need to learn how to think from the activists' point of view to estimate the reputational risk for the company and its brands. The chapter concludes with a detailed discussion of Wal-Mart's strategic adjustment in response to activist threats.[4]

Corporate scandals are reputation killers for companies and for their managers and board members. Chapter 4 investigates the impact of corporate scandals, with an emphasis on executive compensation, drawing on lessons from moral psychology to explain the outrage evoked by corporate decisions that, from a purely economic point of view, appear to be immaterial. Examples discussed include the AIG bonus case, Tyco, Merrill Lynch, and pricing for AIDS drugs. We also discuss relevant differences between nonprofits and corporations.

Improving reputational equity is not easy. Frequently, this requires an integrated approach and changes in business practices. But sometimes opportunities present themselves. The focus in Chapter 5 is on the paradigmatic case of disaster response and the opportunity for companies to occupy the role of hero. The leading example in this case is Wal-Mart's response to Hurricane Katrina, which triggered the turnaround in its corporate reputation. We develop general approaches to how to respond to disasters and discuss the relationship between corporate social responsibility (CSR) and reputation management.

Next to outrage, fear is the second major driver of reputational challenges. Customers and other stakeholders tend to perceive risk in very different ways from experts. The severe overestimation of personal risk can lead to fear. Research in cognitive psychology has identified many of the factors that shape risk perception and may lead to fear. Yet, most business strategies ignore them. Chapter 6 discusses these factors in the context of biotechnology and other emerging technologies, such as nanotechnology, energy, and social networking. Finally, we will draw some conclusions for investors in emerging technologies.

Chapters 7 to 9 systematically develop an integrated reputation management system and its core components: (1) mindset, (2) processes, and (3) values and culture. Chapter 7 focuses on developing a strategic mindset. The key focus of this chapter is to show that reputation management needs to be integrated into corporate strategy. The goal is for each employee and manager to consider herself the steward of the company's reputation. The lead example is the invention of life insurance–backed securities, a lesser-known cousin of mortgage-backed securities. The business context is a market-entry challenge. We will discuss the approach used by Prudential in entering this controversial market. This demonstrates the need for leaders to integrate reputation management into corporate strategy and day-to-day decision making.

Chapter 8 focuses on building a reputation management process. A reputation management process consists of a decision-making system and an intelligence system. The decision-making system needs to span the businesses and integrate the various corporate functions. We discuss various examples from leading corporations to show the importance of integrating the reputation management system with the core strategic process. We argue that, unlike other corporate capabilities, an intelligence system is an essential, not an optional, component of a reputation management process.

The last chapter focuses on the importance of values and culture for a proper reputation management system. Using the Arthur Andersen case as our lead example, we discuss the intersection between people and reputation management processes. The key insight here is that company values and culture must be actively protected and maintained—a slow erosion of a culture of integrity over a period of years can lead even the strongest of companies to the brink of disaster. Andersen had experienced a largely undetected shift away from its core values; and when the company faced a major crisis, the Waste Management scandal, management learned the wrong lessons and ignored the slow deterioration of values. This led directly to the mismanagement of the Enron crisis and the subsequent collapse of the firm. As a secondary example, we also discuss the differences between GE and Siemens in the context of corruption scandals.

The Conclusion summarizes the main insights of the book and discusses the integration of the reputation and people management processes. It highlights the importance of a strategic perspective and the dangers of falling into the expert trap.

A word to the reader who does not live in a traditional corporate environment, but perhaps works in a nonprofit organization or a government agency: to introduce and discuss our toolbox, I am using mainly examples from the corporate world, especially from publicly traded companies. The reason for this focus is simple. Public filing requirements provide better access to information, and a company's stock price provides a simple measure of impact. That said, the content developed in this book applies to other entities, whether privately held companies or nonprofits, government agencies, political parties, even individuals for whom maintaining a strong public reputation is critical.[5] From time to time some modifications will be necessary, and I will point them out as we move forward.

CHAPTER 1

THOMAS OFF THE RAILS

The Decisive Moment and How to Miss It

As for leadership, I have to hold myself accountable for the positives and negatives. We did a good job managing risk; but we did a less good job managing our reputation.

—**Lloyd Blankfein,** CEO Goldman Sachs, May 21, 2010[1]

Reputation is to companies what health is to individuals; we may claim that it is our most important possession, but we pay little attention to it until a crisis hits. In this spirit, we will begin our examination with reputational crises. This is the moment when companies must pay attention. Nothing focuses the mind better than a near-death experience.

You have probably never heard of RC2 Corporation, a midsized toy company from the Chicago area. In 2006, RC2 had around $519 million in annual revenue and a little over 800 employees. However, if you have children, you probably know who Thomas the Tank Engine is. Popularized through a well-known children's book series, television shows, the Internet, and toy stores, Thomas and Friends found their way into numerous homes, to the delight of young children everywhere. The talking trains underwent mild adventures that taught them about friendship, telling the truth, and other moral lessons. All was well until the summer of 2007, when Thomas came off the rails.

In June, RC2 voluntarily recalled 1.5 million units of its Thomas the Tank Engine toys (roughly 4 percent of the total it had sold in the United States), reporting that the red and yellow paint used in the factory in China that built the tank engine toys might have been lead-based.[2] Lead-based paint carries serious health risks—especially to young children—including kidney and nerve damage, learning disabilities, attention deficit disorder, and decreased intelligence. These dangers have led to regulatory responses all over the world. The U.S. government, for example, created laws regarding the use of lead paint and the disclosure of possible exposure to it in 1978.[3] Upon learning of RC2's problems, the U.S. Consumer Product Safety Commission issued a stark warning to parents, telling them to "not delay in getting these toys away from their kids."[4] A second recall of five additional Thomas and Friends products two months later that affected 200,000 units did not help matters.

Despite similar problems across the industry,[5] RC2 paid a particularly severe economic price for the recall. Three years to the day after the announcement of the recall, the company's stock price was still down by 60 percent.

Recalls need not always have such a lasting negative impact, as demonstrated by the classic Tylenol crisis. In the fall of 1982, seven Chicago-area residents died after taking Tylenol, which at the time was the leading over-the-counter painkiller. Tylenol had a market share of about 37 percent at the time, more than its next three competitors combined, and accounted for approximately 8 percent of Johnson & Johnson's total sales and 19 percent of its corporate profits.[6]

Police investigators quickly concluded that an unknown suspect had taken at least three bottles of Tylenol capsules from stores, laced them with cyanide, and returned them to store shelves, a fairly easy task in a time before the innovation of tamper-proof containers. Indeed, the Tylenol crisis led directly to the development of tamper-proofing. The incident created tremendous media interest, generating more than 125,000 stories, at the time making it the most documented media event since the assassination of John F. Kennedy.

The discovery prompted Johnson & Johnson to issue a nationwide recall of Tylenol products on October 5, 1982, five days after the deaths became known. The company assisted health departments with nationwide public service advertisements warning against consuming Tylenol capsules, and created a toll-free hotline. In addition to recalling more than 31 million bottles of Tylenol capsules, Johnson & Johnson offered to exchange tablets for all Tylenol capsules already purchased.

The immediate cost of the recall topped $100 million, while estimates of the total cost of the crisis—which included temporarily depressed sales and the short-term loss of the company's liability insurance—range from $500 million to more than $1 billion. Throughout the crisis, Johnson & Johnson CEO James E. Burke served as the voice of the company. A month later, he introduced the tamper-resistant packaging at a press conference that was covered live by satellite. The new packages would have three modifications: glue-sealed boxes, a plastic seal over the neck of the bottle, and a foil seal over the opening.

These examples suggest that the important issue is not just whether a crisis occurs, but how it is managed: for every Thomas, there is a Tylenol. Understanding the sometimes subtle differences between effective and ineffective management of reputational crises is critical.

THE DECISIVE MOMENT

We make our first mistake in the very way that we think about crises. Intuitively, we characterize them as purely negative events. Terms like *damage*, *stress*, *pressure*, and *disaster* naturally come to mind.[7] Instead, we should recognize that how we conceptualize a problem determines what counts as a good solution. If we face a potential catastrophe, walking away with merely a black eye or avoiding getting hit by the bus surely looks like a good outcome. If we think only about damage, then damage control is the best we can hope for; all these expressions suggest a defensive attitude. The important but unstated assumption is that the best one can hope for is to get as close as possible to the precrisis state.

Suppose we have some measure of performance, as expressed by the wavy line in Figure 1-1. This can represent a company's stock price, its revenue, its market share, or any other operative measure. Now, assume that a crisis hits that leads to a collapse in that measure. A damage control approach will then try to get as close as possible to the precrisis state.

Figure 1-1 **The Concept of Damage Control**

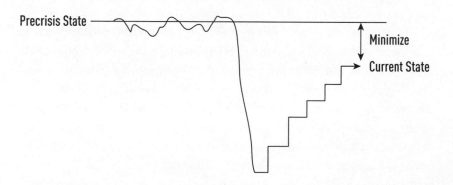

However, crises almost always present opportunities as well, sometimes significant ones. In other words, the postcrisis state can be *better* than the precrisis situation, as pictured in Figure 1-2.

Figure 1-2 **Crisis as a Decisive Moment**

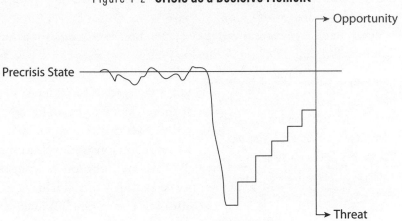

According to this approach, we can conceptualize crises as *decisive moments, turning points for better or for worse.*[8]

What distinguishes a crisis from a particularly bad day at the office or any other important decision? What makes the moment truly "decisive"? And why are the stakes so high? Various answers come to mind. Crises frequently happen without warning and under extreme time pressure. Decision makers drown in information overload, yet truly vital information is not available.

All this is true, but in the case of *reputational crises*, there is another issue, and one that is frequently overlooked. In a crisis, *people are paying attention*; it is as if the company is on stage, the lights are bright, and everybody is looking at management's next move. Among those who are paying particularly close attention are customers (as in the case of lead paint in toys), employees (as in sexual harassment lawsuits), investors, suppliers, and other business partners, and also third parties such as competitors, advocacy groups, politicians, and regulators. There is hardly ever a crisis without the media lighting the stage, and once there

> A reputational crisis can be a near-death experience for a company. The key is to turn such a crisis into an opportunity to improve your company's reputation. These crises are decisive moments, not just exercises in damage control.

is a stage, jumping onto it may prove irresistible for anyone with an agenda and a desire for attention.

When people pay attention, they remember, sometimes for a very long time. The case of Thomas the Tank Engine is already a few years old, but the company has not yet recovered. The Tylenol case is more than 28 years old, but it still yields positive reputational benefits for Johnson & Johnson. To this day, Johnson & Johnson ranks among the world's most admired companies.[9] Tylenol has maintained its sales position among over-the-counter medications, and according to a recent study, it is the second most purchased over-the-counter brand (after Nicorette antismoking gum).[10]

> How your company handles the decisive moment will have a lasting impact on its reputation. Rarely will others pay as much attention as they do when a company is on stage during a reputational crisis.

An even more illuminating piece of evidence is a marketing approach chosen by Johnson & Johnson operating company McNeil Consumer Healthcare, the manufacturer of Tylenol. On January 21, 1999, McNeil introduced a new over-the-counter sleep aid called Simply Sleep into the U.S. market. While the market for sleep aids had been booming, customers remained concerned about not only whether the drugs were actually effective, but also whether they were habit-forming.[11] Nonetheless, McNeil put a big, bright yellow sticker on the blue package with the wording "from the makers of Tylenol."

Not only did McNeil not shy away from association with the Tylenol incident, but it *reminded* customers of it. This decision should surprise us only if we are still stuck in the damage control paradigm. If we think about the underlying business problem, properly managing reputational crises may result in increased brand equity and trust. Companies can then leverage that brand equity for various business purposes, in this case, the introduction of another brand. Simply Sleep is now the second most popular brand after Pfizer's Unisom brand. Together, they command more than 40 percent of the over-the-counter sleep-aid market.[12]

We can think of McNeil's strategy as a test case for evaluating the success with which a reputational crisis was managed after the fact. Think back to the last incident you or your organization faced. Would you mind if it came up in a job interview? Would you hope it came up?

Would you want to be known as "the makers of Tylenol"? If not, you or your company has failed the Tylenol test.[13]

Of course, we are familiar with similar phenomena in "normal times," when the company is not facing a crisis. For example, even customers who are aware that a generic and a branded painkiller are identical except for the price still frequently prefer the branded product. This effect is more pronounced when their symptoms are severe, and it becomes dominant when the customer buys the medicine for a spouse or a child.[14]

Sadly, most companies forget these lessons during a reputational crisis and focus solely on technical and legal issues. In other words, they forget the very basis of their business model: the need to maintain customer trust.

Things don't always go as well as they did in the Tylenol case. Whenever I teach a reputation management class, I play a simple association game with my students. "Here is how it goes," I begin. "I will tell you the name of a company, and you will please shout out the first thing that comes to mind when you hear it. Are you ready? Here it is: Exxon!"

Invariably, among the first three answers is *"Valdez"* or "oil spill." In case you do not remember or were too young, the *Exxon Valdez* oil spill occurred more than 20 years ago, yet it is still a core component of Exxon's reputational profile. On March 24, 1989, the *Exxon Valdez* and the 53 million gallons contained within its hull slammed into the Bligh Reef in Prince William Sound in Alaska. Approximately 11 million gallons of oil spilled from the tanker, decimating the fish, seabird, and mammal populations that inhabited the sound.[15]

> Take the Tylenol test. Recall your last reputational crisis and how you handled it. Now ask yourself: Do you hope people will forget about the incident? Or do you hope they will remember it?

The disaster became front-page news across the country, and Exxon became the focus of much negative publicity and even the butt of jokes on late-night talk shows. Much of the criticism revolved around the company's lagging response time and subsequent cleanup efforts. Although company officials arrived soon after the accident, Exxon executives did not comment on what had happened for almost a week, and when they did, their information often contradicted information from other sources.[16]

Exxon's communication approach came across as defensive, arrogant, and evasive, an attempt to shift blame to the Coast Guard, Alaskan officials, and the ship's captain. Six days passed before Exxon's chairman made his first comments in response to the accident, and sixteen more passed before he actually arrived on the scene. CEO Lawrence G. Rawls had earlier stated that because of the crisis, he had no time to visit Alaska, but that the team of Exxon experts on location was doing an excellent job. The *Valdez* accident led to significant regulatory changes[17] and cost Exxon approximately $4.3 billion in cleaning expenses, legal costs, and compensatory and punitive damages; the exact amount is still being determined by the courts, more than 20 years after the accident.[18]

To be sure, Exxon (now ExxonMobil) is a successful company by any standard, having made frequent appearances at the top of *Fortune* magazine's Fortune 500 list and never falling below the top three since the rankings were first released in 1955. The *Exxon Valdez* incident served as a wake-up call for the company, prompting a complete reorganization of its environmental, health, and safety policies. Amy Myers Jaffe, an energy expert at Rice University, recently called Exxon "the safest oil company there is."[19] For its efforts, Exxon has thrice received the British Safety Council's "Sword of Honour" and has won the U.S. Coast Guard's William M. Benkert Gold Award for marine environmental excellence.[20]

Nevertheless, Exxon remains a target of activist groups, reinforced by its reluctance to address global warming. In 2002, Stanford University accepted ExxonMobil's gift of $100 million to fund a Global Climate and Energy Project, only to be greeted with student protests and the revocation of gifts from other major donors.[21] Despite the company's apparent shift in February 2007, when CEO Rex Tillerson publicly acknowledged that developing climate policy would be "prudent," the company continues to face intermittent accusations of sabotaging efforts to battle global warming.[22]

In future years, Exxon's place in the popular imagination is likely to be replaced by BP and its Gulf of Mexico oil spill. Estimated at more than 18 times the size of the *Valdez* spill, the Deepwater Horizon catastrophe temporarily halved BP's market value, cost CEO Tony Hayward his job, and poisoned the company's relationship with U.S. consumers and government officials, in a market that accounts for 40 percent of BP's total revenues. The crisis has proven so devastating that BP's very survival as an independent company was in doubt.[23]

Tellingly, the American media savaged Hayward's performance during the crisis. BP's board subsequently ordered the CEO back to London and turned to Robert Dudley, a U.S. native from the Gulf region and the former head of BP's Russian joint venture. Dudley was widely credited for improving relations with the U.S. government and the general public, leading to the ultimate prize: his appointment as BP's next CEO.

What distinguishes success from failure in managing reputational crises? How do we identify opportunities when the world (or at least our business or career) seems to be coming to an end? Living through a crisis can be an overwhelming experience. On the one hand, we experience information overload. On the other hand, critical information is not available. Everybody wants to be updated and reassured, but there is not even time to draft a first response to media inquiries.

Crises almost always present complex decision problems. On top of the need to reassure customers, they may involve complex engineering problems, operational issues, supplier and employee relations, or regulatory and legal challenges, to name just a few. In this environment, decision makers can easily lose their bearings and focus on the wrong problem. Therefore, the first strategic task of crisis leadership is to *identify the business issue*. Rather than focusing on assigning fault, identifying legal liabilities, or arguing who is right or wrong, the key question is how the ensuing crisis is connected to the company's business model, its value proposition, its brand, and its relationship with customers and other stakeholders.

In comparing Thomas and Tylenol, we can clearly see this difference. RC2 focused too much on the question of who was at fault (in this case, the most likely candidate would be the Chinese supplier or its subsupplier), while Johnson & Johnson

> During a reputational crisis, task number one is to identify the business issue. How is the incident connected to the company's business model, its value proposition, its brand, and its relationship with customers and other stakeholders?

paid hardly any attention to the question of fault. After all, the tampering was done by a serial killer. Instead, Johnson & Johnson clearly identified the core business issue: customers were in danger of losing trust in the brand, and required reassurance. Everything Johnson & Johnson did served exactly this goal of defending the Tylenol brand and rebuilding trust. By going far beyond what was expected, Johnson & Johnson demonstrated that it put the health and safety of its customers first, as mandated by its value statement, the famed Johnson & Johnson Credo.

It is very easy to mismanage these situations, especially when companies change their business model or strategy. This is true even for Johnson & Johnson and Tylenol. During 2010, Johnson & Johnson's McNeil unit recalled more than 40 over-the-counter products—including leading brands such as Tylenol, Motrin, and Benadryl—after an FDA investigation revealed "deficiencies" in a manufacturing facility. This marked the beginning of an *annus horribilis* for the company.[24]

> Managers frequently get sidetracked by the question of who is at fault. But this is not the business issue. Companies need to focus on defending the brand and rebuilding trust.

During the subsequent hearing and investigations, FDA inspectors found contamination and other quality problems at an additional manufacturing facility. Perhaps most alarming, the company faced charges that in some cases it had used paid contractors to buy up contaminated products from retailers rather than issuing a proper recall. As a consequence, the FDA was considering taking civil action against the company, while the U.S. House of Representatives held hearings in which lawmakers chastised the company for its lax standards and inappropriate business practices. In late 2010, the company started to take action and allocated more than $100 million to upgrade its manufacturing plants, appointed a new manufacturing executive, and engaged in a broad quality improvement process. Johnson & Johnson's CEO, Bill Weldon, was widely criticized for his slow reaction and for being invisible during the crisis. It is one of the supreme ironies in the history of reputation management that the company that gave the world the "gold standard" in crisis management is now viewed as falling short of its own standard.

Reputational risks can be elevated as a result of a shift in corporate strategy. Any given strategy carries its own reputational risk, and over time, the company's reputation management capabilities tend to match that risk profile. In the case of changing to a strategy with a higher level of risk, existing approaches and capabilities are likely to be inadequate, and this may trigger a crisis. Such deficiencies are very difficult to spot before things go poorly because of the unfamiliarity of the new environment. Moreover, once an incident occurs, the company's instincts are to use its established approaches, which are ill suited to its new strategy and therefore may even exacerbate the crisis.

Intel's Pentium processor crisis presents a great example of this dynamic.[25] In June 1994, Thomas Nicely, a mathematics professor from Lynchburg College, noticed some discrepancies in his research results on computational number theory. He had used a PC powered by the new Pentium processor, which at the time constituted a breakthrough in personal computing, as it allowed users to run computationally intensive problems, including Professor Nicely's research project on enumerating large prime numbers. After spending the next few months trying to pinpoint the problem, he finally discovered a flaw in the chip in October. He notified Intel's tech support on October 24, 1994. A week later, he still had not received a response, so he dispatched an e-mail inquiry to a number of individuals and groups, including authors of textbooks and various trade journals such as *InfoWorld* and *PC Week*.[26]

In early November, Intel acknowledged the flaw in its chips and said that it had discovered the problem independently. However, the company had dismissed the problem as being "not serious" because Intel's experts estimated that the average user had only a one in nine billion chance of encountering an inaccurate result because of the error, and thus it was of no noticeable consequence to businesses and home users. The problem had been identified in June, but the company not only had felt that a recall was unnecessary, but had also continued to send the faulty chips to client computer manufacturers while production of the bug-free chips was taking place. The company had only just begun providing the revised chips to its biggest customers.[27] This response was consistent with Intel's typical approach as a supplier to large corporate customers: it would replace chips on a case-by-case basis, and only after the customer had requested an exchange.

However, Intel no longer operated exclusively as a business-to-business (B2B) supplier, and the rules in the mass consumer products market were vastly different. CNN and other major news networks picked up the story, and the *New York Times* published it on the front page of its business section, causing a public outcry that was quickly echoed by Intel's customers. Intel's CEO, Andrew Grove, responded by advising customers via an Internet notice to call the company if they wanted a replacement chip, explain how they were using their Pentium, and then wait for the company to decide whether or not a new chip was warranted.[28] The replacement policy ignited a firestorm of criticism that quickly turned to mockery as customers and Internet users chided the company: "At Intel, quality is job 0.999999998" and "I heard that Intel lost one of its divisions today."

In mid-December, IBM announced a halt on all shipments with Pentium processors, claiming that the flaw was more common than Intel had originally stated. The toll-free telephone line that Intel had set up to answer concerns became flooded with inquiries, and over the course of the next week, Intel's share price dropped by almost 8 percent.

On December 17, Intel CEO Andrew Grove called an all-day meeting to change Intel's policy on Pentium replacements, and three days later, the company offered to replace any flawed processors—no questions asked.[29] The total cost of the recall, estimated from an announced pretax charge against Intel earnings in January 1995, was $475 million.

The puzzle here is not why Intel got into trouble and mismanaged the situation—by this point such patterns might be sounding familiar. What is more puzzling is why an approach that had been effective for many years suddenly stopped working.

Shortly before the launch of the Pentium processor, Intel had dramatically shifted its marketing strategy. Previously a technology-focused B2B company, Intel had begun marketing itself directly to consumers with the 1991 introduction of its "Intel Inside" campaign. The campaign proved to be a brilliant move, as a comparison between Intel and its closest competitor, AMD, clearly shows; Intel resonated with consumers,

> Changes in business strategy are prone to trigger reputational crises. Why? Existing reputation management capabilities have not been updated to address the new risk environment. The results are crises and puzzlement as to why the old strategies have stopped working.

connoting images of cutting-edge technology, while the name AMD meant little or nothing to all but the most tech-savvy users.

Once it had positioned itself as a consumer-facing brand, Intel had to play by different rules. The established engineering-based approach simply ceased to work, as it presupposes a technically sophisticated audience. With the "Intel Inside" campaign, the company had made a promise to its customers that Intel processors were of particularly high quality. When this was combined with the fact that consumer brands— particularly those supported by extensive advertising—attract more media attention and scrutiny, Intel faced dramatically raised stakes for a successful reputation management response.

To be sure, there is nothing wrong with business models based on a relationship of trust. Their downside is that the mere perception of quality problems makes customers feel misled and betrayed, with dramatic consequences for the company. If you live by the brand, you die by the brand.

THE TRUST RADAR

Trust is the magic word in managing reputational crises, and it is the first issue upon which companies should focus. But how do we reassure customers and other constituencies? Many factors influence trust. Some are based on rational, cognitive factors, such as a record of reliable service and quality, or endorsements by credible third parties. Others are based on nonrational, emotional factors, such as tone of voice, perceived sincerity, or even facial features.[30] These emotional factors, while important, are difficult to operationalize in a complex decision problem. The *Trust Radar* shown in Figure 1-3 serves this purpose by reminding us of the four most important factors in building or maintaining trust.

Starting at the right, the first factor is *transparency*. This should not be confused with full disclosure; transparency does not mean that everything that is known must be revealed. In many cases (such as when privacy or trade secrets need protection), full disclosure is impossible. A well-known former head of communications for a major multinational firm once told me that "in sticky situations, I am 80 percent forthcom-

Figure 1-3 **The Trust Radar**

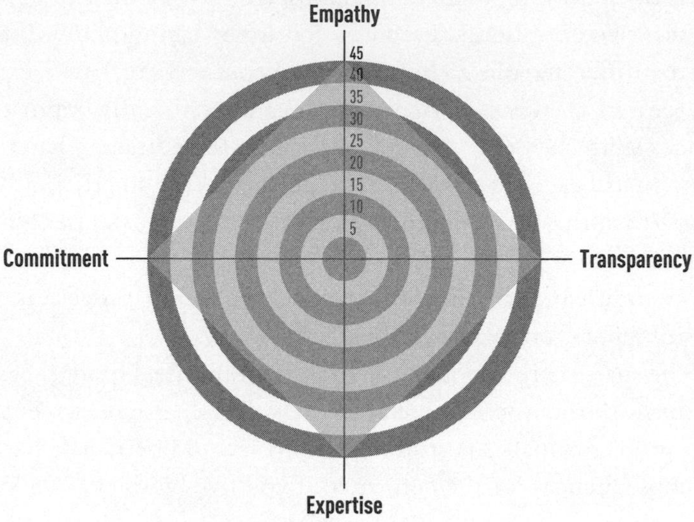

Empathy

45
40
35
30
25
20
15
10
5

Commitment

Transparency

Expertise

ing and 100 percent transparent." Transparency is violated when the relevant audience believes that relevant information has been willfully withheld, as in the case of a noncommittal "no comment" statement. That does not mean that "no comment" should never be used, but managers must understand that it carries a significant cost. A good way to achieve transparency is to tell the audience what you do know, what you do not know, and when you will follow up.

An important and frequently overlooked component of transparency is being understood. The public will not consider technical mumbo-jumbo or "legalese" transparent, even if it discloses relevant information. They will instead assume that a company is hiding behind incomprehensible jargon instead of speaking plainly and in a straightforward manner.

> Relationships of trust have both rational and emotional foundations. Maintaining and enhancing trust is the most important task during a reputational crisis. Transparency, expertise, commitment, and empathy are the key factors in building trust during such a crisis.

Continuing clockwise, our second factor, at the bottom, is *expertise*: "We know what we are doing, and we have a team of experts that will fix the problem." The audience needs to be convinced of the organization's competence. With few exceptions, corporations do not struggle with a perceived lack of competence, since we rarely doubt that a company *can* do the right thing. More likely, we believe that it *chooses* not to do so. In the case of ensuring safer products, we may suspect that the company does not want to do so because that would cost it money. In other words, we usually do not doubt a company's capabilities, but we do doubt its motivations.[31]

That is not the case for nonprofits and some government agencies. Institutions are sometimes viewed like people. While for-profit companies are seen as being competent, but not necessarily caring, nonprofits are seen as being caring, but not always competent.[32] The reputational catastrophe suffered by the Federal Emergency Management Agency (FEMA) during Hurricane Katrina stemmed not from the belief that FEMA had bad intentions, but from the belief that it lacked competence. Nonprofits in the disaster management field frequently face this problem. The Red Cross's "Means-to-Recovery" program, for example, faced criticism that it was underpublicized and highly bureaucratic.[33]

If customers perceive a lack of expertise, bringing in third-party experts with credibility is a simple way to address this concern. In some cases, the board may need to nudge management in this direction, as a CEO may fear looking incompetent or weak if he admits to needing the assistance of an outside expert. In this context, a board member or other trusted advisor may want to point out that what matters most is addressing the perceived lack of expertise, regardless of its accuracy or inaccuracy.

Continuing clockwise, our third factor is *commitment*: communicating that a problem is being addressed or that a process for improvement is moving forward. In many cases, commitment is signaled most effectively by senior management. A former fire commissioner once expressed this to me as follows: "When the house is on fire, people want to hear from the guy in charge!"

The most powerful and direct way to signal commitment is for senior management to show up and take charge. It demonstrates accountability and sends the message that nothing is more important than resolving this particular crisis. When a Virgin train from London bound for Glasgow crashed after derailing as a result of a line defect, the company's CEO, Sir Richard Branson, not only cut short a family vacation to help handle the situation personally, but also visited crash victims in the hospital and praised the train driver's courage and actions that saved more lives.[34] In contrast, the fact that it took more than a month and a formal request from the U.S. House of Representative's Oversight and Reform Committee for Akio Toyoda, Toyota's president and grandson of the company's founder, to visit the United States following the January 2010 discovery of a flaw in the accelerator pedal mechanism of a wide range of vehicles created the appearance of a lack of accountability. It did not help that in the early days of the recall, Mr. Toyoda continued to attend the World Economic Forum in Davos, Switzerland.[35]

Exxon CEO Lawrence Rawls's failure to immediately visit the disaster area in Prince William Sound further undermined the public's trust in the company. To an efficiency-minded CEO, such rituals may look like a waste of time, the most precious resource during any crisis. After all, what is gained by flying to Alaska and looking at dead birds? Ironically, it is exactly this "inefficiency" that creates the strong symbolic value. By showing up, a CEO signals that taking care of this crisis is the company's absolute top priority, demonstrating a sense of commitment.

Does it always have to be the CEO? No; the appropriate level of commitment depends on the perceived magnitude of the crisis. To use the fire commissioner's metaphor, when the burning house is just a small building on a neighborhood block without victims, the local fire lieutenant will do just fine, but if the Empire State Building bursts into flames, nothing less than the fire commissioner will do, even if operational control is located at a lower level in the hierarchy. When in doubt, use someone a little higher in the management hierarchy than necessary, even if the executive may not direct the operations. Toyota's use of the U.S. head of sales during the accelerator crisis was one or two levels too low to inspire public faith in the company's commitment. Aiming too low in the hierarchy is easily misinterpreted as carelessness or disinterest.

The importance of demonstrating commitment also casts doubt on the extensive use of PR professionals as spokespeople. The problem with such professionals is that they do not have operational responsibilities; they are not in charge, and the audience knows it. In a crisis, people want to hear from leaders who have the power to resolve the issue.

The final component, *empathy*, is perhaps the most important factor of the four and the easiest to overlook.[36] Empathy is not the same as an apology, although an apology can express it. However, an apology that appears formulaic and insincere does more harm than good, because it may appear cynical and calculated. On the other hand, a leader reaching out to perceived victims with warmth and authenticity can be very effective, regardless of whether it is accompanied by an apology.

In response to Virgin's train accident, Sir Richard Branson expressed sorrow for the loss of life ("It is a very sad day because of the loss of one life and the injuries caused to other people"), while also supporting the driver whom he called a "hero" for helping the passengers survive the crash ("He is definitely a hero. In the sober light of day, we will have to see if he can be recognized as such"). In a crisis context, we view corporations less as impersonal purveyors of goods and services and more as members of the community. Members of the community are presumed to care; if they do not, they look monstrous and out of touch.

Let us now apply the Trust Radar to two classic examples: Johnson & Johnson's Tylenol response and the *Exxon Valdez* (Figure 1-4).

From a purely operational perspective, the Tylenol recall was far from flawless. The company took a few days to respond, and its initial response proved inadequate. In the graph, we can capture this less-than-stellar execution with a medium expertise score. However, its performance on the other three factors, especially the committed and empathetic engagement of the CEO, more than compensated for this shortcoming. Exxon's response, on the other hand, exhibits the typical focus on expertise alone, to the exclusion of the other factors.

Such an exclusive focus on expertise is quite common. Toyota's initial reaction to the accelerator crisis is typical. Eleven days after the recall of more than 2 million vehicles because of a sticking gas pedal, Toyota issued a press release with a fix for the issue, stating that adding a small metal reinforcement bar to reduce friction would prove "both effective and simple."[37] This wording indicated that Toyota viewed the problem as predominantly an engineering problem, and for an engineering problem, a metal bar would be a sufficient solution. Toyota

Figure 1-4 **Exxon versus Johnson & Johnson**

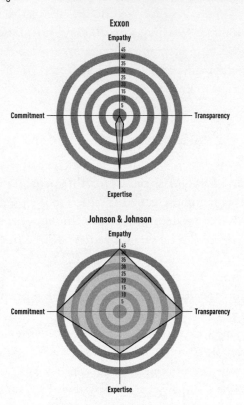

overlooked its deeper problem, however: the damage done to its brand, a brand that was defined first and foremost by quality. Customer doubts as to whether Toyota had sacrificed safety and quality to accelerate its growth could not be put to rest with a simple metal bar.

A year after the incident the company continues to struggle in its efforts to rebuild trust with its customers. Toyota recalled 7 million vehicles in the United States in 2010, and it was the only major car-maker whose sales here declined while sales for the rest of the industry rose 13.4 percent. The influential product rating magazine *Consumer Reports* recently stated that 19 percent of respondents listed Toyota as having the highest quality in the 2010 survey, down from 30 percent a year ago. During an interview at the 2011 Detroit Auto Show, Toyota's head, Akio Toyoda, vowed that the company would put its "heart and soul" into every vehicle, "just as mothers make rice bowls for their children."[38]

As a second example of an exclusive focus on expertise, consider Goldman Sachs. On Friday, April 16, 2010, the U.S. Securities and Exchange Commission (SEC) filed civil charges against Goldman Sachs & Co., accusing the firm of fraud for selling mortgage investments (so-called synthetic collateralized debt obligations, or CDOs) without telling the buyers that the securities had been crafted with input from a client who was betting on them to fail. According to SEC Enforcement Director Robert Khuzami, "Goldman wrongly permitted a client that was betting against the mortgage market to heavily influence which mortgage securities to include in an investment portfolio, while telling other investors that the securities were selected by an independent, objective third party."[39] After the civil charges were filed, Goldman responded with a statement denying the allegations as "completely unfounded in law and fact."

The SEC also quoted several Goldman Sachs e-mail records obtained during the investigation. A Goldman vice president and the creator of the CDO in question, Fabrice Tourre, was quoted in a January 2007 e-mail to a friend describing himself as "the fabulous Fab standing in the middle of all these complex, highly leveraged, exotic trades he created without necessarily understanding all of the implications of those monstrosities!!" In a March 2007 e-mail, Tourre characterized the U.S. subprime mortgage market as "not too brilliant." He also wrote that "according to Sparks," presumably referring to Daniel Sparks, who led Goldman's mortgage business at the time, "that business is totally dead, and the poor little subprime borrowers will not last too long!!!"

On April 27, 2010, the Permanent Subcommittee on Investigations, part of the U.S. Senate Committee on Homeland Security and Governmental Affairs, followed with a hearing investigating Goldman's business practices. Although it was technically independent of the SEC investigation, it also focused on sales and marketing practices related to CDOs. Throughout the hearings, senators pressed the Goldman executives on whether they felt a sense of responsibility or duty of care toward their clients, as in the following excerpt:

Senator Tester (D-Montana): Do you think Goldman Sachs did anything wrong in this whole process of these synthetic CDOs?

Daniel Sparks (former Goldman Sachs managing director and head of the mortgage department): Wrong to me has some qualitative comment about doing something inappropriate . . . um . . . that doesn't mean we didn't make mistakes or do deals that didn't turn out the way we had hoped they would.

These carefully worded responses did not reassure their intended audience. Immediately following the hearing, outraged legislators called for additional investigations into Goldman's activities, and news leaked that federal prosecutors had begun conducting a criminal probe into whether the company or its employees had committed securities fraud, sending Goldman shares plummeting.

During an interview on National Public Radio, CEO Lloyd Blankfein reflected on the SEC hearings, saying, "It was quite a humbling experience to be in a position where Goldman Sachs, which prides itself on the role it performs in the U.S. economy . . . [had] to defend itself against some of the charges that were made."[40]

On July 15, Goldman Sachs settled civil charges with the SEC for $550 million and agreed to make changes to its marketing and compliance practices. Goldman's shares rose, adding about $5 billion to its market capitalization, which nonetheless remains more than $20 billion below its level at the beginning of the crisis.[41]

Goldman Sachs subsequently conducted a detailed internal investigation of its business practices. In January 2011, the company released a report outlining 39 recommendations intended to bolster internal controls, increase transparency, and improve its reputation. "Goldman Sachs has one reputation," the report said. "It can be affected by any number of decisions and activities across the firm. Every employee has an equal obligation to raise issues or concerns, no matter how small, to protect the firm's reputation."[42]

So far, we have focused largely on corporate leaders, but as discussed earlier in the context of the Katrina disaster, the Trust Radar is just as useful for nonprofits, public agencies, and politicians. For example, former New York City Mayor Rudy Giuliani received widespread praise for his leadership after the 9/11 terrorist attacks. It was his career's decisive moment.

It is worthwhile to remember that before the attacks on 9/11, Giuliani's career had been in a tailspin. After initial success, his tenure as mayor had lost its luster and become mired in controversy. Several police brutality and shooting incidents had led to lower popularity ratings, and Giuliani had become known for lashing out at members of the media that criticized his administration. In the spring of 2000, the combination of his diagnosis with prostate cancer, the media coverage of his extramarital affair, and his subsequent nasty divorce from his wife forced him to withdraw from a bruising battle for the New York Senate seat that Hillary Clinton later captured.

> The principles of reputation management do not apply only to corporations. They also hold for nonprofits, government agencies, politicians, celebrities, and many others.

All of this changed with Giuliani's response to the September 11 attack on New York's World Trade Center. Upon learning of the attack, Giuliani immediately raced to the scene to meet with his police and fire commissioners. A lasting image showed Giuliani, his hair and clothes still covered with ash, emerging from the smoke and rubble of a severely damaged city office.

His next actions perfectly capture Giuliani's leadership during the 9/11 crisis. He comforted a police officer and then made a statement to a TV crew. "Today is obviously one of the most difficult days in the history of the city," he began. "The tragedy that we are undergoing right now is something that we've had nightmares about. My heart goes out to all the innocent victims of this horrible and vicious act of terrorism. And our focus now has to be to save as many lives as possible." When asked about the number of casualties Giuliani responded, "The number of casualties will be more than any of us can bear."[43]

This combination of calmness, candor, and compassion became the defining characteristics of Giuliani's leadership approach. In the days and weeks following the disaster, Giuliani repeated his message of recovery through unity when he praised New York's police, fire department, and other emergency responders, and mourned those who had perished. Despite little or no sleep, he kept attending funerals, in some instances five per day, and spoke frequently to the city. He met with a psychologist to determine the best way to continue communicating in a comforting fashion but honestly with a city that was still reeling from the tragedy. This authentic incorporation of the four factors of the Trust Radar not only provided much-needed leadership for the city (there was never any question as to who was in charge), but also transformed his career from that of an ill-tempered politician in decline to "America's Mayor."[44]

Compare this to the performance of President George W. Bush after Hurricane Katrina. It took the president three days to visit the disaster site, and his flight over a flooded New Orleans and Louisiana created an impression of disengagement and lack of involvement. Katrina fatally damaged the Bush administration's hard-won reputation for crisis management, earned during the aftermath of 9/11.[45] The administration looked incompetent, symbolized by President Bush's comment regarding FEMA director Michael Brown: "Brownie, you're doing a heck of a job."[46] (Brown would resign under intense criticism just 10 days later.) Reflecting on Katrina, former Bush aide Scott McClellan said, "One of the worst disasters in our nation's history became one of the biggest disasters in Bush's presidency."[47]

These brief remarks show that the tools for managing reputational crises are as useful to government organizations and nonprofits as they are to corporations. The Red Cross, the U.S. Marine Corps, the FBI, and the Mayo Clinic are brands that are every bit as powerful as Apple, McDonald's, and Coca-Cola. They stand for a set of values and a distinct purpose. If these brands are under threat, they need to be managed just like those of any other entity that has a reputation to uphold. The case of personal reputations—especially for actors or other celebrities with a strong public presence—is analogous. Examples ranging from Martha Stewart to Michael Vick to Tiger Woods make this point self-evident.

THE TASTE OF WATER

These examples, old and new, successful and unsuccessful, nicely illustrate the mechanisms that drive perception during a reputational crisis. To understand these processes in more detail, a rigorous approach using controlled experiments is helpful. The approach is similar to the market research studies that are conducted when companies design or evaluate brands.[48]

Subjects read little vignettes of fictitious newspaper articles that describe a crisis. For example, a food manufacturer may be accused of using a potentially harmful food additive (the made-up ingredient "glo-actimate") in order to increase the shelf life of its products, or the company may be involved in a nasty sexual harassment lawsuit. In addition to this background information, subjects are also provided with a statement by the fictitious company.

The company could respond in one of three ways. In the case of an "engaged response," the company voiced concern about the allegations, expressed its empathy toward customers, and committed to conducting an investigation into the allegations. In short, we made up a corporate statement that captured all dimensions of the Trust Radar. In the case of a "defensive response," the company disputed the allegations, showed no empathy, and highlighted its expertise. This was a stylized version of a typical corporate response, with its focus on the problem's technical aspects. Finally, to capture the advice typically given to avoid legal liabilities, we added a "no comment" response.

We first asked our subjects to express their opinion of the company. The subjects responded as predicted, viewing the engaged company significantly more positively. Interestingly, their responses exhibited no significant difference between a "no comment" response and a defensive response. In other words, when a company is silent, subjects view it as defensive. We also found that an engaged response increased the respondents' belief that the company was warm and caring toward others, although it did not increase their trust in the company's competence and reliability.

This is consistent with our observation that customers' trust in the company's expertise and capabilities is far less fragile than their trust in the company's motives. Previous virtuous acts by the company did not affect their opinions. For example, a company that had funded cancer research would still be viewed as negative if it adopted a defensive posture. Previous philanthropic actions mattered only when the company was silent; here, a "moral bank account" seemed to maintain some trust among its customers.

These reactions were not limited to the case of potentially harmful food additives, but also occurred in the case of an alleged sexual harassment incident. Moreover, negative reactions were not limited to the corporate image, but also applied to the evaluations of logos, bottle designs, or products.

Perhaps the most striking example occurred in a variant of the experiment in which customers were asked to evaluate the taste of a product, here bottled water. We gave subjects the same fictitious vignettes and responses and then had them taste-test water from the company that was in trouble and compare it to a competitor's product. Of course, the water in both cases was identical. The results showed that the mere accusation of sexual harassment led customers to rate the taste of the company's product lower.

Even more striking, subjects drank less water from the company that was in crisis, suggesting that the response is visceral and goes beyond a conscious evaluation. As before, the style of response (engaged, defensive, or no comment) mattered. Taste evaluation and quantity consumed were higher for a company with an engaged response, while there was no significant difference between companies offering defensive or no comment responses.

What makes these findings important is that a corporate response, even to an unrelated event such as a sexual harassment accusation, can have a direct and measurable impact on the evaluation of core brand attributes. Designing these attributes correctly is a core challenge for brand managers, but they can be easily undermined by the negative spillover from a mismanaged corporate reputational crisis.

Corporate executives are only partially aware of these effects. When we asked corporate executives to predict how public attitudes would be affected by these same scenarios, the executives correctly predicted that an engaged response would be viewed more favorably than a defensive response, but they were overly optimistic about the public's ability to refrain from forming opinions when the company offered "no comment." That is, executives assumed that such a response would be viewed more positively than a defensive response, when in fact this is not the case.

> Corporate reputation strategies have direct and measurable effects on the evaluation of core brand attributes. They can affect overall customer perceptions, evaluations of corporate logos, and even opinions of product taste and levels of consumption. Corporate executives are largely unaware of such effects.

Perhaps this is one reason why executives in so many real-world cases adopt a "no comment" approach.

A QUESTION OF GUILT

The skeptical reader may suspect that there is another important difference between Exxon and Johnson & Johnson and between Giuliani and Bush: guilt. In the Tylenol case, it quickly became clear that the deaths were the act of a serial killer, not the consequence of a manufacturing defect or quality problem, whereas blame for the *Exxon Valdez* clearly lay with Exxon and its employees, even though the magnitude of this responsibility has been heavily contested. In the 9/11 case, New York City clearly was the victim, whereas in the case of Katrina, the federal government bore at least some responsibility for the deterioration of the dams in New Orleans and the slow speed of the federal emergency response, even though that responsibility was shared with the city and with the state of Louisiana.[49] However, the importance of guilt is overrated. Let's consider the following example.

On an icy day in the winter of 2005/2006, amidst heavy winds and nearly blinding snow, Southwest Airlines Flight 1248 attempted to land at Chicago's Midway Airport. The seasoned pilot and crew appeared to have made a safe and successful landing, but then were unable to stop the plane. It skidded beyond the end of the runway, through the airport perimeter fence, and onto an adjacent roadway, where it collided with a car. The accident left 21 people with minor injuries, 1 person with serious injuries, and six-year-old Joshua Woods dead when his family's car was crushed by the plane's fuselage.[50] It was the first fatal accident in Southwest's 40-year history.

Southwest Airlines has been the greatest success story in the U.S. airline industry over the last four decades. Posting its first profitable year in 1973, Southwest has enjoyed consistent revenues and profitability for 38 consecutive years, never once engaging in layoffs despite operating in a highly competitive, cyclical industry. Indeed, according to a much-quoted article, Southwest Airlines was the best-performing stock among *all* publicly traded companies from 1972 to 2002.[51]

Known for its affable staff, no-frills service, and use of secondary metropolitan airports, the airline steadily grew to become America's largest (and the world's third largest) airline in terms of passengers carried. Despite its success, Southwest remained steadfast in its commitment to being a "fun" airline, as reflected by its corporate culture, its approach to customer service, and its humorous advertising campaigns. In addition to customer satisfaction and loyalty, Southwest received widespread acclaim in 1988 by becoming the first airline to ever win the "Triple Crown" of awards for the Best On-Time Record, Best Baggage Handling, and Fewest Customer Complaints in the same month.

Southwest Airlines reacted swiftly after Flight 1248's failed landing. Within a few hours of the accident, CEO Gary Kelly addressed the public at an early morning press conference in Dallas. Formerly a CPA, Kelly had been appointed CEO, president, and chairman of Southwest in 2004. Kelly made some brief remarks outlining his assessment of the situation before boarding the next plane to Chicago, following an earlier plane, which had arrived just eight hours after the failed landing, carrying 94 Southwest employees who were prepared to assist with the developing situation in Chicago.

> Executives focus too much on questions of guilt. Maintaining trust is usually more important than showing who was at fault.

Eighteen hours after the failed landing, Kelly gave a second press conference in Chicago, expressing his sympathy to the family and friends affected by the accident. "There are absolutely no words to accurately state our grief and our sorrow over this tragedy." Kelly cautioned that it was too early to determine whether the weather had affected the landing, and rejected suggestions that Midway's shorter-than-average runways were to blame: "I think it's inappropriate to suggest that the airport is not safe," he said, noting that there are other airports with "runways much longer than at Midway that have had more accidents." He further endorsed Midway's safety record, pointing out that it was "properly certified by the FAA, and . . . other airlines have flown jets to Midway for decades with few accidents." He also addressed the possibility of pilot error, but indicated that there was no reason to suspect the airplane's crew as a cause of the accident.

In addition to the airline's efforts to assist those immediately affected by the crash, Southwest promptly set up a customer service line and Web page for families looking for information and updates on their loved ones. Southwest staff members worked overtime to contact each person affected by the accident and to comfort those who had been injured.

Two weeks after the accident, Kelly granted various interviews in which he emphasized the company's grief over the death of Joshua Woods. To keep Southwest employees informed and morale high, Kelly continued to send personal notes, cards, e-mails, and telephone messages offering perspective, gratitude, and encouragement. Kelly assured the public of the company's full cooperation with regulators such as the National Transportation Safety Board (NTSB) and the Federal Aviation Administration, as well as Midway Airport. He also personally sought out information from company pilots to learn more about the aircraft systems relevant to the investigation while stressing the company's priority of "[pinpointing] the cause or causes of this accident and making any necessary corrections."

Kelly handled this crisis about as well as anyone could given the circumstances, demonstrating all four factors in his crisis management strategy. Kelly repeatedly informed both the general public and Southwest employees of what the company knew or didn't know, showing transparency. He utilized Southwest's considerable expertise on safety matters effectively, going beyond the government investigation, and he exhibited contrition and empathy that struck observers as genuine and authentic.

Most important, observers never wondered who was in charge. Kelly remained deeply involved, leading the company through the crisis from the first day to the safety hearings. He recognized the crisis for what it was: a test case for Southwest's core values and its promise to customers. Notice also his reluctance to assign blame, either to the pilots or to Midway. Both were key constituencies, in addition to customers, that needed reassurance. Midway International Airport, for example, is Southwest's second most popular destination, behind McCarran Airport in Las Vegas, and it plays an intricate role in Southwest's strategy of serving lower-cost secondary airports.

All too often, companies forget about their people and their business partners when they are managing a crisis, instead getting too caught up with the media and other external constituencies. Employees, suppliers, and other stakeholders are paying just as close attention during a crisis, and will surely remember just as well as customers and members of the media. Through his personal notes and direct expression of gratitude,

Kelly made sure that Southwest's employees felt recognized in their extraordinary efforts, a gesture that they are not likely to soon forget.

The public response to Southwest's handling of the accident was forceful and overwhelmingly positive. Industry observers told the *Chicago Tribune* that "the company offered a coordinated, polished response" and added that it may "set a new standard for how airlines deal with crisis."[52] Perhaps even more notable was the response of the marketplace: Southwest's passenger miles and average number of occupied seats increased, and the company's stock price never faltered.[53] In my classes, I show my students Southwest Airlines' stock price over the course of a year, and ask them to guess when the accident took place. They cannot. Try it yourself; Figure 1-5 is the company's stock price chart over the relevant period. Remember that the accident took place in the winter, which in truth does not narrow it down much in Chicago.

Figure 1-5 **Southwest Airlines' Stock Price over the Crisis Period**

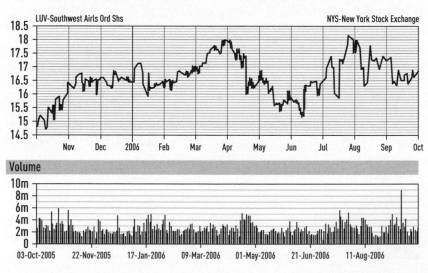

The actual date of the accident? December 8, 2005. As you can see in Figure 1-6, based on the (modest) change in share price and trading volume, it was a nonevent.

Notice that throughout the entire episode, the question of guilt was of little importance. First, fault in this case was difficult to establish.

Figure 1-6 **The Midway Accident**

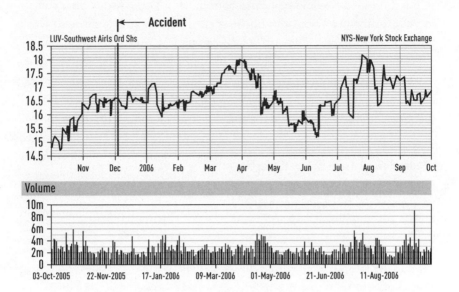

The initial NTSB hearings painted a complex picture, as is typical in airplane crashes. It involved subtle issues of pilot judgment, communication between air traffic control and the pilots, training of airport employees, safety procedures at Southwest, and even forecasting by the National Weather Service. Issued more than two years after the crash, the final report received little media attention, although it ultimately attributed the crash largely to pilot error and training.[54]

Notably, Southwest was very careful not to blame Midway or its lack of extended buffer zones (a consequence of the space constraints of its urban location). The company's relationship with Midway is worth considering in more detail, as it relates to a more general critical difficulty in reputation management. Suppose for the sake of the argument, and (as far as we know) contrary to fact, that the lack of buffer zones had been the real cause of the fatal accident. Should Southwest have changed its crisis response? The answer is no. First, Southwest needed to consider the importance of an ongoing business relationship with Midway. More important, blaming the airport would not have solved any of Southwest's problems, as the next question would have been: "If you had these concerns about the airport, why did you continue to land there? If you did not know, wasn't it your duty to verify that the airport was safe?" In other words, Southwest would be held accountable not only for its own behavior, but for the behavior of its business partners, because it chose to work with them. *Reputational risk extends beyond the legal boundaries of the firm.*

The same issue applies to RC2 in the case of Thomas the Tank Engine. The company, in vain, tried to blame its Chinese contract manufacturer for the problem. This does not work, because customers justifiably ask, "Why did you choose to outsource manufacturing to China in the first place? To save money? Aha—so you are sacrificing the safety of our children for profit!" *Companies can outsource operational, financial, and even (to a large extent) legal risk, but they cannot outsource reputational risk.* This issue is particularly important for companies with strong brand names. If a brand is a promise, customers will feel a sense of betrayal if that promise appears to be broken, even if the actions causing the breach were, strictly speaking, beyond the control of the firm.

> Reputational risk extends beyond the legal boundaries of the firm. It can come from suppliers, customers, or business partners. And you cannot outsource reputational risk.

There are many examples of this phenomenon. Global supply chains are perhaps the most obvious examples, with issues ranging from manufacturing quality and supply chain integrity to privacy and data protection in service outsourcing. Regardless of where the breakdown occurs, the branded company will be held accountable, because it is the one that made the promise that was broken.

A particularly striking example of this phenomenon occurred in the context of the BP oil spill. Although BP owned the well, the Deepwater Horizon rig was owned by Transocean, a contractor that had leased the rig to BP. In its immediate response, BP tried to shift some of the blame to its contractor, without success. CEO Tony Hayward, for example, stated, "The drilling rig was Transocean's drilling rig; it was their equipment that failed, it's their systems, their processors that were running it. . . . We are responsible for the oil and for dealing with it and cleaning the situation up."[55]

The strategy backfired, as the media and the Obama administration criticized the company for trying to evade responsibility. President Obama remarked, "I have to say, though, I did not appreciate what I considered to be a ridiculous spectacle during the congressional hearings into this matter. You had executives of BP and Transocean and

Halliburton falling over each other to point the finger of blame at somebody else."[56]

Similar troubles can originate downstream in the value chain as well. Athletic wear companies suffer when their spokesperson athletes behave badly, as was the case in the recent scandals involving Tiger Woods and Michael Vick. An insurance company's reputation will suffer if its agents use predatory marketing techniques, even though they may be independent contractors, and an accounting firm's reputation may be hurt when its clients commit fraud, even if the fraud was concealed from the auditors. The impact can be substantial. In the case of the Tiger Woods scandal, researchers have estimated a 2 to 4 percent drop in the stock price of Woods's main corporate sponsors.[57]

This insight has important consequences for reputation management for B2B companies. Consider the case of a paper company supplying a well-known brand, such as FedEx or Staples. The paper business faces many environmental challenges, ranging from the issue of sustainable forestry to water pollution. If the business practices of the paper company cause a reputational crisis, it will immediately spill over to the high-profile customer. Indeed, the high-profile customer may be the origin of the crisis in the first place. In the case of Nike's issues with child labor, the better-known brand created a much higher-profile "stage" than the little-known supplier.

From the point of view of the high-profile client, the B2B service provider can increase the client's reputational risk through questionable business practices, or it can provide "reputational insurance" through responsible business practices and excellent relations with regulators and other stakeholders. As an example, consider a privately held data entry company in India that provides data entry services for financial services companies. Now suppose that because of some complicated breakdown in data security (Was it the client? Was it the outsourcing company? Will we ever know?), confidential customer financial data were lost. The reputational risk for the outsourcing company will be much greater if the client is Citigroup than if it is an unknown regional bank, even if all other aspects of the incident are identical. This means that the service provider may inherit much of the reputational risk from the client company, even if the supplier is little known.

Managing reputational risk is particularly difficult when the client is a well-known brand, for the brand will have a strong incentive to sever ties with the offending supplier to protect its own reputation. If the service provider is disproportionately reliant on the large client for revenue, this can even spell the end of the supplier. B2B companies can insure themselves against these risks by monitoring the reputational risk profile of their clients and by aligning their business practices accordingly. For example, International Paper supplies McDonald's, Wal-Mart, Revlon, and Johnson & Johnson and has made a strong commitment to environmentally responsible business practices, making it more attractive for clients with vulnerable reputations.[58]

In sum, while managers naturally focus on the question of guilt during a reputational crisis, this can easily distract the company from focusing on the business challenge of reassuring customers, employees, suppliers, and stakeholders. In many such cases, the question of ultimate responsibility is unknown or unclear at the time when the critical decisions are being made.

> Suppliers inherit the reputational risk of their customers. Suppliers can be reputational assets or liabilities for their clients.

Ironically, this is less difficult in cases where the company recognizes that there was a problem. The most difficult crises are those in which the company believes that it has done nothing wrong, but everyone else thinks it has. Not only must management avoid being distracted by questions of guilt, but it frequently must also overcome internal resistance to its efforts, as a significant portion of the company—especially those with operating responsibility for the product in question—is likely to feel defensive and even victimized. It takes both strong leadership and strategic sophistication to move beyond these understandable but unproductive emotional reactions and adopt a clinical approach that defines the problem for what it is: a crisis of trust.

THE FIRST 24 HOURS

There is a more practical reason why questions of guilt or fault lack relevance during a crisis: there is simply no time to find out. It took the National Transportation Safety Board more than two years to publish its final report, but Southwest had to make its decision within a few hours. This situation is typical. Decision makers are drowning in facts, many of them irrelevant, but they lack the critical information that is needed to get to the bottom of the problem, and all the while a decision has to be made quickly. The fact that time is the most precious resource during a crisis is well known, but why?

There are many causes of extreme time pressure, but in a reputational crisis, everything hinges upon the need to capture the decisive moment: that short time span during which customers and other stakeholders are paying attention. In most cases, this window is no longer than a workday in the relevant news market. Shaped by 24-hour news channels and newspapers, the market's attention quickly moves on to the next item of interest. For example, business-related stories account for roughly 18 percent of the agenda in a typical issue of the *New York Times*, but less than 5 percent of front page coverage. The only times these percentages of coverage converge are the rare instances of major scandals, such as during the peak of the Enron crisis.[59]

This pattern is typical. During a crisis, news coverage increases dramatically during the first hours, only to drop off almost as quickly. Quantitative studies of online news stories suggest that the typical window is only eight(!) hours; 20 percent of all news stories on a given issue are published within an eight-hour period.[60] Only in the rare cases of major crises will the news cycle lengthen.

These dynamics encourage a familiar response from CEOs and other senior executives. The gut reaction of a CEO is often to say to the head of corporate communications: "Get me out of the headlines." This desire for the crisis to end quickly is completely understandable, as crisis situations are extremely stressful and

> The global news cycle has shrunk to eight hours. Companies need to reassure their customers before they know the facts.

carry reputational risks not only for the company, but also for the CEO and his family. However, companies need to realize that "getting out of the headlines" is not the same as resolving a reputational crisis successfully. The speed with which the crisis is ended is far less important than whether customers and other key constituencies remember the company and its management in a positive or negative light. Companies need to realize that in their daily lives, customers rarely pay conscious attention to a company.[61] What should guide decision making, therefore, is taking advantage of these situations to leave a lasting, positive impression in customers' minds, not attempting to end a crisis as quickly as possible. Simply getting out of the headlines quickly is a very bad idea if the last thing customers remember about a company is that it doesn't care about them.

There is an important difference between the dynamics of attention in a corporate crisis and those in a political crisis, and awareness of these differences is crucial for CEOs and board members. Many crisis management professionals and advisors come from the world of politics and, naturally, apply the instincts and frameworks developed there to the corporate world.[62]

A common tactic for surviving a political crisis is to wait it out.[63] After all, media attention will soon move to a different topic, and one can hope that by Election Day, voters will have long forgotten about this particular incident. Even major crises may fail to make a lasting impact on subsequent elections. I was struck by this in 2004, when two major crises dominated the headlines.

In April, members of the 372nd Military Police Company along with members of other U.S. agencies were charged with the physical, psychological, and sexual abuse of prisoners held at the Abu Ghraib prison in Iraq.[64] Pictures of U.S. personnel demeaning prisoners and committing acts of torture were widely circulated on the Internet and through news channels such as *60 Minutes* and *The New Yorker*.

A few months later, the insurance brokerage industry faced the biggest crisis in its history when then New York Attorney General Eliot Spitzer charged Marsh & McLennan with steering clients to insurers with which it had commission agreements. The charges also stated that the lead brokers had tried to arrange rigged bids for insurance contracts from those insurers. The charges resulted in the ousting not only of Marsh CEO Jeffrey Greenberg, but also of his father, insurance industry legend Maurice "Hank" Greenberg, who had led AIG for 37 years and had transformed it into the world's largest insurance and financial services corporation. Moreover, business practices in the industry changed forever, with significantly higher restrictions on the acceptance of so-called contingent commissions and greater disclosure requirements concerning how brokers are compensated.[65]

What about Abu Ghraib? Two congressional hearings were held, in January and September of 2005, respectively. Eleven soldiers were court-martialed and faced charges of dereliction of duty, along with various other charges. Some of the soldiers received prison sentences, but none of the officers were convicted. Most important—and in sharp contrast to the insurance brokerage scandal—there were no resignations among the political leaders. A similar incident would almost certainly have cost the CEO of a corporation his job. Imagine for a moment a corporation in the prison management business that was confronted with similar pictures; no CEO could have survived such a scandal, but Abu Ghraib played hardly any role in the subsequent U.S. presidential campaign, and it was never mentioned during the candidate debates between President Bush and Democratic challenger John Kerry.

"Waiting things out" works in politics for many reasons. Voters cast ballots only every few years, they have few choices (frequently there are only two major competitors who split the market for votes), and vote decisions are driven by many considerations, including expectations about future policies and conduct. In this choice process, even a significant crisis is only one factor among many, and

> Corporate and political crises follow different rules. Customers rarely pay attention to companies, but if they do, it matters. Getting out of the headlines is a good thing only if the last impression is positive.

is perhaps only dimly remembered by voters when they are casting their ballots. More important, this approach works so well because the public pays *constant* attention to politicians, attention that increases in intensity during a campaign. Since one story quickly follows another, any particular story is less likely to take firm root in the public's imagination. This approach *does not work* in the corporate context, because customers rarely pay the same sustained attention to a company. When they do, however, they do so with heightened focus, so the impact on the company's reputation can be profound and permanent.

There is a final reason why speed matters. We mentioned earlier that failing to respond to a crisis is interpreted as having something to hide and reinforces a perception of guilt, violating our expectation of transparency. Various experiments have shown that speed takes on even greater importance in highly charged ethical decision contexts. Subjects in experiments judge decision makers as increasingly less moral the longer the decision maker takes to decide. In effect, mere consideration of acts that are perceived to be unethical leads to moral outrage, even when the decision maker ultimately makes the "right" moral decision.[66]

The need for speed creates a serious quandary. On the one hand, a slow response by itself will lead to negative impressions. On the other hand, it is impossible to obtain even a general overview of the situation in 24 hours, let alone in 8. Managers will be dealing with information overload even while truly critical facts remain unknown. Recall that in the Southwest Airlines crash, it took more than two years to finish the final report on the incident.

What is a manager to do? The key to solving this dilemma is counterintuitive: do not focus on finding a solution, because you won't find it. Instead, focus on creating a trusted process for getting to a solution, as Southwest Airlines did. Reputational crises are almost always about trust, so the goal during the first few hours should be to reassure customers and other constituencies in order to maintain and enhance trust in an environment of fear and skepticism. Delaying will decrease the company's perceived transparency, empathy, and commitment, eroding trust very quickly. Management assessments of the situation that later turn out to be false will do the same, prompting perceptions of incompetence. CEO Tony Hayward's early claims that the environmental impact of the spill would be modest quickly undermined trust in BP.[67] Conversely, maintaining trust will give companies much-needed room to maneuver, which is possibly the most important goal during the first 24 hours.

CRISIS LEADERSHIP

This chapter has outlined an approach to managing reputational crises. It has identified the importance of capturing the decisive moment that will shape the perception of the relevant audiences. We have developed an approach that is focused on maintaining and enhancing trust, the most important task during a reputational crisis. We have also seen many examples proving that these strategies are frequently not adopted. Why? If these approaches work, why aren't corporate leaders using them?

We can identify three possible reasons for that. The first reason is based on a mistaken belief. CEOs

> Executives operate under the mistaken belief that the public trusts them. But CEOs are among the least trusted professions, just barely ahead of used-car dealers and politicians.

may systematically overestimate the trust reservoir that they have with the general public. Recall the shockingly low trust scores for various industries from the Harris Interactive poll cited in the Preface. This holds not only for companies, but also for senior executives as compared to other professions. In a recent Gallup survey, CEOs were ranked among the least trusted professions, roughly at the same level as lawyers and stockbrokers, and only slightly above used-car salesmen, the least trusted profession. To put this in context, 84 percent of the surveyed respondents trusted nurses (the most trusted profession), while only 12 percent trusted executives, and only 7 percent trusted used-car salesmen.[68]

In spite of that distrust, CEOs act as if they can depend on a substantially larger reservoir of public trust than they actually have. This may stem in part from living in an environment that is rich in positive feedback not only from staff members and colleagues, but also (if the company performs well) from customers, suppliers, and investors. In a reputational crisis, however, more skeptical audiences are involved, and they are far more reluctant to bestow praise upon these same CEOs. In my advisory work, I am always astonished at the genuine surprise and hurt that CEOs express in response to hostile media coverage. It simply does not square with their self-image.

Unfortunately, the factors that drive self-perception and those that shape the perception of others—the relevant category in reputation management—are very different. In general, people are more likely to attend to negative information than to positive information. They find it difficult to withhold judgment, even when they are faced with contradictory and incomplete evidence, and they weigh negative information more heavily than positive information when they are forming opinions of others.[69]

Complex explanations of perceived wrongdoing are thus unlikely to gain traction with your audience. The deck is particularly stacked against companies that are intrinsically for-profit entities. Even in cases of socially responsible actions, many will still suspect for-profit companies of harboring self-interested motives for engaging in prosocial acts—for example, making large charitable donations to obtain a good reputation or tax benefits rather than because of a genuine desire to help. These biases probably contribute to the fact that corporations are among the least trusted groups in the United States. A 2010 Harris poll revealed that only 15 percent of Americans said that they had "a great deal of confidence" in the people in charge of running major companies, while 27 percent claimed to have "hardly any." Only 49 percent of those surveyed reported having a positive image of "big business."[70]

During reputational crises, leaders must be cognizant of these biases. Incorporating them into decision making requires a high level of strategic sophistication—here, the ability to view a familiar situation from the point of view of a usually less knowledgeable, more suspicious audience. These factors may explain why companies struggle more with a crisis when the company believes that it has done nothing wrong, while everybody else believes that it has done something, as in the earlier example of Goldman Sachs. Overcoming this sense of victimization creates an additional obstacle, one that is not faced when a company immediately senses its own culpability.

The second factor is emotional. Reputational crises are extremely stressful events, and in such situations, our field of vision tends to narrow. Evolutionary development has equipped us with mechanisms that both grab and direct our attention in times of danger or stress. At the same time that the speed of processing for *non*-threat-related stimuli decreases, the processing speed of threat-related stimuli actually increases, effectively consuming the vast majority of our attentional resources.

The capacity to process multiple things at once, however, tends to suffer during periods of high stress. Think of how easy it is to drive in your neighborhood while listening to the radio or to someone chatting in the backseat, but how difficult multitasking becomes when you are trying to find a new building in an unfamiliar neighborhood, or you are on a busy street during rush hour. In the latter situation, if you're like most people, the radio gets turned down, the cell phone conversation is ended, and backseat riders are silenced. Dividing our attention draws excessively on our cognitive resources. Optimal processing occurs when we can focus our resources on the source of threat or stress.[71]

Focus in times of stress is undoubtedly desirable and has provided an advantage in many contexts encountered during human evolution. However, in some situations, a tighter focus may be suboptimal. This is well known in group interactions under severe time constraints, a situation that is typically encountered by crisis teams. In such settings, groups often focus on a smaller range of task-relevant cues at the expense of considering other alternatives, which may undermine the quality of the decision arrived at by the group.[72] Group consensus becomes a premium for members, which can also lead to pressure on dissenters and the suppression of contradictory (but potentially useful) information. This stands in contrast to situations without lingering time constraints, in which groups are more likely to reach a creative, well-thought-out decision, without one dominant individual deciding alone.

> Stress narrows our field of vision. The desire to "duck and cover" is natural, but it needs to be actively resisted.

In the leadership context, this typically means that leaders fall back into their comfort zone, usually their area of expertise. Crises are typically experienced as a loss of control, so sticking to one's area of expertise reestablishes the sense of control. After all, expertise means that the expert knows more about an area than the general public. But, as we saw in the context of the Trust Radar, expertise is only one of the factors that build trust. By focusing on expertise alone, the leader is likely to find herself in a worse position tomorrow than she is in today.

Resisting this pull requires emotional fortitude, especially in a context in which the leader's advisors are being driven by the same emotional factors. During a reputational crisis, the leader's mindset needs to broaden, not narrow. The evidence suggests that few leaders are capable of this.

The third factor is institutional. Imagine Southwest's CEO in a meeting with his executive team in which he expressed his wish to visit the family that had lost its boy in the airplane crash. We don't know what happened in the Southwest Airlines meeting, but the typical scenario would have the company's general counsel strongly voicing reservations about this decision. After all, an apology can always be interpreted as an admission of guilt, which could increase the company's legal liability. General counsels will often recommend saying nothing, or as little as possible, as the prudent course of action.

All too often, the discussion ends there. The CEO will simply defer to the general counsel, who handles the crisis henceforth. We have seen earlier that "saying nothing," while tempting, not only undermines trust in the company, but affects people's evaluation of the company's logo, products, and brand. Companies are perceived as being guilty until proven innocent. In other words, a "no comment" comes at the significant cost of undermining trust in the company.

A CEO needs to balance many risks, but in a reputational crisis, two of these are usually particularly at odds: legal and brand risk. To make this clear, remember that the Southwest brand stands not only for "low-cost fares" (in the sense of good value for money, not low quality) and "operational excellence," but also for "friendly" and "fun." The message is that customers will be treated as people, not as bar codes. Suppose for a moment that Southwest had chosen a defensive or "no comment" position. This would have damaged the brand that the company had worked so hard to build over the previous four decades. From this perspective, the increased legal risk seems like a minor concern.

In some cases, of course, the legal risk will clearly dominate, possibly making a "no comment" response entirely appropriate. Crises involving financial reporting sometimes have this characteristic, as any acknowledgment may lead to a tidal wave of shareholder lawsuits. Therefore, the general counsel should always play an important role during a reputational crisis. The problem, rather, lies in the CEO's mindlessly abdicating his responsibility to the legal department. In other words, good crisis management teams have a strong, opinionated general counsel, while poor crisis management teams are run by the general counsel. Crisis management is a management responsibility, while the job of the legal counsel is to minimize the legal risk.

Despite the overlap between the two, crisis management should never be delegated entirely to the legal team. The CEO must weigh the various risks (customers, competitive, financial, and legal) and then make the decision. Of course, in a real decision, these risks will never be neatly identified or quantified, but a decision must nevertheless be made. Simply handing the problem over to Legal is not a decision; it's avoidance. The final irony of this common but ineffective approach is that many general counsels resent this shift of decision-making authority. Good counsels recognize that a decision that focuses predominantly on the legal risk is likely to be skewed, and will lack the tight integration with business strategy that is the hallmark of good crisis management.

There is another problem with the "legal risk first" approach. It may be based on a false premise: the belief that showing empathy with a victim or apologizing necessarily increases legal risk. There is surprisingly little evidence for this belief.[73]

THE DECISIVE MOMENT AND HOW TO MISS IT   49

One area in which this issue has been studied extensively is the area of medical malpractice. Contrary to common belief, physicians that maintain an authentic relationship with patients and their families based on empathy are much less likely to be sued,

> Management of a reputational crisis should never be delegated to the corporate counsel. Crisis leadership is a senior management responsibility. Good reputation management teams have a strong corporate counsel; bad ones are run by the corporate counsel.

and when they are sued, their settlements are lower on average. As a consequence, many hospital systems—including Harvard Medical School and the University of Michigan Health System—now encourage their physicians to maintain an affective bond with the patients and their families.[74] These policies originated not from some abstract desire for better patient management, but from the data-based calculations of risk managers, who simply realized that they could reduce risk by switching from a legalistic to a trust-based approach.

This section is entitled "Crisis Leadership." You will now appreciate why. Effective, tested approaches need to be implemented by people who find themselves in highly charged emotional situations. This is one of the many intersections between the people process and the reputation management process. Leaders may delay a response by waiting for more data, may wish to move the decision making to functional experts and external advisors, and most important, with all the bullets flying, may forget the source of their company's success: the trust of its customers. They must still exercise leadership along cognitive, emotional, and moral dimensions, or, more succinctly, logos-pathos-ethos. These dimensions are always important, but in a reputational crisis, they become essential.

LESSONS THAT THOMAS CAN TEACH

RC2 did not capture its decisive moment. The company's initial response was evasive and focused largely on the culpability of its suppliers. It failed to reassure customers and did not utilize the four factors of trust. Moreover, RC2 handled the actual mechanics of the recall poorly. When angry parents demanded refunds, the company instructed owners of the tainted products to mail them to the company, at which point the company would send a replacement Thomas, as well as separately mailed reimbursement of the estimated shipping costs and a "free gift"—the Toad vehicle.[75]

The story did not end there. Two months after RC2's first recall, the company initiated another recall of five new toys that were possibly contaminated with lead paint. The list of recalled products included the all-black cargo car, the olive-green Sodor cargo box, the all-green maple tree top, signal base accessories . . . and the Toad vehicle, the free gift from the first recall! The company issued an apology to previous recall participants, along with instructions on how to return the potentially contaminated Toad vehicle. Having learned its lesson from the first recall, this time RC2 sent prepaid shipping labels to each customer.

RC2 was savaged in the media. A quick scan of business pages found headlines like "Thomas the Poisonous Tank Engine Recall Fallout Continues" and "Engine of Destruction: Lessons from the Thomas the Tank Engine Debacle." Soon after, a Seattle-based law firm filed a class-action lawsuit against RC2 on behalf of Illinois mother Channing Hesse, who had bought seven recalled toys.

In January of 2008, RC2 agreed to settle a class-action lawsuit for $30 million. The terms of the settlement ordered the company to provide, at the customer's request, either replacement toys or cash reimbursements, along with a bonus toy and an agreement to implement new safety standards. RC2 subsequently adopted new policies to improve its safety systems: the Multi-Check Safety System, which provided for more rigorous testing of incoming products and adopted a zero tolerance policy for contaminations.[76]

RC2 has yet to recover from the Thomas crisis. RC2's stock price, which had reached an all-time high in June 2007, now hovers at around one-third of its precrisis value. Immediately following the crisis, the company lost 33 percent of its value in just a few weeks. Currently, the company faces new troubles, as its license to produce all the Thomas and Friends railway products other than those pertaining to the wooden track system expired in the first quarter of 2010. RC2 faces the potential loss of the remaining Thomas and Friends line in 2012. In the meantime HIT Entertainment, which owns the Thomas brand, has reached a deal with competitor Mattel to license the Thomas image and take it in a new direction.[77]

THINGS TO REMEMBER

Heart attacks can teach us to take better care of our health. Crises can teach a business to take better care of its reputation. Understanding reputational crises is important for two reasons. First, a company's conduct during a crisis will have a major impact on that company's reputation. Second, understanding the forces that drive reputational crises provides the right perspective for managing reputational equity proactively and strategically. Here are some of the main lessons to take to the next chapters.

- Reputational crises are a time when companies must act to protect their reputational equity. But too often, crises are conceptualized only as threats and dangers. This leads executives to focus exclusively on damage control and miss the opportunity to improve the company's reputation.

- Reputational crises are best seen as decisive moments, turning points for better or worse. How a company handles such a decisive moment will have a lasting impact on its reputation.

- During a crisis, companies are on stage. Everything they do is highlighted, and people are paying attention. But when people are paying attention, they remember, sometimes for a very long time.

- The global news cycle has shrunk dramatically. Companies need to act before they know all the facts; if they do not, they will miss the decisive moment. Getting out of the headlines is a good idea only if the last impression is positive.

- Building and maintaining trust is the most important task during a reputational crisis. Questions of guilt are secondary. Corporations and CEOs frequently have no trust reservoir to draw upon. Trust must be earned through decisive action.

- The Trust Radar identifies the four major factors that restore trust: transparency, expertise, commitment, and empathy. Executives tend to focus only on expertise. This narrowing of focus is typical and predictable, but it is not effective.

- Managing a reputational crisis is the responsibility of business leaders, not legal or public relations experts. These specialists can play a critical role in a crisis team, but responsibility should not be delegated to them. The focus always needs to be on the business issue at stake, not just the legal or technical dimensions.

Decisive moments can be missed, resulting in reputational damage. In the next chapter, we will discuss how reputations can be rebuilt. That requires a keen understanding of how public perception is shaped.

CHAPTER 2

MERCEDES AND THE MOOSE

Brand Management beyond Customers

"8. We got a nice thank you from the Toyota people."

—"Top 10 Things Overheard at BP Headquarters"
from *The Late Show with David Letterman*,
May 5, 2010[1]

A TOAST IN TOKYO

I t was the best of times. On October 21, 1997, Daimler-Benz AG's top management congregated at the Tokyo Auto Show to raise a toast.[2] They had a lot to celebrate. Over many years, Daimler's Mercedes division had delivered consistent profits as one of the world's iconic luxury brands. During the mid-1990s, Mercedes led the European luxury market with about 25 percent market share, followed by BMW and Audi. In addition, Daimler had announced the introduction of two new brands, the ultra-luxury Maybach and the hip, urban Smart Car, the product of a joint venture between Daimler and the Swiss watchmaker Swatch. Perhaps most important, just three days previously, its Mercedes brand had successfully completed what was arguably the most audacious strategic gamble in its history: the introduction of the A-Class.

The product development process had lasted almost four years, and Mercedes had refurbished a production plant exclusively for the A-Class, bringing the total development and production costs to an estimated $1.4 billion. Mercedes also had run an 18-month, $115 million marketing campaign, with extensive ad placements and a series of special public events in 19 European cities called the "A-Motion Tour," which attracted more than a half million Europeans.

The creation of the A-Class represented a huge strategic gamble for Mercedes. It was originally conceptualized as a response to what Mercedes perceived as the primary strategic shifts in the car industry: the increased importance of economies of scale and scope, driven by globalization and technologies. In addition, Mercedes was starting to feel pressure from competitors, who were driving down the margins of the luxury car segment with aggressive pricing. Daimler's head of car operations, Jürgen Hubbert, claimed, "We were in danger of falling into a positioning trap. If we had been content with the small number of sales for the S-class (49,996 in 1996), we would end up in the same corner as Rolls-Royce—an existential crisis for the corporation."

Mercedes's solution to this conundrum was the A-Class, which was intended to attract a new customer segment: younger drivers, especially women and young families. Mercedes expected that 80 to 90 percent of A-Class customers would be new to the franchise, and that 50 percent of them would be women, compared to 10 to 20 percent of existing customers. The key was Mercedes's belief that the strong brand loyalty of its present customers would extend to these new customers, leading them to trade up to higher-margin products over their lifetime: from the A-Class to the C-Class and E-Class, and possibly even to the S-Class. The automobile industry generally believed that customer acquisition cost six times more than customer retention. In other words, the A-Class, as the name makes plain, was designed and marketed as an entry-level car. Completing the portfolio with a smaller car would also help Mercedes meet companywide environmental regulations and better position it in various emerging countries in Asia and Latin America.

Mercedes wanted to offer a product "with the size of a small car, the space of a middle-market limousine, the security of a middle-market car, and the versatility of a van, all supported by the renowned Mercedes quality." From a practical point of view, the car had to be affordable and compact for use as a "city car," since much of the target customer segment lived or shopped in urban environments. To appeal to this new customer segment, Mercedes downplayed certain aspects that were typically associated with the brand—like luxury and prestige—and instead emphasized innovation, future orientation, and an urban lifestyle, with themes like "Drive the future of the automobile," and "We believe in the next generation." Some advertisements featured drawings of A-Class cars by young children. All in all, the campaign represented a radical departure from typical Mercedes advertising, which usually focused on luxury, prestige, technology, and safety.

This down-market strategy had obvious risks. To make the car affordable for its intended customer segment, the A-Class had to be priced under $20,000 without compromising Mercedes's core values of quality, safety, and innovative technology. Any customer perceptions of such a compromise—factual or otherwise—would undermine the Mercedes brand as a whole, not just the A-Class product. To deal with these challenges, Mercedes adopted a new design and manufacturing process, reducing development time from the usual 59 months to 47 through the extensive use of computer simulations as a complement to real-conditions driving tests.

The development process included several innovations, such as the "sandwich concept," which was Mercedes's solution to the typical safety problems associated with compact cars. In frontal-impact crashes, the lack of a sufficient crumpling zone in compact cars can lead to severe injuries to the driver and the passengers. The sandwich concept was a computer-generated process that caused the engine to collapse and slide under the driver's and passenger's seats in the event of a frontal crash, minimizing their injuries. For this concept to work, the new design required a higher seating position—comparable to that of a minivan—and a slightly elevated center of gravity.

The car was an instant success. According to surveys, 86 percent of Germans had heard about the A-Class, creating the product awareness necessary for a successful launch. With rave reviews in the European motor press and preorders approaching 100,000, Mercedes management looked forward to toasting the "Baby Benz" as its crowning victory.

Suddenly, disaster struck. During the Tokyo Auto Show, Mercedes executives received an urgent phone call. Earlier that day, Swedish journalist Robert Collin had used an A-Class vehicle in a so-called Moose Test,[3] which consists of a rapid lane change within a specific distance at an approximate speed of 65 kilometers per hour without braking. This swerve and then return to the original lane of travel simulates the avoidance of an obstacle that appears suddenly, such as a moose wandering into the road. Moose accidents are a frequent cause of highway fatalities in countries such as Sweden, Finland, and Canada.[4]

In Collin's test, the A-Class had rolled over, causing a minor injury to one of the passengers. Although the Moose Test was not required for vehicle certification in any European country, similar tests were compulsory, including various avoidance maneuvers that permitted braking; the A-Class had passed all of these mandatory tests. However, on September 23, 1997, an A-Class test car had lifted two wheels from the ground in a different driving test. Despite numerous attempts, the Mercedes experts had been unable to reproduce the same test results, and concluded that the A-Class design was sound.

Collin included a report of the rollover in a review for the Swedish car and technology magazine *Teknikens Värld* ("World of Technology"). Because of the enormous buzz surrounding the launch of the A-Class, news of the rollover spread rapidly through major European newspapers, forcing Daimler's management to make a rapid decision.

In Chapter 1, we discussed how to manage a reputational crisis. One of the main lessons is that leaders need to focus on the main business problem and not get sidetracked by the overwhelming complexity of the challenge. In reputational crises, the business problem typically consists of retaining and reassuring customers and other stakeholders.

Done right, this can actually increase trust, a reputational asset that can be leveraged for other business purposes. With its key elements of expertise, commitment, transparency, and empathy, the Trust Radar can help companies capture these opportunities. However, things do not always go as planned.

Minutes after Mercedes's management had first received the information regarding the Moose Test, Mercedes's head of public relations, Wolfgang Inhester, made a first statement to waiting journalists in Tokyo. "At this point we do not know any of the details," Inhester said. "The management board cannot give a statement just because somewhere a car flipped over. Otherwise, we would have to comment on everything. Once we know more, we will be happy to comment on the incident." The German newspaper *Die Welt* later summarized the statement as, "The management board does not see the necessity to give a statement just because a car flipped over somewhere." In response to journalists in Tokyo, the head of the Mercedes passenger car division subsequently stated that "based on the available data, it would be brain-dead to stop the production of the A-Class at the present time."

On October 23, 1997, two days later, Mercedes headquarters released an official statement announcing that "the company believes that the incident in Sweden was due to extreme driving conditions that pushed the laws of physics. Experts from our product development teams have been sent to Sweden to conduct a detailed analysis of the incident." Mercedes also suggested that faulty or the wrong type of tires had been used in the test.

Mercedes based its reaction on its belief that the Moose Test was flawed. The test was not standardized, and Mercedes engineers suspected that almost any car would fail the test under the conditions that prevailed: a heavily loaded vehicle, a very sticky surface (airbase asphalt), an unrealistic situation (avoiding objects without braking, an unnatural reaction for all but specially trained drivers), and a demanding steering wheel rotational speed obtained only by professional drivers, who cross their arms to improve rotational speed. Mercedes also speculated that the Moose Test failure could be attributed to the tires supplied by Goodyear. Because the tires were believed to be too "sticky" in terms of grip to the road, they might have led to sliding when friction was suddenly lost. The tires were designed to be especially soft to enhance driving comfort, but in extreme steering situations, this softness could lead the rim to touch the road briefly, causing the car to tilt. Goodyear, however, stated that it had supplied the tires precisely to Mercedes's specifications, and could thus be expected to contest a tire-based explanation.

The response from Mercedes represents a classic version of the expertise focus discussed in the previous chapter. The company offered little transparency with its initial "no comment" statement, and correspondingly little commitment or empathy. Instead, it focused entirely on the technological aspects of the incident. In its statements, we hear a lot of confidence in the quality of the car—even some arrogance.

The public reaction was predictably negative. Various journalists interpreted the "pushing the laws of physics" comment as a challenge and attempted to replicate the Moose Test. While the A-Class passed most of these tests without difficulty, it did fail some of them. For example, the mass publication *Auto-Bild* conducted a test in which the A-Class vehicle rolled over onto its roof. Not until a few days after the result had been widely reported in the press did it become known that *Auto-Bild* had inadvertently used the wrong kind of tires. The German media began publishing jokes and cartoons that mocked both the Moose Test and Mercedes.

Because of existing contracts, Mercedes ads continued to run in German movie theaters, a common form of advertising for new cars and other consumer products in Germany. Whenever the ad slogan "We believe in the next generation" appeared, the audience burst out laughing. During this period, Daimler's stock fell from $77.18 on October 15 to $68.50 on October 27, a drop of more than 11 percent.

BEYOND CUSTOMERS

Mercedes missed its decisive moment; rather than quickly rebuilding trust, it worsened the crisis. The company came across as arrogant and lacking in empathy, and the last thing customers remembered about the Moose Test was the image of a flipped A-Class. The Mercedes case provides a nice insight into how easily this can happen. After all, the company did examine the issue quickly and truthfully report what it found: there was no problem with the car, but instead the test was flawed. We now appreciate that this is insufficient. Companies need to connect with their customers and the public on dimensions besides expertise, including empathy, commitment, and transparency. Note that this is a situation in which the company felt that it had done nothing wrong, but everybody else disagreed. This can lead to both defensiveness and a lack of internal alignment, as internal constituencies (e.g., Mercedes engineers who believed that they were receiving unfair blame for producing an unsafe automobile) may push back if the company takes a more conciliatory approach.

Mercedes had lost control over its most precious asset—its brand—but how could the company regain that control? Typical solutions were unlikely to work. An advertising campaign would have lacked credibility. Mercedes's credibility had been severely undermined by the combination of its initial "limits of physics" statement with pictures of a flipped-over A-Class. Any suggestions that these tests might have been as flawed as the original Moose Test disappeared in the media storm. Letters to customers or other direct forms of communication might have proved more persuasive, but they would have reached only existing customers, a trivial number compared to the potential customers who had been unsettled by the media coverage.

Finally, educating the media would have been a difficult, thankless task. After a few weeks, the story had lost its urgency, and its technical complexity made it unlikely to capture the attention of media outlets. Even a highly engaged effort might have reached only a small subsegment of the many news outlets.

The strategic challenge was significantly more severe, as Mercedes had to reestablish control over its brand and restore customer trust, not only in the A-Class, but in the Mercedes brand as a whole. In other words, to rescue the A-Class, Mercedes had to shift public perception from negative to positive. It had to do right by its customers, and it had to get credit for doing so! This required a radical strategic shift. The key insight is that Mercedes's relationship with its customers was no longer bilateral. When we think of brand management, we usually think of it as a relationship between the firm and its customers. In

> When companies lose control over their brand, typical solutions, such as advertising campaigns or letters to customers, are not enough. Customers are more likely to be influenced by the media and third parties. This requires a strategy that is consistent with the incentives and capabilities of such third parties.

a reputational crisis, however, media influence will play an important role, with customers receiving news and editorials not just from the company, but from third parties. This mix of information and opinions shapes consumer attitudes toward the company. We are moving from one channel of influence to many, most of which the company cannot control.

We can hardly overstate the importance of this point. Most practicing managers still believe that a good reputation is a consequence of consistently delivering high-quality goods and services to their customers—essentially, that reputation is based on actual experience with the company. This approach may have worked a decade ago, but it no longer applies. I would guess that most of the readers of this sentence are not clients of Goldman Sachs, but that they still have an opinion about the company and its business practices. Similarly, the biggest problem for McDonald's reputation is not that Mom and her daughter had a bad experience at a McDonald's restaurant when a server was rude. The biggest problem is that on her way to work, Mom may have heard on the radio that French fries may increase the risk of breast cancer.[5] Reputation is public opinion applied to companies, opinion that may or may not be based on actual experience. Therefore, focusing on experience and other direct channels will be insufficient for protecting or rebuilding reputations. This insight is captured in Figure 2-1.

Figure 2-1 **Beyond Customers**

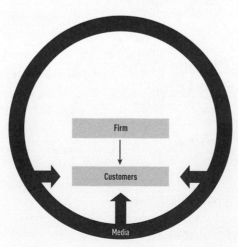

Figure 2-1 emphasizes the importance of indirect, uncontrolled channels. These can consist of the media (including social media) or peer-to-peer influence.[6] How do we navigate this treacherous environment?

REPUTATIONAL TERRAIN

In his classic treatment on military strategy *The Art of War*, Sun Tzu includes a magnificent chapter on the importance of terrain. He distinguishes different forms of terrain and develops suitable strategies for each one, with an overall lesson that the strategy must fit the terrain, and if terrain conflicts with strategy, terrain wins. We will adopt the same approach to understanding the media. The first and most important insight is that the media are not a single entity. Media coverage comes in many shapes and forms; it creates a media landscape with different segments, which gives rise to *Reputational Terrain*. Our first goal is to orient ourselves in this terrain, and our second goal is to develop strategies that fit the terrain.

David Baron's theory of the media provides a useful tool that we will adapt for our purposes.[7] News coverage is largely driven by two forces: (audience) *interest* and (societal) *importance*. The consumer of news determines audience interest, which drives the amount and likelihood of coverage. Societal importance shapes an issue's coverage: whether it is purely factual or includes commentary and advocacy. Producers of news make this determination as journalists and editors. It follows that various outlets will differ on what they consider important. A story that is important to a mass-market broadsheet like the British daily the *Sun* may be irrelevant to the *Wall Street Journal*. This should not be confused with *media bias*, which reflects a particular political ideology. Rather, it incorporates the editorial decisions on what to cover, how to write, what to put on page one, what to cover in the back of the paper, and so forth. Explicit or implicit political bias would shape these decisions, of course, but we should recognize that not everything that happens can be printed or covered, and so selection (and thus a judgment on what is important) takes place even when a media outlet scrupulously tries to avoid any slant. This is simply a consequence of managing limited publishing space and prominence of placement.

> News coverage is largely driven by audience interest and societal importance. Issues will fall into different regions along these dimensions. Communication strategies need to fit this Reputational Terrain.

By *advocacy*, we do not mean only editorials or other forms of direct commentary; we also include articles that quote experts who may be highly critical of a company. In other words, from a customer's point of view, it makes little difference whether criticism of Mercedes comes from a *Financial Times* editorial or a safety expert who is quoted in the paper. Both examples make a negative impact on the customer's mind. In fact, the opinion of the quoted expert may make a far greater impression, because it has higher credibility. Within the professional code of newspapers, the distinction between editorial comment and news coverage is critical, but customers do not necessarily make the same distinction, and therefore both can be equally damning.

Figure 2-2 uses these two dimensions to map out Reputational Terrain.

Figure 2-2 **Reputational Terrain—Coverage**

Let us take a tour of this Reputational Terrain. In the low-interest/ low-importance quadrant (the lower left in Figure 2.2), much of the coverage is purely factual, typically provided by wire services or appearing on the back pages of the business press. In this segment, a company's appropriate strategies include clarifying facts and pointing out inaccuracies. For example, a company can clarify an erroneous story about a planned bond offering with a simple press release. Most companies spend almost all of their lives in this area.

As audience interest increases, we move toward live coverage, such as on cable news. In many cases, this type of coverage is still factual, but it is now also visual, ongoing, and combined with extensive commentary. Take hurricane coverage as an example; the typical news channel will place a reporter or anchor on the scene (an "embedded" reporter) to comment live on the events as they unfold. Much of the coverage has little content and sometimes states the obvious (e.g., describing the weather as we see it in the background), but it is frequently emotionally engaging and can have a breathless quality.

Most companies will never find themselves in this quadrant. Rare exceptions include industries with large audiences, such as entertainment and sports, or some rare moments of high drama like the fall 2010 rescue of the Chilean miners. For a few organizations, this quadrant is typical. The Federal Bureau of Investigation (FBI) is one such example. The FBI is constantly located in a space of high audience interest, not only because it appears in a never-ending supply of TV shows and movies, but also because it is reinforced by live coverage of a hunt for a serial killer and other such high-profile investigations. For an organization located in this region, the main peril is not a sudden jump in audience interest (the characteristic risk for companies that spend most of their lives with far less attention) but the unexpected introduction of an issue that is of social relevance into an environment that already has high audience interest. In the case of the FBI, this could be a concern over privacy or civil rights in the context of an investigation.

Celebrity athletes also present classic examples of these dynamics. Star athletes constantly face major media scrutiny, but that interest is usually relegated to the sports or gossip pages. Only in certain cases does it become front-page news, as when an event in the life of a celebrity touches on a broad issue of social significance. In the dogfighting scandal involving NFL quarterback Michael Vick, the issue was cruelty to animals, while issues of morality, marriage, and the ever-present question of whether star athletes are held to a different ethical standard amplified coverage of Tiger Woods's divorce. Woods is a particularly interesting case study, as his "brand"—with its core elements of excellence and perfection—had transcended the typical sports market, attracting not just the usual athletic sponsors like Nike or Gatorade, but also the consulting firm Accenture and telecom provider AT&T. These nontraditional sponsors dropped Woods first as news of his infidelities surfaced, while Nike (as of the writing of this book) stood by his side.

In the low-interest/high-importance quadrant (upper left), we deal with sophisticated, in-depth coverage intended to convey the complexity of an issue and explore its various dimensions. The trade press and certain high-quality publications such as *The Economist* fall into this category, and they typically enjoy small audiences. *The Economist* has a North American circulation of just over 820,000 self-selected, sophisticated readers who want news coverage that goes beyond the obvious.[8] Its news coverage features detailed discussions, figures, tables, and even references to academic papers. Analysis and interpretation rule this region, and companies can shape the discussion by providing strong supporting data and constructively engaging in a debate among experts.

As audience interest increases, we move toward a mass audience, and from print to TV. In the high-interest/high-importance area, we find hard-hitting TV news programs that address controversial social issues in a format that is attractive to a mass audience. The U.S. television show *60 Minutes*, with an average of 14 million viewers, is the archetype of this format.[9] It focuses on drama, compelling individuals, easily understood moral conflicts depicting good versus evil, and testimony, rather than data. During football season, the show immediately follows six hours of NFL coverage, but it has remained on the air for over 40 years. To attract a large audience, mass-market TV shows must be highly visual, easy to understand, and gripping, which they accomplish by telling a good story. By focusing on individual cases and how these individuals are affected by an issue, *60 Minutes* builds dramatic tension around a few key characters, often including a victim, a villain, and a hero.

Although companies may perceive themselves as the victims of hostile media coverage, the general public rarely shares this perception. Companies are not typically the object of empathy, even when they lose a lot of money or their stock prices drop dramatically. The public does not feel sorry for powerful organizations, especially when they are perceived as wealthy and profit-motivated. Of course, the public may empathize with individual workers who have lost their jobs, but the emotional reaction does not easily carry over to the company as a whole. The same is true of shareholders who are perceived as wealthy, greedy, and anonymous; losing an investment does not elicit the same amount of sympathy as being the victim of fraud. The public's unwillingness to accept companies as victims implies that companies have only two available roles: hero or villain, differentiated by their relationship to the victim. Heroes act on behalf of and in the interest of the victim, while villains work at cross-purposes.

Complicated arguments like the statistical properties of effective safety technologies are very difficult to convey quickly and coherently to an audience that is not prepared for them, so approaches that focus solely on technical or legal aspects will almost always fail. A company that responds to an injured child by referring to its exemplary safety record is perceived as uncaring, even monstrous. Instead, the company must tell a compelling, credible story that can stand up to images that have direct emotional impact. Appropriate strategies first express direct and personal empathy for the victim, and then commit the company to getting to the bottom of the problem.

We can summarize effective strategies in Figure 2-3.

Despite its apparent simplicity, the Reputational Terrain is a very versatile tool.

You may recall from the previous chapter that one of the defining characteristics of a reputational crisis is that people are

> The potential for media advocacy is highest when interest and importance are both high. In this segment, news is conveyed as a story: emotionally engaging, simplified, and with heroes, villains, and victims. Companies usually have only the choice between hero and villain—few people have sympathy with corporations. To become the hero, the company has to identify the perceived victim and save it.

paying attention because the company is on a stage, so that its every move is highlighted. What factors determine whether people are paying attention? The Reputational Terrain can help us understand this issue.

Suppose a hedge fund must cease its operations. Such stories will usually be found in the lower left corner. If the hedge fund has many

Figure 2-3 **Reputational Terrain—Strategies**

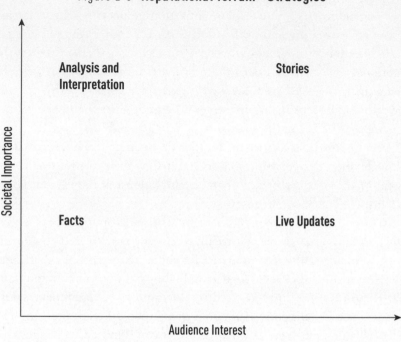

billions of dollars of assets under management, it may move up on the societal importance dimension; if its failure involved fraud, it may move up even more.

Somewhat paradoxically, however, other seemingly irrelevant factors can move the story up and toward the right, such as the names of its clients. Disgraced investment manager Bernie Madoff's high-profile clientele, which included Jewish human rights activist and Nobel laureate Elie Wiesel, moved the case to the extreme top right corner. The collapse of the hedge fund Lipper Convertibles L.P. presented another example when former investors sued the fund and some of its investors for unjust enrichment, alleging that they had withdrawn their funds in anticipation of the collapse and thus avoided the losses suffered by other investors. Typically, such an allegation of "front running" would barely make headlines, but Lipper's investor base of actors Sylvester Stallone, Julia Roberts, and John Cusack, as well as former Disney CEO Michael Eisner and former New York City Mayor Ed Koch, made it front-page news.[10]

Name recognition or celebrity status is not the only factor that will move an issue to the forefront, as anything that increases the likelihood of the issue's making a "good story" has relevance. Examples include the presence of an identifiable, sympathetic victim or victim group (particularly one that is viewed by society as deserving special protection, such as children, the elderly, or the poor), the availability of striking visuals (like the Abu Ghraib photos or a video of rats at a Taco Bell restaurant),[11] a well-known brand (like the Thomas the Tank Engine example from Chapter 1), or a connection to a particularly controversial issue (like the "morning-after pill" and the abortion debate).

Reputational Terrains are not static, but can change over time. Understanding these shifting dynamics is critically important for reputation management, in the context of both managing challenging situations and adopting proactive strategies, a topic that will occupy us in Chapter 7. The history of bariatric surgery over the last few years provides an instructive example. Colloquially referred to as "weight-loss surgery," bariatric surgery was developed to combat long-term health risks in severely obese individuals, which include high blood pressure, high cholesterol, type 2 diabetes and its complications, coronary heart disease, stroke, gallbladder disease, osteoarthritis, sleep apnea, and respiratory problems, along with various forms of cancer. In 2008, the U.S. Surgeon General estimated that 112,000 preventable deaths occurred as a result of obesity. In the beginning, the 1991 National Institutes of Health Consensus Conference Statement on Gastrointestinal Surgery for Severe Obesity governed decisions on when to conduct the fairly complex procedures, whose typical costs ranged from $20,000 to $35,000.[12] Mortality rates were at about 0.5 percent on average, but varied by procedure, patient, and provider.[13]

For more than a decade, bariatric surgery was treated no differently from any other medically necessary surgery. Things changed dramatically in 2002, when the number of Americans seeking weight-loss surgery increased from 63,100 in 2002 to 103,000 in 2003 and 140,000 in 2004.[14] One of the driving forces behind this spike was the significant media coverage of the *Today Show* weatherman Al Roker's bariatric surgery in March 2002.[15] Other celebrities followed, producing two major effects. First, the coverage massively increased awareness of the surgery, which led many more patients to consider it. Second, and just as important, however, it also changed the public

perception of bariatric surgery; it quickly went from a pure medical necessity to a weight-loss strategy in the mind of the public, who
came to see it as an alternative to dieting and exercise, moving it to
the realm of *People* magazine. This shift in perception dramatically
increased the demand for bariatric surgery.

The story does not end there. Even with a constant mortality rate
(which is statistically unlikely, since increased demand would attract
new surgeons to the discipline, some of whom may not have sufficient
training and expertise), increased demand for surgeries will lead to a
higher number of complications and fatalities—in other words, victims.
Suddenly, the procedure became connected to the important social issue
of patient safety. A highly critical one-hour special on the hard-hitting
TV news show *48 Hours* followed, complete with interviews with surgery victims and their families and footage of unscrupulous surgeons
hiding from cameras. During the special, *48 Hours* correspondent Har-
old Dow explained: "Here's the problem—the demand is creating a gold
rush, with doctors and hospitals racing to get in on this lucrative business. Surgical weight loss centers are sprouting up all over the country,
but many of the surgeons being recruited just don't have the specific
skills, experience, and training needed to perform the new procedure
safely."

Bariatric surgeon Dr. Julie Ellner concurred. "Unfortunately, there
are a lot of training courses out there where surgeons can learn how to
do this in a weekend, and then go back to their home institutions and say
that they're laparoscopic surgeons and try to start up a program," she said.
"These are some of the highest-risk patients you could possibly operate
on, and if you aren't appropriately trained, you can kill people."[16]

Figure 2-4 illustrates how the issue moved through the reputational
landscape. It started as a technical issue, largely confined to the medical community. The name of a celebrity patient dramatically increased
audience interest, shifting it to the right, but then that increased demand
created more victims, which led to concerns about patient safety and a
vertical shift up along the social importance dimension. With sustained
high audience interest as a result of the celebrity dimension, the issue
moved squarely into the upper right corner, complete with both victims
(the bariatric surgery patients and their families after the surgery has
gone wrong) and villains (unscrupulous and unqualified doctors).

Figure 2-4 **Reputation Dynamics: Weight-Loss Surgery**

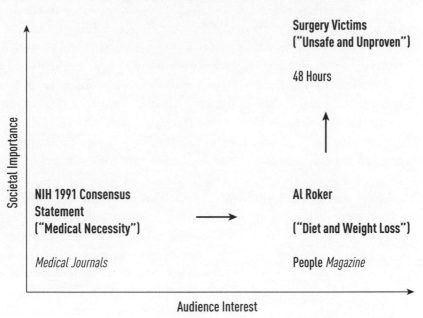

Where did the hero come from? It came from an unlikely corner: health insurance companies. As mentioned in the Preface, health insurers and HMOs have some of the lowest trust scores for any industry, only slightly higher than those of tobacco companies. In this case, however, the denial of a surgical procedure could be viewed as protecting patients from an unsafe, unnecessary, and untested procedure. In early 2004, Florida's major insurance carriers began to eliminate coverage of gastric bypass surgery. "Gastric bypass surgery is an extremely risky procedure that is of questionable benefit to the patient," said Dr. Robert Forster, Blue Cross's vice president and chief medical director. "We are concerned at the growing numbers of these procedures while significant questions remain regarding quality of care, safety and long-term consequences."[17]

If the surgeons wanted to strike back and improve public trust, what approaches would work? Under the logic of storytelling, the key is to be viewed as the hero, not the villain. The difference, of course, is that the hero saves the victim. In order to win the battle for public perception, the surgeons would need to focus on a different victim: the morbidly obese patient whose life could be saved by the surgery. To make this work in the upper right corner of the Reputational Terrain, the surgeons would have to focus on individual, sympathetic patients, rather than on numbers and statistics. Patient testimony and biographies would prove particularly effective. A pure communication approach, however, is unlikely to be successful without addressing the issue of patient safety, perhaps through changes in industry practices, such as the use of certification or other forms of self-regulation. The process of integrating reputation management and business practices will play a central role in later parts of the book.

In the case of bariatric surgery, the industry was in the midst of rapid change, which led to corresponding changes in its reputational environment. In other situations, the issue context can be changing even though a company's business practices and other industry characteristics remain constant. A food company that hears about the problem of lead paint in toys might react by breathing a sigh of relief that it is not in the toy business, but this is shortsighted. The issue that has grabbed media attention is not just about toys, but about manufacturing quality in China in general, an issue that could have severe consequences for the food industry, given its globally integrated supply chains.

> Reputational Terrains are not static; they shift in response to new events. These events can seem unrelated, even trivial. Nevertheless, they can dramatically alter a company's reputational risk environment. Common examples are celebrity involvement, powerful visuals, and adjacent industries or issues.

Sure enough, a similar scandal hit the food industry a year after the RC2 recall, generating headlines regarding milk products and infant formula that were contaminated with melamine, a basic chemical compound that is used to make flame-retardant plastic and cleaning products. Melamine is banned from use in food production because of its link with renal and urinary problems, but Chinese milk producers had used it to create an illusion of higher protein counts in dairy products. More than 300,000 babies fell ill, with six infants dying from kidney-related problems.[18]

Once an issue enters the public consciousness, journalists will pay attention to adjacent industries and companies when they face similar problems. Companies may not view these issues as related, but as long as journalists and the public do, the companies' reputational risk will increase.

Consider the case of Internet gambling. In normal times, this is an issue that is of moderate importance and interest, largely driven by moral concerns and questions regarding gambling addiction. These concerns are fairly constant and can easily be anticipated. Suppose, however, that you read a report about children being lured to Internet gambling sites; the involvement of vulnerable populations would move the issue to the upper right quadrant. Then suppose that reports surface alleging the use of Internet gambling to launder drug money. The issue moves still further up and to the right. Finally, suppose a news report mentions that Internet gambling has been used for money laundering by terrorists: red alert. Note that this is a threat not just for the operators of Internet gambling sites, but also for their service providers, including payment processors such as credit card companies and PayPal. Indeed, when the U.S. government outlawed Internet gambling, it specifically targeted service providers to enforce the ban.[19]

In a similar recent example, payment service companies such as MasterCard, Visa, and PayPal decided to terminate their relationship with WikiLeaks. The companies formerly had allowed donors to make contributions to WikiLeaks but suspended their services in early December 2010 when WikiLeaks founder Julian Assange came under fire from the U.S. government for publishing thousands of classified documents and was arrested for sexual misconduct in Sweden on an international warrant. The payment companies subsequently came under attack by a loose group of hacker activists calling themselves "Anonymous" as part of "Operation Payback." During the so-called "denial-of-service" attacks, computers flooded a server to prevent the display of Web pages.[20]

The involvement of governmental actors raises an important issue. Once there is a stage, the company will rarely occupy it alone. Some actors will jump onto it to advance their own agendas; others will be dragged onto it kicking and screaming. That includes advocates and experts, but also regulators and politicians. Consider a safety issue such as the lead paint on toys case or the recent Toyota recall. First, the company gets into trouble. Media attention focuses on its response to the crisis and how it will address customer concerns. Journalists then examine what caused the crisis. When did the company know, were warning signs ignored, what processes did the company have in place, and were those processes applied consistently? Attention will then shift to the regulators, with the public and politicians asking why the regulators did not anticipate the problem. Were early warning signs ignored? Is the level of expertise and staffing appropriate to monitor these issues and take decisive action? In other words, were the regulators asleep at the wheel? The regulators will face tremendous pressure from the media and from politicians, who will take tough positions either of their own volition or because their constituents are concerned; either way, they can position themselves as protectors of the public. Tough hearings for both the CEO and the regulators result, with the regulators now needing to protect their own reputations.

The best way to do this is to come down hard on the company. Many of my clients have had a disturbing experience in such cases. They have cultivated a collaborative relationship with regulators, always resolving ongoing issues in a constructive fashion, with mutual respect between experts. Suddenly, a reputational crisis hits, and the very same officials will no longer pick up the phone for fear of appearing soft. Executives often find this reaction disturbing at a personal level, but they must nevertheless anticipate it by understanding the incentives for regulators and politicians, who respond to significant shifts in public perception. Smart regulators will understand this and take a proactive stance. Otherwise, politicians with oversight responsibility will turn on the heat through public hearings, funding choices, or the replacement of the regulator. In other words, *the positions of public officials on an issue are not fixed*; they will change in response to public opinion, and these changes can be mutually reinforcing. This is illustrated in Figure 2-5.

Once companies lose the battle for public perception, they not only lose the trust of their customers, but invite a hostile response from regulators and other public officials. Once the company is portrayed as a villain, many public officials will vie for the role of the hero.

The recent difficulties faced by Goldman Sachs provide an illustrative example. You may recall the reputational crisis that Goldman faced after the SEC filed charges against the company on April 16, 2010, related to its synthetic CDOs. The goal here is not to discuss the validity of the charges against Goldman. The point of this example is that public outrage after the financial crisis created pressure to act for both regulators and members of Congress, especially the Democratic majority

Figure 2-5 **Public Opinion and Public Agents**

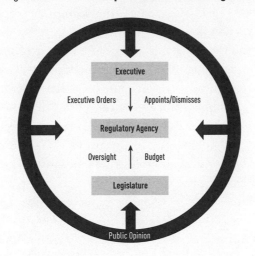

and the presidential administration. By targeting Goldman, both groups relieved the pressure on themselves and changed public sentiment in a way that was more conducive to stricter regulation of the financial services industry, resulting in the passage of a sweeping financial regulatory bill. Senate Majority Leader Harry M. Reid summarized the sentiment as follows: "When this bill becomes law, the joy ride on Wall Street will come to a screeching halt."[21]

Goldman's original combative approach played right into the hands of its accusers, adding fuel to their fire. In an acerbic column, *New York Times* columnist Frank Rich sarcastically encouraged the company to "Fight on, Goldman Sachs!"[22] The company quickly adjusted and settled the charges for $550 million, but the political landscape had changed for good.

> Public actors such as politicians or regulators will respond to shifts in public opinion. In the event of a crisis, they need to protect their own reputations. A common response is to come down hard on the company.

A NOTE ON SOCIAL MEDIA

Many people have suggested that the "old media" are ceding their influence and impact to bloggers, Twitter, Facebook, and other forms of social media.[23] In the context of reputation management, this shift has been more subtle. The mass media—including newspapers, cable and broadcast news, and radio—fulfill two different roles: origination and amplification. On the one hand, the news media originate news, with the classic example being investigative reporting, as in the case of the *Washington Post* and the Watergate scandal. On the other hand, the news media serve as an amplifier, bringing the story "into the living room" and creating a public event. As an example, consider election coverage, where panelists and commentators discuss electoral results as they are being reported by pollsters and forecasters, or a natural disaster, where the media are reporting live from the scene.[24]

User-generated media are playing an increasingly important role in originating news, as the professional media are beginning to get more of their stories from Facebook, YouTube, or Twitter. United Airlines's "Guitar-Gate" represents such an example. Singer Dave Carroll's Taylor guitar was reportedly damaged by baggage handlers at Chicago's O'Hare Airport. After a year of communication with United, the company denied Carroll any recompense for the damage, which he had spent roughly $1,200 repairing. Carroll warned the company that he would write three songs and produce three videos about the incident. He indeed released the first video on July 6, 2009. It quickly emerged as an Internet hit, attracting more than 3.5 million views on YouTube and becoming one of iTunes most downloaded songs the week after its release, while receiving coverage from news outlets worldwide. The uproar prompted the airline to try to make amends, ultimately donating $3,000 to a music charity at Carroll's request.[25]

Any disgruntled customer or employee with a computer, a camera phone, and an Internet connection can potentially create a serious problem for a company, a problem that will stay on the Web forever. That having been said, even a damning video is just one of millions of postings and is unlikely to attract a customer's attention unless she is actively searching for it. All this means that without an amplifier, a user-generated news item is likely to have only moderate influence.

Recent quantitative research paints a nuanced picture of the interaction between mainstream news media and user-generated media. A team of computer scientists from Cornell and Stanford recently developed a clever way to study the dynamics of the news cycle.[26] They tracked the diffusion of short phrases of text—so-called memes—

across news media and blogs over the period from August 1 to October 31, 2008, scanning some 90 million documents and capturing a significant part of the U.S. presidential campaign. Examples of memes are quotes from some of the presidential candidates, such as Senator McCain's quote that the "fundamentals of our economy are strong." Indeed, the meme with the highest frequency was the infamous "lipstick on a pig" line that made headlines in September 2008. First, the team found that most of the stories still originated in news sites before percolating to blogs, with an average time gap of about 2.5 hours. By comparison, only about 3.5 percent of quoted phrases moved from blogs to news sites. So, by this measure, news organizations are still the main originators of news. Second, news volume increases at a faster rate than blog volume, but also decreases at a faster rate. In other words, blogs keep issues alive much longer than the typical media news cycle. Third, the interaction between blogs and news media can be quite subtle. In the typical pattern, the news media break a story, then a group of early bloggers picks up the story *before* the majority of news sites jump in. After the news sites have moved on, bloggers continue to respond to the story, keeping it alive in the blogosphere for a much longer period.

In summary, the demise of the news media as the driver of public reputation has been greatly exaggerated. While an increasing number of stories originate in user-generated media, the overall fraction remains quite small. However, what blogs and other forms of nontraditional media still lack in news origination, they may make up for in sustainability, as they continue to comment on a story, keeping the issue alive long after the news media have moved on.

MERCEDES EMBRACES THE MOOSE

Let us now apply these ideas to the Moose Test that caused Mercedes to lose control of its brand, with all of its core brand attributes (quality, safety, and technology) under attack and with potentially disastrous consequences not only for the newly launched A-Class, but for all Mercedes models. Mercedes's initial reaction to the test focused largely on technical details, a response that customers considered arrogant, eroding their trust in the company and its management.

Mercedes realized that a traditional advertising campaign would not be sufficient. This was due in part to Mercedes's shaken credibility, and in part to the strategic reality that Mercedes needed to reach a much broader audience, including both existing and potential customers, in order to rescue the A-Class from disaster. This meant turning media coverage from negative to positive. The first task was to locate the issue in the Reputational Terrain; the Moose Test clearly resided in the upper right quadrant, with high audience interest and high social importance. After all, it had dominated headlines and news shows for days.

Upon closer reflection, however, we have a puzzle. Quality problems during the introduction of a new car typically do not make the front page unless they cause a string of serious injuries or fatalities, and no such injuries occurred in the A-Class case; the only injury was a minor one to one of the journalists. Mercedes's initial reaction ("The management board cannot give a statement just because somewhere a car flipped over. Otherwise we would have to comment on everything.") perfectly illustrates this line of thinking. Compared to typical cases this did not look like a big deal . . . but this was not a typical case.

As an iconic brand, Mercedes should have expected that some people would express *Schadenfreude* (taking pleasure in the misfortune of others) at seeing the proud company stumble. Moreover, Mercedes had spent a fortune on an extensive promotion campaign, so that everybody knew about the A-Class. Additionally, the A-Class was intended as a car for young families, so the fear of an unsafe automobile created with it the textbook potential victim: young children. Perhaps most important, the name of the test (the Moose Test) resonated with the general public. Had the test been called the "3G4SX Test," I doubt that it would have generated nearly as much media interest. Instead, the Moose was everywhere, adding a healthy dose of ridicule to the grim difficulties faced by Mercedes. From a safety engineering perspective, the name of the test is totally irrelevant, but from the perspective of reputation management, it ensured that the story captivated an audience that stayed attuned to Mercedes's growing brand perception problem. These dynamics can be nicely illustrated in the Reputational Terrain chart, now applied to the Moose Test.

Figure 2-6 **Reputational Terrain—The Moose Test**

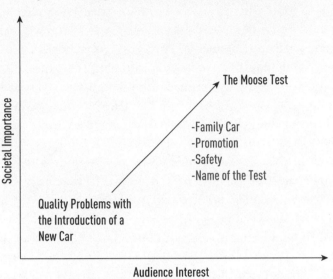

We can now identify the correct strategy for the given terrain. In the high-interest/high-importance segment, this means telling a story. Step 1 is to identify the victim. This is easy: the families that are worried about the safety of their young children. Step 2 is to become the hero who saves the victim, here by making the car *safer*. Notice that making the car safer does not mean convincing the driver that his fears are misguided; it is far too late for Mercedes to rely on its technical expertise alone. Instead, it means taking concrete and easily verifiable steps to improve the car's safety. For this to work in the correct Reputational Terrain, Mercedes's actions must be easily understandable and credibly communicated to an unsophisticated mass audience. After all, Mercedes needs to win the battle on the terrain where it is located: in the upper right corner. In other words, the task is to do the right thing *and* get credit for it.

The stakes were tremendous. "We have one more shot, and it must be 100 percent on target," Director of Marketing Communication Jochen Pläcking later said, describing the atmosphere of the meeting in which Mercedes decided on a bold move. On November 11, 1997, three weeks after the Moose Test, Daimler organized a press conference with hundreds of journalists present. "We have taken the public criticism and the concern for our customers to heart," CEO Jürgen E. Schrempp began in his opening statement. "Nobody regrets more than us that in extreme driving tests, the A-Class has exhibited a weakness. Our engineers have worked day and night to look for an optimal solution. We have found it. . . . We don't want to deliver any vehicle that we know we can improve and build better." Mercedes announced that it would recall all 18,000 already produced A-Class vehicles, 2,600 of which were already on the road. All cars would undergo various modifications and, most important, would be retrofitted with the brand-new Electronic Stability Program (ESP) system, which Mercedes had recently introduced as a standard feature on Mercedes luxury cars.[27] (The company had planned on offering it only as an option on the A-Class starting in mid-1998, at a price of about $1,300.) The ESP provided extra safety in crucial situations and significantly reduced the danger of skidding during turns. Even though Mercedes engineers believed that the additional benefits provided by the ESP would be negligible with respect to the Moose Test, and that minor modifications to the car would be sufficient, Mercedes recognized that minor modifications would fix the minor technical problem, but not the major reputational problem that it had caused.

Mercedes estimated the cost of the recall at $57 million for 1997 and $114 million for 1998, mainly for the installation of the ESP system. The company started a new ad campaign in 180 newspapers, directly addressing the issue by describing the Moose Test positively, directly, and in a relaxed fashion. The text explained that the company wanted to end the discussion about the A-Class problem, and described the functional details of the ESP system. Meanwhile, the company sent letters to its customers and launched an information campaign via the Internet, telephone, and personalized letters. About a month later, as the recall was winding down, Mercedes invited the four journalists who had experienced rollovers with the A-Class (including Robert Collin, the Swedish journalist who had started everything) to test the stability of the refurbished A-Class in a Mercedes testing facility in Spain, and brought in former Austrian Formula 1 race car champion Niki Lauda as a test driver. The car passed all the driving tests, during which Niki Lauda called it "the safest car in its category." Mercedes later used pictures of the tests and interviews with the drivers involved in a two-minute television ad that mimicked the look and feel of a German news feature. The company purchased advertising time to show the spot right before or after the German prime-time TV news, and then launched hundreds of print ads to inform the public about the spots. Six weeks later, while officially relaunching the A-Class, Mercedes invited 450 auto journalists to a driving workshop on Goodyear's test track in Montpellier, France. The journalists were invited to test the safety of the car on 11 different drives, each one simulating a different real-life driving situation. Mercedes also launched two new ads showing German tennis champion Boris Becker, a major celebrity in Germany, with quotes from his tennis career when he had to learn from mistakes.[28] As its crowning gesture, customers picking up their refurbished A-Class found a stuffed moose waiting in the passenger seat. Mercedes had embraced the Moose Test, and, at least for a while, transformed itself into "the maker of the Moose Car."

Mercedes's strategy for rebuilding trust had worked.[29] In February 1998, Mercedes started delivering the A-Class again, with an *increased* preorder list, now for 120,000 cars. The company sold 136,000 A-Class vehicles in Europe in 1998, and the car soon became the bestselling Mercedes model in Germany.

The story of Mercedes's turnaround is remarkable, not because of its happy ending, but because it involved a complete strategic reversal from Mercedes's original position. Mercedes abandoned its focus on engineering issues and concentrated on the main challenge of rebuilding trust with its customers. This meant engaging in an extensive and highly publicized recall strategy, despite its belief that the public's safety concerns were ill-founded and the gains from its response were modest at best. Notice how this time, Mercedes made sure that it hit all four elements of the Trust Radar. The involvement of Daimler's CEO demonstrated the company's full commitment, whereas earlier, during the first weeks of the Moose Test crisis, Schrempp had made no public statements, inviting criticism from the German media. The November 11 press conference changed all this and sent a clear signal as to who was accountable. In the words of the German press, the Moose Test crisis had finally become "a CEO matter" (*Chefsache*).

In internal communications, Schrempp not only underlined the seriousness of the situation, but also emphasized the importance of viewing the Moose Test crisis as both a threat and an opportunity. "In every crisis there is an opportunity," Schrempp told his team during the crisis. "We must concentrate all our energy to identify the opportunity in this crisis. I don't know yet what it is, but I know it is there." Schrempp also constantly reminded management not to focus solely on the technical aspects of the crisis. "In such a situation, it is important to realize that not only technical but also psychological aspects matter. It is important to view the situation from somebody else's point of view," he stated in a later interview.

We have focused on customer perception, but reputational challenges involve multiple constituencies, each with its own concerns or agendas. Unlike in other safety crises, the involvement of politicians and regulators was muted for Mercedes, largely because the rollover had not caused any serious injuries. Employees and Mercedes dealers were a much more significant issue. To alleviate their concerns, management complemented its public relations strategy with an internal communication strategy, with Schrempp and Hubbert sending e-mail messages and letters about the recall and its implementation to Daimler's employees and dealers. "We had certainly wished for a different start for the A-Class," Schrempp wrote in the internal company newspaper *Headline*. "But it is important to see how we dealt with this issue. We admitted that we had a problem and that we regretted it very much. We also have a solution. And I think that in the long run, we will come out stronger from this temporary weakness." The company also organized an internal ad campaign in coordination with its main union, IG Metall, to motivate and reassure Mercedes-Benz employees at the A-Class plant in Rastatt regarding their job security. Daimler also decided not to fire any members of the management team because of the Moose Test. Dieter Zetsche, then head of marketing and now Daimler's CEO, faxed guidelines for dealing with the recall and the suspended deliveries to all European dealers, who reportedly perceived the suspension decision as courageous, appropriate, and necessary to regain customer trust.

To coordinate these various decisions, Mercedes set up a 10-person crisis task force, nicknamed the "A-team," a tongue-in-cheek reference to the popular TV series. Headed by Volker Stauch, head of Global Services—Passenger Cars, its members represented various company divisions (Development, Purchasing, Sales, Logistics, Production, Controlling, and Communication). In creating the task force, Mercedes could not rely on an existing crisis management plan, as management had not developed detailed plans for potential recalls. Daimler's CEO Schrempp was not a member of the task force, but was kept constantly informed about the team's activities. The team focused on analyzing the crisis and designing possible solutions, with a dual mission to focus on both the technical aspects and the communication strategy. It adopted the motto, "We will make the A-Class a Yes-class again," a pun in the original German.[30] Throughout the crisis, the team met daily at 7 p.m., often until 3 or 4 a.m. Fifty-five task-force meetings took place, with more than 100 people assisting the team internally.

The operational challenges of the recall proved substantial, as Mercedes had to refurbish 18,000 cars in three months, roughly equivalent to Porsche's annual production at that time. To accomplish this task, Mercedes set up four retrofitting centers across Europe from scratch. The company pulled staff from all over Europe, a seemingly insurmountable logistical challenge, exemplified by the difficulty of something as simple as obtaining hotel accommodations for 1,000 employees per center on short notice. Nonetheless, the A-team performed in exemplary fashion. In the course of one evening, engineers designed a new component to hold the ESP, complete with drawings, the construction plan, and the materials needed. A few hours later, a supplier had already manufactured the first prototype, compressing a development process that usually took three months into just 24 hours.

Perhaps the most remarkable aspect of Mercedes's approach was its relaunch strategy. The company's initial attempt to argue that the safety concerns were mistaken had failed, as its attempt to supply technical information to prove its assertions reflected a belief that it faced a mere engineering challenge. Upon recognizing the problem as one of brand reputation, Mercedes completely reversed its approach and focused on the more fundamental business challenge of defending its brand and rebuilding trust with its customers. To do that convincingly, Mercedes had to shift public perception and flip hostile media coverage, becoming the hero rather than the villain. Using all factors on the Trust Radar represented step 1; the dramatic recall was step 2. Mercedes had done the right thing by its customers; it needed to ensure that it would get credit for its actions.

To understand this challenge, let us revisit the Reputational Terrain. Three months after the initial test, interest in the Moose Test had waned (see Figure 2-7), and it was no longer making headlines. Most CEOs would view this as good news, as criticism of the company had subsided as well. This is misleading, as we discussed in Chapter 1, because leaving the headlines is a good thing only if customers and other stakeholders are left with a positive impression. That was not the case here, for the last thing customers remembered about the A-Class was the image of a flipped-over car. Mercedes had to replace this image in the mind of its customers, but nobody was paying attention anymore, and the stage was no longer lit.

Figure 2-7   **Reputational Terrain—The Moose Test, Four Months Later**

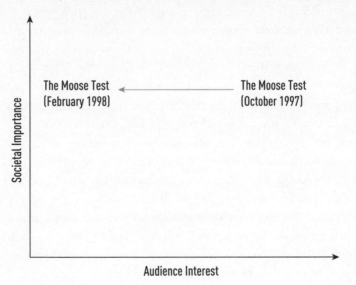

Mercedes had to relight the stage and rekindle audience interest if it was to have a second chance at making a first impression. All of Mercedes's actions pursued this objective: the ad campaigns, the test drives with journalists, and the use of celebrity drivers. Notice the peculiar structure of the celebrity test drive. It resembled a stunt rather than a proper test drive, and with all due respect to Niki Lauda, he was not trained as a professional test car driver. Never mind. The goal was never to convince the technical safety testing community, but to convince the general public, and to accomplish this, Mercedes had to move the issue back up to the upper right quadrant. Incidentally, immediately after it had learned of the Moose Test, Mercedes had asked the well-regarded German testing association TÜV to conduct a Moose Test. During the October 29 press conference, the head of TÜV's car division showed a video in which an A-Class vehicle had passed the test without difficulties. But these results never resonated with people who were gasping in shock at the front-page pictures of a flipped-over Mercedes-Benz.

Why did the Niki Lauda test work so much better? It was the name of the test car driver! By increasing audience interest, the Mercedes message landed in the right terrain (see Figure 2-8). Therein lay a certain irony, for it was the name of the test that got Mercedes into trouble, and the name of the test car driver that got the company out of it.

Figure 2-8 **Reputational Terrain—The Moose Test, Relighting the Stage**

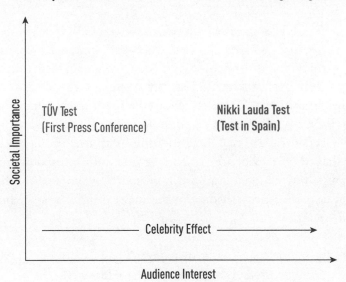

Throughout this crisis, Mercedes never tried to play down the Moose Test. It wanted its customers to remember the test, not to forget it. Like Johnson & Johnson advertising subsequent products as coming "from the makers of Tylenol," Mercedes embraced being known as the "maker of the Moose Car." After its initial stumble, Mercedes conceptualized the test both internally and externally as an opportunity to demonstrate the company's commitment to its core values and its ability to learn, and it wanted its customers to know this. Mercedes would certainly have preferred to avoid this ordeal in the first place, and yes, it would have been both cheaper and more effective to capture the opportunity to demonstrate greatness during the first 24 hours. Nevertheless, the tale of the Moose Test provides some hope.[31] Reputations can be rebuilt, but doing so requires a sustained effort that frequently involves adjustments to the business process. A successful strategy requires not only money and management time, but more important, the ability to correctly spot the relevant business problem among all the technical details, and the mental agility to look at the problem from another person's point of view, even (or especially) if we believe that point of view is incorrect. In other words, it requires strategic sophistication—and that is a rare currency indeed.

THINGS TO REMEMBER

In the early stages of the Moose Test issue, Mercedes lost control of its most precious asset, its reputation. But Mercedes was able to recover from initial missteps. Doing so required a sober assessment of why its original approach had not worked, followed by a radical shift in strategy. Mercedes realized that its relationship with its customers was now being shaped by outside forces. Rather than becoming defensive, the company's leadership embraced this perspective and dealt with it in a clinical fashion. Here are some of the main insights that helped it to solve the puzzle.

- Reputations are public by nature. They are not just the result of serving customers and other stakeholders well.

- Customers and the public will form attitudes toward companies that are based not on experience, but on a mix of opinion and fact provided by the media and other third parties.

- Strategies need to fit the terrain. Managing reputations requires understanding the reputational landscape. Reputational environments are not fixed. They change in response to emerging issues, developments in related industries, or the policy context.

Apparently trivial developments, such as the involvement of a celebrity, can dramatically alter reputational risks.

- The Reputational Terrain helps companies to attain situational awareness. Audience interest and social importance are the key factors that shape how an issue will be covered in the media and which strategies will work.

- The most challenging area of the Reputational Terrain is where both audience interest and social importance are high. In this area, news coverage needs to appeal to a mass audience. The consequence is a focus on storytelling.

- Good stories need compelling characters: hero, villain, and victim. No matter how executives may feel about being attacked by the media, companies are not well cast as victims. Leaders should not count on much public sympathy. That means that companies have only two roles available to them: villains or heroes. The default is the role of the villain. Becoming the hero requires identifying the victim and then saving it.

Mercedes intuitively followed these steps. This allowed the company to "embrace the Moose," fully take advantage of the stage, and reinforce to customers and the public what it stood for when the chips were down.

So far we have focused on issues that are closely related to a company's core strategy and identity. But reputational challenges can come from everywhere. Indeed, sometimes they are strategically manufactured by third parties. This is the topic of our next chapter.

CHAPTER 3

SHELL TURNS ON THE WATER CANNONS

The Growing Impact of the Second Circle

"The short-term impact on business is as serious as anything that has happened in the recordable history of this company."

—**Peter Duncan,** CEO, Shell Germany, 1995[1]

TROUBLE IN THE NORTH SEA

n September 1991, Shell UK—a member of the Royal Dutch Shell Group of Companies—had a problem. It operated a large oil storage facility and tanker loading buoy in the North Sea called the Brent Spar, a cylinder that stood 463 feet high (more than twice the height of Big Ben) and weighed about 14,500 tons.[2] An internal review had concluded that the company could not economically justify the refurbishing that the facility needed, and so Shell UK decided to decommission the Brent Spar. First, however, the company had to figure out a way to dispose of it.

As is common in these cases, Shell UK evaluated its options based on engineering complexity, risk to public health, workforce safety, environmental impact, cost, and other such factors. International regulatory principles govern the removal of offshore petroleum platforms, and in the case of the Brent Spar, they determined that the British Department of Energy was the relevant regulatory authority. Other European countries could voice opinions on the matter, but they could not veto or change a decision by the British government.

To gain approval from the government, Shell UK had to submit its preferred disposal option, the Best Practical Environmental Option (BPEO). The company hired a team of researchers at Scotland's University of Aberdeen and the consulting firm Rudall Blanchard Associates to prepare reports weighing the various options.[3] The field licensee—in this case, Shell UK—would bear the costs of abandonment, with part of the cost (50 to 70 percent) qualifying as tax-deductible. Historically, the approval process had been straightforward and fairly routine, but this time there was a catch. The Brent Spar was the first of many deepwater installations—50 in U.K. waters alone—and would therefore set a precedent for those that followed. Any installation in shallow water required complete removal and onshore dismantling, but deepwater installations, if approved, could be disposed of at sea.

After a two-year evaluation process, two options survived the initial screening process: horizontal onshore dismantling and deepwater disposal. The former alternative consisted of rotating the buoy to a horizontal position, transporting it to shore, and dismantling it. The latter involved towing the structure to a deepwater disposal site in the northeast Atlantic and sinking it. The Aberdeen study commissioned by Shell

UK concluded that deepwater disposal was preferable on the grounds of engineering complexity, risk to health, safety of the workforce, and cost (about £12 million for deep-sea disposal versus £46 million for onshore dismantling).[4] Shell UK also consulted with various stakeholder groups, including the Scottish National Heritage, the Joint Nature Conservation Committee, various fishermen's associations, and British Telecom. In February 1995, the British government announced its approval of the deep-sea disposal plan and informed European governments of its decision, giving them three months to voice their opinions. While some of the European governments—including Germany's—had criticized deep-sea dumping, no government officially protested, and Shell UK scheduled the towing of Brent Spar to the disposal site in the North Atlantic for mid-June.

However, at least one organization refused to let this occur without a fight. Founded in 1971, Greenpeace International had grown to become the world's largest multinational environmental group. In 1995, it had about 3.1 million contributors, worldwide offices located in 30 countries, a full-time staff of about 1,200, and a budget of nearly $150 million. Over the years, Greenpeace had developed the capability to operate globally, with four seafaring vessels, a helicopter, and modern communications equipment at its disposal. Most important, Greenpeace could draw on a vast network of thousands of volunteers, nowhere more than in Germany, where it had one of its largest and most active constituencies. Greenpeace enjoyed high acceptance and popularity among the German public, and it had frequently captured center stage through spectacular actions. Greenpeace Germany alone contributed more than 40 percent of the total budget of Greenpeace International and served as the home for its North Sea logistic center.[5]

Despite this popularity, Greenpeace had faced some recent challenges. The organization had opposed the first Gulf War, prompting dramatic declines in contributions in the United States. In 1994, Greenpeace had been forced to cut its budget by about 10 percent, dismiss more than 20 staff members, and close its offices in Boston and Fort Lauderdale.[6] In addition, Greenpeace found itself mired in a strategic identity crisis, known as the "wet suits" versus "dry suits" debate. Traditionally, Greenpeace had positioned itself as confrontational and action-oriented, with a shrewd ability to create publicity. One of Greenpeace's principal strategies was to attract the public's attention through high-profile, confrontational acts that Greenpeace's own photographers and film crews covered, resulting in dramatic footage. "We try to keep it simple," said Steve D'Esposito, an American who served as executive director of Greenpeace International at the time. "One, we raise environmental awareness. Two, we want to push the world toward solutions, using the most egregious examples. The whole point is to confront; we try to get in the way. Confrontation is critical to get coverage in the press or to reach the public some other way." More recently, however, some members of Greenpeace had wanted to move toward more constructive engagement and even possible partnerships, especially with large corporations.[7]

Greenpeace had learned about Shell UK's plans concerning the Brent Spar in the summer of 1994 and decided to commission a policy study to consider the arguments for deep-sea disposal. The study strongly favored onshore disposal and rejected deep-sea dumping on environmental grounds, especially because of concerns about toxic residues. Greenpeace elected to run its campaign opposing the deep-sea disposal out of its North Sea Operations Center in Hamburg, Germany.

The campaign against Shell lasted from April 30 to June 20, 1995. Greenpeace activists occupied the platform repeatedly, first by boat and later, in dramatic fashion, by helicopter. The initial occupation lasted for three weeks, until Shell decided to use water cannons to clear the platform. Journalists stationed on a nearby Greenpeace vessel filmed these confrontations and broadcast them by satellite. The campaign received little media attention in the United Kingdom, but German television broadcast extensive footage of helicopters dodging water cannons and soaked activists on the platform. The head of the campaigns section of Greenpeace Germany, and organizer of the Brent Spar landing, Harald Zindler, recalled, "We were very happy when Shell decided to clear the platform. It portrayed Shell as an unresponsive and inconsiderate big business." Expressions of outrage and protest in Germany and the Netherlands grew in response to the media coverage. Members of all German political parties and Angela Merkel (the German minister of the environment at the time) condemned Shell's decision to dump the rig in the deep sea. On May 22, even the worker representatives on Shell

Germany's supervisory board expressed "concern and outrage" at Shell's decision to "turn the sea into a trash pit."

Under pressure, Shell Germany executives met with Greenpeace representative Jochen Lorfelder, who argued that 85 percent of German motorists would participate in a boycott if Shell attempted to go through with its plan for deep-sea disposal. He told Shell executives, "In the four weeks it would take to tow the Brent Spar to its dumping site, Greenpeace would make life a nightmare for Shell." The chairman of Shell Germany explained that Shell UK's studies indicated that deep-sea disposal actually represented the best alternative for the environment, but Lorfelder answered, "But Joe Six-Pack won't understand your technical details. All he knows is that if he dumps his can in a lake, he gets fined. So he can't understand how Shell can do this." In its media campaign, Greenpeace successfully appealed to the German enthusiasm for recycling. In their homes, many Germans separated garbage into bags for metal, glass, paper, aluminum, plastic, and organic waste.

In the meantime, the Fourth International North Sea Conference met on June 8 and 9, with the disposal of petroleum facilities as one of its main topics. Several European countries called for onshore disposal for all oil installations, while the United Kingdom and Norway (the countries with the largest and most difficult deepwater structures) called for evaluations on a case-by-case basis. During the same period, calls for an informal boycott of Shell by German motorists mounted, with support from members of all German political parties, unions, a motorists' association, and the Protestant church (including the former chief justice of the German Constitutional Court, Ernst Benda).

Despite the growing protests and repeated occupation attempts, Shell began towing the Brent Spar rig to its planned dumping site on June 11, causing a fierce, instantaneous public backlash. Shell sales dropped by up to 40 percent at German gas stations, and the mayor of Leipzig barred city vehicles from using Shell gasoline. Boycotts also spread to the Netherlands and Denmark. During the G7 Summit in Halifax, Canada, German Chancellor Helmut Kohl criticized Shell and the British government for persisting with the proposed deep-sea dumping. Two days later, a firebomb exploded at a Shell gas station in Hamburg. In the United Kingdom, members of Parliament repeatedly attacked Prime Minister John Major, but he refused to reconsider the government's decision to approve Shell's proposal.

Finally, on June 20, 1995, Shell gave in. After a meeting of the Royal Dutch Shell Group's managing directors in The Hague, Shell UK chairman Christopher Fay announced that Shell would abandon its plans to sink the Brent Spar oil rig. Fay stressed that he still believed that deep-sea disposal offered the best environmental option, but he admitted that Shell UK was in an "untenable position" because of its failure to convince other governments around the North Sea. Shell UK would attempt to dismantle the platform on land and seek approval from Norwegian authorities to anchor Brent Spar temporarily on the Norwegian coast. Three years later, Shell converted the Brent Spar into a port landing facility in Norway, a recycling solution whose final cost Shell estimated at £60 million.

The story does not end there. After Shell UK had decided to abandon deepwater disposal, Greenpeace commissioned an independent Norwegian inspection agency called Det Norske Veritas to resolve the issue of the remaining oil sludge. Shell had previously estimated that the Spar contained about 100 metric tons of sludge, a fraction of Greenpeace's estimate of 5,000 metric tons. On September 5, the executive director of Greenpeace UK, Lord Peter Melchett, admitted that Greenpeace's significantly higher estimate was inaccurate, and apologized to Fay. Shell UK welcomed the apology and announced its intention of including Greenpeace among the stakeholders that it would consult in its review of options and the development of a new disposal strategy.

Although Greenpeace called the Brent Spar affair a victory for the environment, the jury is still out in many quarters, with some scientists and environmentalists affirming that deep-sea disposal would have been environmentally acceptable. In a June 1995 issue of *Nature*, two British geologists argued that the environmental effects of Shell UK's decision to dump the Brent Spar rig in the deep sea would "probably be minimal."[8] Indeed, the metals of the Brent Spar might even have proved beneficial to the deep-sea environment, and the rig might have created an artificial reef for fish. Making matters worse, the onshore disposal of the Brent Spar could actually pose greater risks to the environment. Robert SanGeorge of the Switzerland-based Worldwide Fund for Nature said, "Deep-sea disposal seemed the least harmful option."

He called the Brent Spar episode "a circus and sideshow that distracted from the big environmental issues affecting the world."[9]

THINKING STRATEGICALLY

The main difference between any of the reputational crises discussed so far and the Shell-Greenpeace confrontation lies in its origin. Rather than being triggered by an actual or imagined quality problem—a "broken promise" to customers or business partners—the Brent Spar controversy resulted from a deliberate attack by Greenpeace. In the absence of the activists' campaign, few customers, if any, would have known or cared much about Shell's approach to decommissioning the Brent Spar. Greenpeace intentionally targeted Shell because the company had the misfortune of being the first to try to scuttle an unwanted oil rig in the North Sea, and Greenpeace wanted to make an example of the company and ensure that other companies would not try to follow suit. Shell was caught unaware and unprepared, and its aggressive stance may have played right into the activists' hands.

Shell's response was typical; when attacked by activists, businesses often become defensive and overreact. These short-tempered reactions only serve to increase media coverage and add fuel to the fire, allowing "David" to score "more PR points than Goliath."[10] This does not mean that fighting back never works or that companies should not seriously consider it as a strategic option, but it does mean that companies must avoid reacting emotionally and should instead treat these challenges for what they are: strategic maneuvers by highly motivated, capable, and savvy agents.

A good way for executives to calm their nerves is to think of Greenpeace as a competitor, not for market share or customers, of course, but for the company's reputation. Getting angry at Greenpeace is no more productive for Shell than getting angry at Exxon Mobil; neither foe will miraculously vaporize as a result.

> Reputational crises can be the result of deliberate attacks. Companies usually react to these attacks in a defensive manner. Such a response plays right into the hands of the attackers. Executives need to avoid emotional reactions and treat these challenges for what they are: strategic maneuvers by highly motivated, capable, and savvy agents.

Anticipating challenges by activists and nongovernmental organizations (NGOs) and managing them effectively requires just as much strategic thinking as handling a traditional competitor. The first rule of strategy is to learn to think like the opponent. World War II British Field Marshal Bernard Montgomery took this practice to the extreme with his habit of collecting pictures of his opponent German Field Marshal Erwin Rommel, known as the "Desert Fox." Montgomery believed that by studying the face of his opponent, he would better understand Rommel's thought processes, allowing him to anticipate Rommel's next move.[11]

In reputation management, thinking like one's opponent means identifying key constituencies and stakeholders, anticipating their motivations and capabilities, and taking appropriate preventive or corrective actions. These constituencies and stakeholders include the media, activists, politicians, and regulators. Frequently, these stakeholders are motivated by political, social, or moral concerns, and take issue with certain aspects of business practices. Managers and corporate councils must take these adversaries seriously, regardless of whether they share the concerns. As the Brent Spar so painfully demonstrates, "being right" does not ensure success; what matters is the public's *perception* of being right.

Many political activists are strategically savvy and have a keen sense of how to use media coverage to their advantage, but managers frequently take a dismissive or defensive stance toward them, especially when the managers feel that they have been unfairly targeted or singled out. A "circling the wagons" response or overly aggressive legal action frequently results. These attitudes play right into the hands of political activists or politicians. Corporate leaders need to understand these interconnections and adjust their actions accordingly.

To see this approach in action, let us borrow a tool from the military: the Red Team–Blue Team war-gaming exercise.[12] The Red Team's job is to conceive of and execute an attack, while the Blue Team's job is to defend against it. Let us assume the role of the Red Team and put ourselves in the shoes of Greenpeace. Six months before the Brent Spar confrontation, it first learned about the Brent Spar from a local activist. As a first step, we need to understand Greenpeace's motivations and capabilities: its purpose, strengths, competitive environment, funding model, and so forth.

As an aggressive environmental campaigning group with a strong global brand, Greenpeace's funding and other resources come largely from donations and membership fees. It relies on a vast network of volunteers whose specific skills can be utilized in a given campaign. Greenpeace views itself as avant-garde, pushing the boundaries of the environmental movement to "change attitudes and behavior," because "this fragile earth deserves a voice" and needs "warriors."[13] Importantly, Greenpeace aims not only to raise awareness, but also to make actual changes in environmental practices. While Greenpeace has targeted both governments and businesses, its recent campaigns have largely focused on corporations, frequently with the goal of shaping industry standards rather than of targeting a particular firm.

Greenpeace occupies one particular niche in the environmental spectrum. Other environmental groups, like Conservation International, are more solution-oriented and less confrontational. Indeed, from time to time, Greenpeace engages in internal debates on finding the right balance between confrontation and engagements, but ultimately one of its greatest strengths lies in staging "high-profile, nonviolent conflict to raise the level and quality of public debate."[14]

To execute its strategy successfully, Greenpeace needs to identify high-profile targets that are highly visible *and* beatable. Generating support for an issue will not suffice; activists also need to create business impact and inflict damage on the company's bottom line. While the Brent Spar certainly qualified on the first criterion, the second one created significant strategic challenges for Greenpeace, because legally the only two institutions that could stop the disposal of the Brent Spar were the British government and Shell UK, which had operating responsibility for the buoy. Other EU governments could comment on the decision, but they could not change it; any influence would be indirect and would be likely to be resisted by a euro-skeptic Tory government. Similarly, given the decentralized decision-making structure of Royal Dutch Shell, any interference from the group level would have been highly unusual and would have set a disruptive precedent.

In effect, Greenpeace had only two targets—Shell UK and the British government—and neither one seemed particularly promising. The British government had publicly supported Shell, and there was no widespread environmental movement in Britain that could have gal-

vanized significant constituency support for a reversal of the government's position. Moreover, the oil industry had created many jobs in the
United Kingdom and provided the British government with significant
revenues from fees and taxes. Finally, the likely alternative to deep-sea
disposal (onshore dismantling) presented significant environmental risk
to the British coastline. For the same reasons, a boycott of Shell UK's
products would probably have had limited success. Some British customers might have participated in the boycott, but the effects would
probably have stayed at a nuisance level, as Shell UK had consulted with
most of the relevant stakeholders and gained their support.

Undaunted, Greenpeace sidestepped the problem and ensured
a greater likelihood of victory for the campaign by targeting Shell's
German subsidiary, along with subsidiaries in other northern European countries. Greenpeace shifted the battle to an arena in which
it enjoyed substantial support; a large, well-organized environmental
movement; and a high level of public awareness. By contrast, Shell
faced a much more tenuous position in the country, as the oil industry
had little economic presence in Germany. To execute this strategy,
Greenpeace shifted its point of attack and targeted Shell's logo (see
Figure 3-1).

Figure 3-1 **Greenpeace's Strategy**

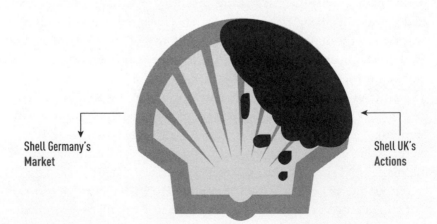

Shell Germany's
Market

Shell UK's
Actions

By attacking one of the world's most recognized corporate symbols, Greenpeace linked Shell UK's actions with Shell Germany's market, moving the confrontation to a battleground where Greenpeace was strong and Shell was weak. This attack caught Shell Germany completely off guard, as it had not been consulted on any aspect of the Brent Spar disposal issue and bore no direct responsibility, legal or operational, for the decision. By exploiting a key component of Shell's market strategy (a global brand with a highly decentralized operating structure), Greenpeace successfully turned Shell's great asset (its brand) into a liability. Shell Germany could not distance itself from Shell UK without undermining the group's core brand management approach. While it bore no responsibility for Shell UK's actions, Shell Germany nonetheless suffered the costs: a boycott that reduced sales by 40 percent.

Let us pause here for a moment to make sure that we capture all the insights. Notice that Greenpeace's targeting strategy resulted entirely from strategic concerns. Greenpeace did not necessarily consider Shell the worst offender among oil companies (some would argue that this honor goes to ExxonMobil); Shell was just a means to an end. Greenpeace recognized and seized an opportunity to generate a public outcry regarding deep-sea dumping leading into the Fourth International Conference on the Protection of the North Sea. The organization understood the magnitude of the Brent Spar disposal, because it would set a precedent for handling other decommissioned rigs in the future.

There are certainly cases in which organizations use a boycott as a punishment against a company. Punitive campaigns commonly arise in the entertainment industry when some population segment takes offense at the content of a movie, a book, or a record. Consider the National Organization for Women (NOW)'s punitive boycott of Alfred A. Knopf, Inc., for publishing the book *American Psycho*, which contained extensive graphic description of violence against women.[15]

Most boycotts do not follow this pattern, however; they are proactive rather than punitive, with the primary goal of effecting widespread change rather than punishing a particular company. Companies that are explicitly targeted may find that this has less to do with specific wrongdoings and more with strategic vulnerabilities that sophisticated activists feel they can exploit.

> Sophisticated activists will select compa-
> nies not to punish them, but to engender
> changes in business practices. Good target
> companies are those that are vulnerable and
> can affect industry standards.

A variety of factors made Shell an attractive target in the Brent Spar case. First, Shell was a well-known consumer brand symbolized by an easily recognizable logo, which made strong media interest in the boycott likely. Second, the Brent Spar was the first of many large North Sea installations that were eligible for deepwater disposal. By creating a strong public backlash, Greenpeace hoped to make an example of Shell and inspire governments to adopt regulations that would prohibit the practice of deepwater dumping. Indeed, no oil company has since attempted deepwater disposal.

At first, companies refrained from pursuing deepwater dumping for fear of becoming the next target. The North Sea countries eventually adopted the 1998 OSPAR Convention for the Protection of the Marine Environment of the North-East Atlantic, which imposed a moratorium on deepwater disposal, effectively ending the practice. In the convention, members accepted the legal obligation "to take all possible steps to prevent and eliminate pollution and shall take the necessary measures to protect the maritime area against adverse effects of human activities."[16] This was Greenpeace's dream outcome. Targeting one company led to a fundamental change in industry practice, first in the form of industrywide self-regulation, then codified by an international convention.

Strategic targeting creates surprise, which in turn compromises adequate responses by companies. When I work with companies that find themselves in the middle of an activist campaign, managers often describe the experience using phrases like "I never saw this coming" and "out of the blue." To grasp this, put yourself in the shoes of Peter Duncan, Shell Germany's CEO. Shell Germany took the full impact of the attack, yet it was *completely innocent*. It had nothing to do with the operating decisions of Shell UK, and the issue went beyond its legal and operational responsibilities. In fact, Duncan told the German magazine *Der Spiegel* that he first heard about the planned sinking of Brent Spar from the media.[17] This is a very important point: *reputational risk transcends the legal structure of the company*. One business segment can suffer because of the activities of another.

Similarly, companies can find themselves held accountable for the business practices of their suppliers, as is evident in the case of the boycott of Nike over global labor practices. A maker of sportswear and related equipment, Nike manufactures its

> Reputational risk transcends the legal structure of the firm. One business segment can suffer because of the activities of another. Companies can also be held accountable for the business practices of suppliers or contractors.

products almost exclusively through independent contractors, the bulk of which (about 70 percent) are located in South and East Asia.[18] The company faced accusations of labor abuse in East Asian factories as early as the late 1980s, and the issue achieved notoriety in the mid-1990s, when the company had to deal with widespread accusations related to the use of child labor, underpayment, and poor working conditions in Cambodia, Pakistan, China, and Vietnam. A BBC documentary fueled passions in 2001 when it revealed the labor practices in a factory in Cambodia.[19] Although the company initially tried to distance itself from responsibility for conditions in the contracted factories, consistent pressure from human rights groups, student activists, and labor organizations ultimately led Nike to ensure that stronger controls for acceptable business practices were in place.[20]

Clearly, reputational risk cares little for organization charts and job descriptions. It arises as a result of forces outside of a company's control, and public perception issues can be reined in only through multidimensional approaches. This reality does not always square well with the typical operating model of most companies, which clearly define areas of responsibility and hold managers accountable only for the performance of their own specific business segments.

THE SECOND CIRCLE

So far, we have focused on the strategic advantages of activists and their ability to select targets, unencumbered by legal and operational constraints. All activists, however, face a significant strategic disadvantage in that they must gain attention for their cause. Space on the public agenda is very limited and highly contested, and activists understand that successful campaigns require media attention. In his handbook for activists, San Francisco low-rent-housing advocate Randy Shaw put it succinctly: "Ideally, tactical activists should use the media both to generate a scandal and then to demand a specific, concrete result."[21] For activists, media coverage has at least four distinct advantages:

- Media coverage provides a cheap means of communicating the activists' message and related information to the public. It creates the stage that leads the public to pay attention.

- Coverage by respected media outlets gives the covered issue some prima facie credibility and puts pressure on the company.

- Visual coverage creates a cognitive and emotional frame for viewers. The use of water cannons in the Greenpeace-Shell confrontation, for example, evoked memories among German viewers of the 1989 Eastern European uprisings against communist regimes.

- Coverage by the mass media may also trigger additional debate in user-generated media such as blogs.

In other words, activists will attempt to use the media to create a reputational crisis for the company, forcing it to change its business practices. That is the nature of the outer circle, illustrated in Figure 3-2.

This tactic is also popular with public officials and politicians. Former New York Attorney General Eliot Spitzer always accompanied his investigations with a press conference at which he presented evidence of questionable business conduct. In many cases, this evidence consisted of embarrassing e-mails or internal memos, which immediately triggered a reputational crisis for the company that was in the spotlight, forcing it to settle and change its business practices. In one such example, Putnam Investments—at the time a division of Marsh & McLennan—lost roughly $70 billion in assets under management as a consequence of a Spitzer investigation. The company eventually paid $110 million in penalties and restitution to federal authorities.[22]

To generate sufficient participation in a boycott, activists need to obtain extensive media coverage that leads to advocacy (the upper right corner of the Reputational Terrain discussed in Chapter 2). This is difficult. Competition for air and print space is fierce, and many

Figure 3-2 **The Second Circle**

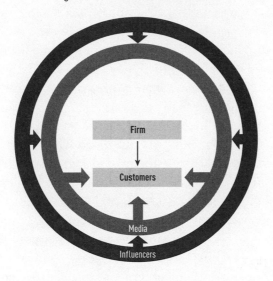

environmental issues, such as the disposal of the Brent Spar, involve complicated, technical concepts that do not immediately resonate with journalists or the public. Indeed, *before* Greenpeace took action, the Brent Spar issue was located in an area that had little or no coverage in the media (the lower left corner of the Reputational Terrain). Greenpeace therefore needed to stage its protests in a way that would increase *both* audience interest *and* social importance. But how?

Successful activist groups distinguish themselves by doing just that. They condense a highly complex issue into evocative images that are easy to understand, emotionally engaging, and connected to issues about which the audience cares passionately. In other words, activists are masters at condensing complicated policy decisions into compelling stories.

Let us see how Greenpeace accomplished this. The Brent Spar occupation provided an ideal means of increasing audience interest by providing drama, high stakes, and spectacular visuals. A Greenpeace occupation looks like a paramilitary opera-

> Activists need the attention of the public. Gaining that attention without the media is very difficult. Smart activists are capable of strategically using media coverage to put an issue on the agenda. Overly aggressive corporate responses will play right into the hands of activists.

tion, which evokes associations of war and conflict, life and death, with Greenpeace activists taking the role of heroes risking their lives in a war to save the planet. By turning on the water cannons, Shell played directly into the hands of the activists. It unintentionally followed their script, assuming the role of the big, evil business that was ruthlessly attacking the selfless defenders of the world's oceans—a perfect example of the villain-victim-hero triad.

Ironically, Greenpeace's initial occupation of the platform generated only moderate media interest. That changed when Shell began firing water cannons. The subsequent drama of soaked activists hanging on to the platform, helicopters dodging water cannons, and supporters flashing victory signs in speeding Zodiacs provided irresistible TV drama.

While using water cannons may seem like an easily avoidable tactical mistake, many companies surprisingly fail to understand this dynamic. For example, they may sue activists for trespassing and other legal infractions, an understandable tactic in response to activists who deliberately break or at least bend the law in executing their campaign. Of course, the activists do this precisely to provoke companies into taking aggressive action, ensuring that the company's role is that of the villain.

Companies must remember that most activist campaigns do not garner media interest, because getting onto the public agenda is hard. Clever activists will select targets accordingly and choose tactics that are intended to maximize media interest. Anything that will increase media interest will do. Activists will simply treat the media drivers identified in the previous chapter as a strategic module. This could be a well-known brand name, a prior incident, or a prominent spokesperson. One reason child labor activists targeted Nike was its celebrity athlete spokesperson, basketball superstar Michael Jordan.[23]

Merely increasing audience interest was not sufficient to ensure Greenpeace's success. The activists also needed to provide the German public with a simple, straightforward reason to act. Ingeniously, Greenpeace framed the whole issue as a recycling issue, something that German citizens cared about passionately (see Figure 3-3). The activists' slogan—"Here I am dutifully recycling my garbage, and there comes big business and simply dumps its trash in the ocean"—made the choice easy for German citizens. Since every upstanding German citizen recycled, Shell, because it was dumping the Brent Spar into the deep ocean, could not be a good *corporate* citizen.

Figure 3-3 **Setting the Stage**

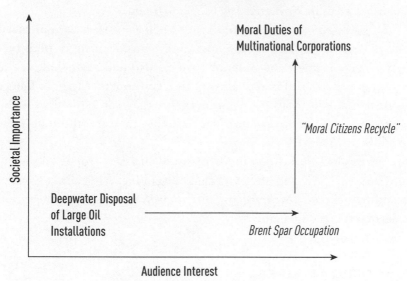

Framing the issue as one involving the moral duties of corporate citizens rendered Shell's scientific arguments powerless. Shell's use of technical language failed to accomplish its goal of justifying deep-sea disposal, and instead looked like a feeble attempt to avoid the onerous duty of being a good corporate citizen. Shell company spokesman Rainer Winzenried underscored this at the conclusion of the Brent Spar battle. "We had to explain the pros and cons of both [disposal] solutions in papers this long," said Winzenried, spreading his arms wide. "They [Greenpeace] had a simple, single-issue message—a poison bomb, the North Sea, and a precedence for 400 other platforms."[24] Taking action against a company resembles a political act: it will work more effectively if it is succinct and connected to issues that are culturally meaningful and evoke a passionate response from customers and stakeholders.

This concludes the Red Team exercise. We now have a good understanding of Greenpeace's strategy, where it will attack, and how it will execute that attack. Greenpeace will focus its campaign on Shell Germany. In addition to its large market and its status as Greenpeace's North Sea Operations Center, Germany has a strong environmental movement and oil companies play only a minor economic role, all in marked contrast to the situation in the United Kingdom. Greenpeace will strike where it has a strategic advantage, not where the legal responsibility lies, establishing this link by attacking the Shell brand.

This strategy puts Shell in a bind. Shell Germany cannot plead innocence in the affair, because claiming that operating responsibility rests with a largely autonomous business will undermine one of the world's most powerful brands and confuse consumers. After all, Shell's global brand aims to assure consumers that they can rely on its high-quality gasoline and superior service, whether they are filling up their cars in Madrid or Moscow.

As a result of the boycott in Germany, Shell's sales dropped dramatically, and Shell UK and Shell Germany began bickering about what to do and who should bear the economic impact. At that point, the group leadership stepped in: game over.

COUNTERSTRATEGIES

Shell clearly did not anticipate the nature and extent of the threat posed by the activists, who considered the fact that the Brent Spar was the first structure eligible for deepwater disposal to be of paramount importance. That meant that by stopping or at least hampering Shell, Greenpeace could set an example for the rest of the industry and raise the cost of using fossil fuels, accomplishing one of its long-term goals.

In addition to its inability to think about the issue from the activists' side (a key capability for strategic crisis management), Shell's internal organizational structure was ill suited for the task at hand. Recall that Shell UK had operating responsibility for disposing of the Brent Spar and thus would have to pay the costs of disposal. Given these incentives, Shell UK understandably focused on the stakeholders in its region (regulators, fishermen's associations, and so on), and based on the responses (concerns about onshore pollution of the British coastline), the company stuck with deepwater disposal. This decision-making structure obviously did not take into account the potential damage to the brand as a whole.

Shell was blindsided by the events that followed and lacked the organizational capability to respond quickly to the threat. Suppose instead that the company *had* anticipated the potential attack. What could it have done differently? It's time to think about counterstrategies.

Playing Tough

A first strategy, favored by many managers, is to play tough, either by ignoring the opposition entirely or by attacking it. Both tactics are based on the intuition that engaging with activists gives them additional legitimacy and attention, which may just add fuel to the fire. Moreover, a willingness to negotiate may be interpreted as a sign of weakness that will just embolden activists; a firm that demonstrates that it is responsive to activist pressure may become a more appealing target for future campaigns, as, some observers have argued, happened to Starbucks.[25] Managers may believe that it is in the best interests of the firm to build a reputation for toughness and to send a message that the company will not be bullied.

This strategy can work in many circumstances, but it needs to be carefully evaluated to ensure that the company is not acting out of anger. In other words, an aggressive response should not be just an extension of an emotional reaction by the CEO or senior management itching to fight back. Neither should companies play deaf if this is merely an excuse for doing nothing. Whether companies choose to engage fiercely or silently, it is imperative that they engage deliberately.

Companies that decide to pursue silence need to be ready for some tough times. While it is true that some activists will simply go away if they are starved for attention, companies will probably need to prepare for an extended period in which some low-grade trouble may flare up from time to time, resembling a chronic condition rather than a crisis.

Consider the case of the Union Oil Company of California (Unocal) in Burma (now known as Myanmar).[26] In 1993, Unocal began developing a $1.2 billion natural gas pipeline to transport gas from rigs in the Andaman Sea to supply much-needed energy for Burma and Thailand. This project looked like a major economic win for the struggling firm, with an expected return of $110 million a year. However, the success of this project relied on the firm's cooperation with the State Law and Order Restoration Council (SLORC), a military junta that had ruled Burma since the late 1980s. The SLORC had been widely reported to have killed thousands of Burmese citizens and had suspended many basic human rights, such as due process and freedom of speech.

The political conditions in Burma led to protests in many Western countries. One advocacy group, the Free Burma Coalition (FBC), based in Madison, Wisconsin, and composed of high school and university students, community members, and Burmese dissidents, had started targeting companies that were doing business in Burma. Through peaceful protests and boycotts, the group pressured many multinational corporations to stop sourcing products from Burma. By 2002, the FBC had convinced more than 30 firms to stop doing business in Burma. However, Unocal, along with a few other firms, had continued operations and even increased its investment.

Unocal's continuing presence in Burma led to increased pressure from the FBC. The protest eventually led to the filing of a lawsuit against Unocal and its parent company on behalf of a group of Burmese villagers, claiming that the company's use of SLORC security forces had resulted in the systematic destruction and relocation of villages, the use of forced labor, and human rights atrocities, including rape and murder. The suit was filed under the Alien Tort Claims Act, which allows U.S. courts to hear human rights cases brought by foreign citizens for conduct committed outside the United States.[27] Unocal decided to appoint a director of corporate responsibility charged with the task of improving the lives of people wherever Unocal worked, but it did not divest its Burmese operations. It eventually settled the lawsuit in December 2004.

A strategy that refuses to engage activists is frequently based on the idea that the activists will eventually come to understand the futility of their efforts and give up. To outlast activists in a war of attrition, management needs to be able to maintain the support of employees, business partners, and suppliers. Employees may be ashamed of the company's actions, may face resentment in their private lives, or may secretly sympathize with the activists. This can breed disenchantment, cynicism, and even security risks such as leaks or unauthorized press contacts. Similarly, customers, especially commercial customers, may fear guilt by association, even if they privately agree with the company's conduct. A well-known branded company, such as The Gap, cannot be associated with suppliers who engage in unfair labor practices. Its reputational risk is just too big.

To avoid this erosion of support, companies must constantly communicate their position to their business partners and their people.

These messages need to be clear and transparent. They should connect the values and identity of the company to maintain a sense of unity, and include an appeal to principles other than material self-interest. This is particularly important for maintaining support among employees, who will be put in the position of needing to defend their company's actions to their spouses, children, friends, and neighbors. A simple "We are doing it for the shareholders," will not suffice.

While taking a tough stance using silence can have its challenges, companies that wish to get tough by aggressively fighting back with lawsuits and other measures must proceed with caution as well. The so-called McLibel incident provides an instructive example. In 1990, McDonald's brought a libel suit against two members of London Greenpeace, David Morris and Helen Steel.[28] Both defendants were unemployed and penniless and were eventually forced to defend themselves. London Greenpeace, a small, radical, anarchist–environmentalist group that had refused to become part of Greenpeace International, had previously started to distribute leaflets accusing McDonald's food corporation of "ruthless exploitation of resources and animals . . . wrecking the planet" and of encouraging tropical rainforest destruction by raising cattle on recently deforested land in Central and South America.

McDonald's was in a strong legal position, because there is no equivalent in the United Kingdom to the First Amendment free-speech protections in the United States. In the United Kingdom, the burden of proof lies with the defendants, who must demonstrate that their claims are essentially true and constitute "fair comment." However, the decision to sue backfired spectacularly. It led to extensive coverage of the case in the London media and created a stage of which Morris and Steel could only ever have dreamed. When the trial finally ended, the "McLibel" trial had

> Confrontational strategies need to be based on a clinical analysis, not on anger or the desire for vindication. Playing tough works best if a campaign focuses on an area that is not central to the company's business model or fails to gain momentum. Companies need to be ready for a long-term war of attrition that requires the ongoing support of key constituencies. Aggressive strategies need to be used with extreme caution, as they may play into the activists' hands.

become the longest case in British history and had turned into a "public relations nightmare for McDonald's."[29]

Playing tough works best when the issue is not central to the company's business model or when the activists' position lacks intuitive appeal. This will be the case if the issue is complex or overly technical. However, if these conditions are not met, other strategies need to be considered.

Credibility Transfer

Companies that become the target of activist campaigns frequently feel that they have been wrongfully accused—they are certain that if they could tell their story, they would win the argument. However, executives need to understand that this is more difficult than it looks. While companies may have a strong reputation for product attributes such as quality, consistency, and taste, they usually do not enjoy similar credibility on issues such as sustainability, working conditions, or animal welfare. Quality, consistency, and taste can be experienced and thus directly tested by customers. If I buy a pair of athletic shoes, I can examine their look, determine how comfortable they feel, assess how long they might last, and so forth. But I cannot verify whether they were made by 12-year-olds in a faraway factory. Customers cannot directly verify whether a company or product makes good on its promise of fair labor standards, sustainable business practices, or commitment to animal welfare. Such dimensions of a product are not based on experience, but must be *believed*; they are known as *credence attributes*.[30]

Examples of credence attributes are labor practices, animal welfare, sustainable business practices, fair trade purchasing, and safety concerns. Even though these attributes cannot be explicitly detected, customers may still feel strongly enough about them to switch to competitive products that have higher credibility in these areas, as is evident from both the Nike boycott and the Brent Spar confrontation.

Companies enjoy far less trust on these dimensions than academic experts, doctors, government agencies, the media, NGOs, and consumer groups do. Moreover, psychological research shows that audiences respond far more strongly to negative news than to positive news. Finally, it is frequently not in the short-term interest of companies to be fully transparent about their business practices, as adopting socially responsible business practices can be very costly and create operational complications.[31]

Taken together, this means that companies will frequently face severe credibility problems on dimensions that are important to activists, even if customers trust their products on experience-based dimensions. Experimental evidence shows that a company that has merely been accused of wrongdoing is not judged differently from a company that has actually been found guilty.[32]

On credence dimensions, customers need someone to believe. If the company is not a source of trust, it must forge relationships with third parties, such as the media or NGOs, that can be called upon as needed to help shape customers' perceptions on issues as they arise. Over the last decade, McDonald's has consistently used credibility transfer with great success.[33] The fast-food giant has fostered relationships with Conservation International and other environmental groups to help mediate sustainability issues, with Dr. Temple Grandin of Colorado State University to assist with animal welfare concerns, and with well-known author Dean Ornish on matters of nutrition. These independent parties, who are all well respected in their sectors, can help to mediate differences of opinion between activists and companies in the eyes of the public, thereby preventing runaway reputational crises. As controversies arise, McDonald's can simply refer to or engage with the expert with the highest credibility level. Customers do not need to understand the details of the issues; they just need to trust the expert. Credibility is then transferred from the expert to the company.

Consider a recent controversy over animal welfare standards. After a nine-year moratorium, the animal rights group People for the Ethical Treatment of Animals (PETA) relaunched its "McCruelty" campaign in 2009 against McDonald's allegedly unethical practices for slaughtering chickens.[34] The reinstitution of the campaign came as a result of McDonald's refusal to insist that its suppliers use controlled atmosphere killing (CAK), which effectively gasses the chickens before attaching them to an assembly line. Although about 30 percent of slaughterhouses in Europe used the method, the technology hardly existed in the United States. McDonald's maintained that CAK has no conclusive advantage over conventional slaughtering methods. But what really made a difference were statements by Dr. Grandin, arguably the country's most trusted expert on humane animal handling.[35]

Dr. Grandin has published several books and was named one of *Time* magazine's 100 most influential people in the world. The award-winning HBO movie *Temple Grandin*, released in 2010, details her struggle with autism. Grandin pointed out various potential problems with CAK, but she did not endorse traditional methods either. Her assessment of the situation diffused some of PETA's momentum and further increased the complexity of the issue.

Companies should not wait for a crisis or campaign to establish a network of third parties. Once a company has been portrayed as the villain, credible third parties will be very reluctant to publicly associate with it. Such outreach requires patience and a long timeline. Credible third parties may be suspicious of the company's motives and need to protect their own reputations. That is, they need to be assured that the company's practices indeed are consistent with their own values and beliefs.

> Companies have less credibility than other parties, especially compared to NGOs. Simply telling its story may not overcome the company's credibility gap. Outreach to credible third parties can solve this problem. This needs to be done well in advance of a problem and requires patience and the willingness to change some business practices.

Any form of financial compensation, direct or indirect, is problematic and will undermine the third parties' independence. At the very least, it should be clearly disclosed. Dr. Grandin, for example, is a member of McDonald's Animal Welfare Council, a group of impartial specialists who offer *pro bono* advice to the company.

Credibility transfer works best if the issues are complicated and the company already has the proper practices in place but has difficulty getting its story across. Good examples are companies that mishandled a previous incident and now, under new management or ownership, are committed to rebuilding their reputation. Credibility transfer is about ensuring open lines of communication and dialogue between companies and stakeholders, but a true dialogue means that both sides are willing to keep an open mind and entertain the possibility of change.

Constructive Engagement

In many cases, stakeholder outreach and communication strategies are sufficient for correcting perception problems; however, companies sometimes also need to make changes in their business practices. For example, McDonald's has modified its business practices in response to activist campaigns and in anticipation of emerging issues. Among other things, McDonald's has changed its conduct in areas ranging from toy safety and sustainability to animal welfare and the introduction of healthier menu items such as salads and apple slices.[36]

Changes in business practices can have various advantages. Ideally, they may remove the main reason for a campaign. But even in the absence of this, such changes may give credence to a communication strategy, facilitate third-party endorsement, or simply add some complexity to an issue to increase the likelihood that analysis and expertise can still be heard. For example, when McDonald's introduced salads and apple slices on its menu, this not only added more healthy items, but also allowed the company to focus on a message of consumer choice.

Such changes can also be implemented on an industry level. In many cases, activists are not merely trying to change the behavior of one specific firm, but want to change industry practice as a whole. When this is the goal, activists frequently select a single firm as their target, thereby reducing participation costs for consumers. If only one oil company is boycotted, consumers can easily buy their gasoline at a nontargeted competitor. Once one firm in an industry concedes, the next can be targeted, and so forth. As a result, targeting firms sequentially can be advantageous.[37] Firms may have an incentive to act as an industry to avoid a race to the top in which sequentially targeted companies adopt increasingly tougher standards. Other firms, however, may not wish to come to the assistance of a targeted firm, perhaps because they want to avoid the heat of a campaign as long as they can or because they have experienced an increased demand for their products. The ability of firms to solve this collective problem will depend on various factors, such as industry structure, consumer demand, and the existing regulatory environment.

While self-regulation can eventually become codified in government regulation, there are increasing numbers of examples in which industries adopt explicit standards of self-regulation without any reference to governmental actors. Perhaps even more common is the tacit abandonment of controversial business practices by groups of firms.[38]

> Constructive engagement can sometimes remove a reputational risk. It also can help to tell a better story should a crisis occur.

WAL-MART AND ITS CRITICS

When companies find themselves the target of persistent activist campaigns, they often experience a corporate version of Elizabeth Kübler-Ross's five stages of grief: denial, anger, negotiation, depression, and acceptance.[39] Few companies have experienced each stage as deeply as Wal-Mart.

In 2004, Wal-Mart had reached the peak of corporate America.[40] It was number one on the Fortune 500 list, America's most admired company, and, with 1.6 million associates worldwide, the largest nongovernmental employer.[41] From the mid-1990s, Wal-Mart had been a pioneer in technology-driven productivity enhancement, extensively using point-of-sale data collection and sophisticated just-in-time delivery systems.[42] Combined with its sheer size (Wal-Mart then accounted for approximately 10 percent of all retail sales in the United States), these technological capabilities enabled the company to exert an unprecedented degree of control over manufacturers, suppliers, and distributors. In practical terms, through its bargaining power, Wal-Mart could force its partners to set prices at whatever levels it deemed desirable.

But all was not well. The company was seeing declining profit margins and a stock price that had lost more than 25 percent of its value since 2000. While much of this decline tracked market conditions, many industry observers believed that Wal-Mart's original formula of cost cutting and rural expansion had reached a point of diminishing returns. Wal-Mart's third CEO and president, Lee Scott, and others concluded that the company needed to develop a more urban strategy, with products for upscale customers in addition to lower-price consumables. One of its most important initiatives was its entry into the grocery market, begun in 1988, which promised to generate conflicts with a number of traditional employee unions in the supermarket chains.[43]

Wal-Mart had always had its fair share of critics. First, the critics alleged that by destroying local "mom-and-pop" stores that could not compete on price, Wal-Mart often turned traditional downtown shopping areas from vital social centers into ghost towns. Second, critics asserted that Wal-Mart's labor practices were unfair. The company should allow its associates to unionize, offer better wages and affordable health insurance benefits, and treat its employees more humanely.[44] Wal-Mart's entry into the grocery industry focused the attention of labor unions, which had traditionally operated in this sector; they viewed Wal-Mart as a threat to the "hard-earned gains" that they had negotiated over decades of labor activism in the supermarket chains.[45]

Third, critics argued, Wal-Mart had to provide a more equitable management of its supply chain, from alleged "sweatshop" workers in China to the company's truckers and its manufacturing partners, which included more than 5,300 factories in 60 countries, virtually all of them outsourced. There were myriad issues associated with the company's supply chain, ranging from child labor to 90-hour workweeks. Though these were subcontractors, critics held Wal-Mart accountable for deplorable working conditions.[46]

Fourth, given the scale of Wal-Mart's operations, critics believed that the company was having an adverse impact on the environment. In the aquatic-farm industry, Wal-Mart created a huge market for inexpensive deboned salmon fillets. To supply this market, entrepreneurs in Chile established salmon farms in the ocean from which they could harvest more than a million pounds of filets per year. This practice generated so much waste from feces and excess feed that huge "dead zones" were observed around these farms.[47]

These criticisms amounted to a repudiation of Wal-Mart's business model. Even worse, evidence suggested that the criticism was resonating with an increasing portion of the public, including growing disapproval by more affluent, middle-class consumers in urban areas—that is, the group that the company had identified as the market that it must enter next if its growth rates were to improve.[48]

Wal-Mart's critics began to mount protest campaigns against the company, which were often spearheaded by union activists. Their tactics included a proliferation of grassroots campaigns, often successful, to block the establishment of new Wal-Mart supercenters in urban areas such as Chicago and Los Angeles; targeted consumer boycotts; a barrage of media attacks (in films and television, on the Internet, and in print); and efforts to unionize Wal-Mart associates. Research studies point out that from 1998 to 2005, Wal-Mart faced protests in one-third of its planned store openings. In two-thirds of the incidents, a store did not open in response to community protests.[49] In addition, the company became the object of a growing number of lawsuits—on average two per hour, 365 days per year, with more than 8,000 pending at any one time—from both current and former employees and customers, including many class-action suits.[50] Activists had become Wal-Mart's biggest business rival.

The Strategy Shift

As media campaigns against the company grew in 2004, Scott decided to mount a counteroffensive. This strategy of responding directly to the claims of critics represented a departure for the company. After hiring the public relations firm Edelman, the company created a new strategic unit at its Arkansas headquarters, which included a campaign-style "war room" to anticipate and respond to stories in the media.[51]

As Scott observed, "When growth was easier, this idea of critics being ignored was O.K." But, he added, the company had to reach out to groups, including antisweatshop groups to improve monitoring of overseas factories, and environmental groups, such as the Natural Resources Defense Council and Conservation International, to improve the company's environmental standards, starting with cuts in paper, plastics, and fuel.[52] The company would, Scott promised, reduce greenhouse gases produced by Wal-Mart stores by 20 percent over the next seven years. Moreover, measures to publicize its improved treatment of its workers were underway: health-care coverage would be provided to Wal-Mart associates for $25 per month. Scott even called on the U.S. Congress to raise the minimum wage. "We have an aggressive vision," Scott explained. "With courage and commitment to change, we will be at our best and remain true to the legacy of the company Sam Walton founded some forty-three years ago."[53]

On February 7, 2007, Scott met with the president of the Service Employees International Union (SEIU), Andy Stern, his fiercest opponent on the issue of unionization, to discuss the issue of universal health coverage. Wal-Mart and the SEIU eventually formed a coalition, along with several other groups that included AT&T, Intel, and the Communications Workers of America, in order to call for high-quality, affordable coverage for all citizens.[54]

Glasnost in Bentonville

Once Wal-Mart had accepted the increased scrutiny of its business practices and conceptualized it as a business challenge, the company increasingly started to spot opportunities to drive down costs and connect with new customer segments. In 2009, with a new CEO and president, Michael T. Duke, at the helm, Wal-Mart embarked on a mission to create an electronic, universal rating system to score products on their sustainability, "the green equivalent to nutrition labels." In the process, the company enlisted the help of scholars, suppliers, and environmental activists. The green labels would take into account not only the impact that products have once they have been used and thrown out, but also the environmental damage accumulated in their manufacturing and shipping—i.e., if a shirt was made from pesticide-sprayed cotton or if excessive packaging was used to ship an item. "We have to change how we make and sell products," said Duke. "We have to make consumption itself smarter and sustainable."[55]

In order to collect sustainability data, Wal-Mart asked 100,000 suppliers 15 questions gauging their products' environmental impact, warning that suppliers that did not participate might be viewed as "less relevant" to the company. John E. Fleming, Wal-Mart's chief merchandising officer, claimed that the company's green label initiative would prove strategically beneficial in the long run, even if environmentally sustainable practices cost the company more at the outset. "These younger consumers, they care deeply about this regardless of what happens in the economy," Fleming said. "When I go around to colleges and universities to recruit, sustainability is tops on their list. So I think this will help us build a better business model."[56] However, Wal-Mart went beyond environmental issues, launching, for example, an exclusive line of fair trade–certified gourmet coffees, called Sam's Choice,[57] and introducing Love, Earth, the first completely traceable jewelry line, developed in association with Conservation International to avoid participation in the conflict diamond trade.[58]

In its ongoing partnership with the Environmental Defense Fund (EDF), an environmental advocacy group, Wal-Mart even introduced staff positions for several EDF employees at its Bentonville, Arkansas, center. According to David Yarnold, executive vice president of EDF, "One reason we are putting a staff position in Bentonville is that we've discovered that when Wal-Mart makes important decisions, the company moves very quickly. . . . [B]y having an office in Bentonville, we'll help assure that the environment is represented."[59]

In its interaction with a critical public, Wal-Mart went from denial and anger to acceptance and proactive management—from threat to opportunity. When Scott retired as CEO of the company in January 2009, Fred Krupp, former president of the Environmental Defense Fund, summarized Scott's contributions:

> You know, it's probably a little bit of an overblown analogy, but I almost think of Lee Scott as a Gorbachev leading Glasnost, because Lee was this figure that opened Wal-Mart's walls up to the outside and changed how they did business.[60]

THINGS TO REMEMBER

Global business has seen the emergence of alternative mechanisms to regulate commerce. Long the exclusive domain of public officials and elected representatives, regulation is now increasingly being accomplished by activists that put pressure on companies to force them to change their business practices. Such forms of "private politics" can have a major impact on a company's reputation. Understanding them properly is an increasingly important capability in today's marketplace. Here are some of the main lessons from Chapter 3.

- NGOs, interest groups, and politicians are competitors in the market for a company's reputation. They will create reputational crises to force a change in business practices.

- Targeting will be driven by strategic vulnerability, not by culpability. Anticipating such vulnerabilities requires thinking from an activist's point of view, even if the company finds the activist's goals or tactics highly objectionable.

- Reputational risk extends beyond the legal boundaries of a company. Strategically sophisticated actors will target a division that may bear no responsibility for the controversial business practices of a sister division. Downstream companies will be targeted to have an impact on upstream members of the value chain, and vice versa.

- Targeted companies need to evaluate their counterstrategies carefully. While a tough response may be emotionally satisfying, it needs to be clinically evaluated in the context of the company's business environment, its vulnerabilities, and its strengths.

- Alternative approaches require some engagement with advocates, either through the use of endorsements or through changes in business practices. These relationships are forms of strategic alliances—but with an advocacy group, not another company—and must be managed in a similar fashion. Creating such alliances takes time and mutual trust. This can rarely be accomplished in the heat of a confrontation, but requires a proactive approach.

Wal-Mart went through all the stages of emotional and strategic turmoil when confronted with this new reality. Targeted by a coalition of activists, the company had to learn to take the increased scrutiny of its business practices seriously and to treat it like any other business challenge from a competitor. Once it adopted a strategic approach, things fell into place. Through some dramatic stakeholder outreach, accompanied by substantial adjustments in its business practices, the company moved from threat to opportunity, from defensiveness to strategy and execution.

CHAPTER 4

OF SHOWER CURTAINS AND WASTEBASKETS

Perks, Scandals, and Moral Outrage

"These guys are doing more to destroy capitalism than Marx."

—**Nell Minow**, cofounder, The Corporate Library[1]

During the height of the financial crisis in November 2008, the CEOs of the "Big Three" American automobile manufacturers—General Motors (GM), Ford, and Chrysler—traveled to Washington to appeal to the U.S. Congress for $25 billion in additional taxpayer funds to help the struggling automakers avoid bankruptcy. As they pleaded their case to the Senate Banking Committee, committee members, political commentators, and the media began questioning why each executive arrived in Washington on a corporate private plane. Experts estimated the price of GM CEO Rick Wagoner's round trip from Detroit to Washington, D.C., at $20,000, while commercial flights from Detroit's metro airport ranged from $288 for coach to $837 for a first-class ticket.[2]

The CEOs immediately realized the damage that their mode of transportation had caused (each one made his subsequent trip to Washington in December by hybrid car from Detroit, and all three companies announced the sale or review of their private jets soon thereafter), but the damage was done. The resulting backlash from the media and lawmakers turned public opinion against the automakers, jeopardizing the prospects for further public aid. GM CEO Rick Wagoner resigned at the White House's request, and both GM and Chrysler subsequently filed for Chapter 11 bankruptcy protection.

A second example also arose in late 2008, when insurance giant American International Group (AIG) posted the largest quarterly loss in corporate history, bringing it to the brink of bankruptcy. The company requested and received an $85 billion federal bailout; less than one month later, it accepted an additional $37.8 billion loan from the U.S. government to stem further erosion of its cash position. That same week, critics pilloried the company for spending $223,000 for hotel and spa services at the exclusive St. Regis resort just days after accepting the first loan. Democratic Congressman Elijah Cummings of Maryland complained that AIG was "getting manicures and massages, while the American people were footing the bill." According to a company spokesperson, one of its subsidiaries had planned the event prior to the bailout as a reward for top-selling life insurance salespeople.[3]

These were but small skirmishes compared to the pitched battle that AIG faced half a year later. On March 14, 2009, after federal aid to AIG had exceeded $170 billion, the company came under fire when reports indicated that it would distribute a second installment of $165 million in retention payments a day later. An explosion of populist outrage battered the company when it became clear that these payments were part of a retention agreement for employees in AIG's London-based Financial Products Division, the same division whose staggering credit default swap (CDS) losses had caused the company's near collapse.[4]

In response, the new AIG CEO, Edward M. Liddy, appeared at a grueling congressional hearing to defend the decision. The retired CEO of insurance company Allstate, Liddy had agreed to his new position at an annual salary of $1. In front of furious members of Congress, Liddy repeatedly pointed out that the contract stipulating the bonus payments had been signed by AIG long before he had taken over the leadership of the company, and that AIG was contractually bound to honor it. Lawmakers repeatedly attacked Liddy throughout the course of his seven-hour hearing. New York State Attorney General Andrew Cuomo followed the hearings with renewed threats for subpoenas of AIG executives, and President Obama encouraged the Treasury secretary to stop AIG from paying the bonuses:

> This is a corporation that finds itself in financial distress due to recklessness and greed. Under these circumstances, it's hard to understand how derivative traders at AIG warranted any bonuses, much less $165 million in extra pay. How do they justify this outrage to the taxpayers who are keeping the company afloat? In the last six months, AIG has received substantial sums from the US Treasury. I've asked Secretary Geithner to use that leverage and pursue every legal avenue to block these bonuses and make the American taxpayers whole.[5]

Following the hearing, several AIG executives received death threats and found their homes vandalized. With Liddy's strong encouragement, 15 of the 20 AIG executives who had received the biggest bonuses voluntarily returned nearly $50 million.

Finally, consider the case of former Merrill Lynch CEO John Thain, who had the dubious honor of being named "The Worst Person in the World" for January 22, 2009, by the news commentary show *Countdown with Keith Olbermann* when it became known that he had spent $1.2 million to redecorate his personal office. Purchases included $87,000 for area rugs, $25,000 for a pedestal table, $68,000 for a nineteenth-century credenza, and $1,400 for a parchment waste can.[6]

Dozens of these examples have dotted the front page of the *Wall Street Journal*. Even admired former GE CEO Jack Welch faced outrage over his retirement package, which became public during Welch's divorce proceedings. His perks included free lifetime use of a company Boeing 737 and a helicopter, tickets for major sporting events and the Metropolitan Opera, fresh flower arrangements, and generous tips for the doorman, among many others. Following the subsequent public outrage, Welch decided to forgo these perks.[7]

All these examples share one common trait: they all created enormous outrage, causing not only embarrassment but also severe consequences for the companies and their leaders. A more careful look will reveal another, more subtle commonality: compared to the amount of money that was at stake, the financial damage done by the actions that caused the most outrage was small—"nonmaterial," in the language of accountants. Even in the case of AIG's $165 million retention bonuses, those payments represented merely 1/1,000 of the total taxpayer investment (see Figure 4-1). Nevertheless, these comparatively small amounts caused substantial damage to individual and corporate reputations.

Figure 4-1 **AIG—Bonus Payments in Comparison**

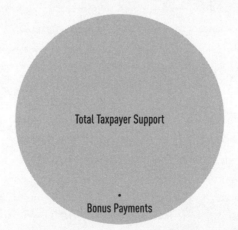

Corporate scandals are reputation killers, and the ensuing outrage is a key driver of reputational crises. Although the global economic crisis probably exacerbated these problems, high compensation for executives

does not enjoy much public support even in good times. In one
study, for example, respondents
suggested an acceptable average
annual salary for CEOs of just
$64,000.[8] These reactions fre-

> Outrage is one of the main drivers of repu-
> tational crises. Outrage can be triggered by
> events that have a small material impact,
> but high symbolic value.

quently blindside executives and board members, who are accustomed
to thinking in terms of efficiency, relative costs and benefits, and market
prices, issues that the public rarely considers when making its evaluation. Instead, concepts of fairness, decency, and other moral dimensions frequently dominate attitude formation, a mismatch that creates
outrage.

SOURCES OF OUTRAGE

On September 30, 2005, the Danish newspaper *Jyllands-Posten* published
12 satirical cartoons by Kurt Westergaard, one of which showed the
prophet Mohammed among other turban-wearing figures in a police
lineup with a witness stating, "I don't know which one he is." Westergaard intended the cartoons as an appeal for free speech in response to
a local Danish controversy. Yet, within hours, protests and riots broke
out in various Muslim communities around the world, causing fatalities in Pakistan, Libya, and Nigeria. The outrage quickly led to calls for
boycotts of Danish products in the Islamic world. Arla Foods, one of
Europe's largest dairy companies and Denmark's biggest exporter to the
Middle East, lost an estimated $1.6 million each day.[9]

Moral outrage is accompanied by powerful emotions like anger,
disgust, and contempt, which in turn may trigger desires of revenge
or disassociation.[10] Situations involving religious values and prohibi-
tions will make these reactions particularly potent, but general corporate misbehavior can evoke similar feelings. Consider, for example, the
controversial advertising used by fashion brands such as Calvin Klein,
Benetton, or Abercrombie & Fitch, or the response to Nike's alleged use
of child labor as discussed in Chapter 3.

Discrimination remains one of the most potent triggers of outrage.
In November 1996, oil company Texaco made headlines when its top
executives were overheard making racially insensitive jokes during a

secretly recorded board meeting. News reports of the so-called black jelly beans tape led to a public outcry and a class-action lawsuit, which the company eventually settled for $176 million.[11]

In such cases, the outrage results from the violation of strongly held norms; an evaluation of consequences, material or otherwise, plays little role. For example, in a series of recent experiments, participants strongly preferred a "misanthropic" manager who treats *all* of his employees badly to an otherwise similar manager who disparaged only his African American employees.[12]

Our immediate response to norm violations is hardwired, and we detect such violations with precision and accuracy. For example, humans typically struggle with logical reasoning; when asked to turn over cards to determine whether an abstract if-then statement is true, subjects generally perform very poorly. That performance improves dramatically when the experimenter instead asks subjects to identify norm violators.[13]

But mental processes can also guide our moral judgment. To experience this, consider the following scenario.[14]

> Suppose a runaway trolley is about to run over and kill five people. Suppose further that you can hit a switch that will divert the trolley onto a different set of tracks, where it will kill only one person instead of five. Is it okay to hit the switch?

The trolley scenario was originally introduced as a moral dilemma, a situation in which different moral intuitions conflict. Ethical intuitions based on maximizing aggregate welfare, such as utilitarianism, imply that the person has a moral obligation to hit the switch. Although this may conflict with a duty to refrain from killing innocents, most people respond that they would hit the switch. Their response changes, however, with the following variant:

> Now, what if the only way to save the five people were to push a large person (larger than yourself) in front of the trolley, killing him but saving the others? Would that be okay?

Now most people say no, even though the consequences in terms of life and death are identical, because there is a basic reluctance to inflict personal harm actively and directly.

Researchers have found increasing evidence that such basic "taboos" correspond to fundamental mental processes. Even infants as young as 10 months old respond to situations representing simple moral situations such as helping or hurting.[15] We make such judgments about norm violations instantaneously and with little effort. Those subjects who followed utilitarian principles by deciding to throw the man onto the rails took significantly longer than subjects who refused to do so; one can overcome basic moral intuitions, but it takes time and effort.[16]

Interestingly, third-party observers expect such immediate responses. In one study, participants were asked to evaluate the resource allocation decision of a hospital administrator who had to choose between spending $1 million to save a child who needed a liver transplant or using the money to purchase equipment and make other hospital improvements that would affect a larger number of patients. Respondents overwhelmingly chose to save the high-cost transplant patient. Moreover, those who chose to use the money for the hospital received negative reviews from observers. Most interestingly, the longer the decision maker deliberated, the more immoral his decision was perceived by observers, who grew increasingly outraged as time went on. In fact, a decision maker who took his time deliberating and then chose to save the patient received more criticism than a decision maker who quickly picked the hospital. In other words, the simple act of deliberating led to negative evaluations.[17]

Moral outrage frequently triggers a desire for punishment, which most people justify as a deterrent of future wrongdoing. However, empirical evidence suggests that the true underlying motive of punishment is to exact retribution; people want to make sure that wrongdoers get what they deserve, even when participation in such punishments involves significant costs.[18]

In cases of moral outrage, the retribution demanded typically remains proportionate to the egregiousness of the violation, and the symbolic aspects of retribution can take on greater importance than pure economic considerations. For example, one study found that participants preferred that a polluting company clean up its own waste rather than clean up more hazardous waste that it had not caused.[19]

Moral outrage will be amplified if it occurs in the context of violated trust. In experiments, respondents favor much harsher punishments for crimes that involved a betrayal, such as a theft committed by the family babysitter. The outrage caused by such deception or other betrayals of trust makes the breach more difficult and more costly to repair.[20]

Businesses that rely heavily on customer trust must pay close attention to this phenomenon, but nonprofits and governments are particularly vulnerable. In contrast to for-profit companies, nonprofits are perceived as being warm and caring.[21] In normal times this is an asset, but it triggers strong emotional reactions of betrayal if it is violated. The scandal surrounding former United Way of America CEO William Aramony demonstrated this, as its legacy has haunted the charity for years. In the early 1990s, reports surfaced about Aramony's lavish spending habits, which included a chauffeured limousine and flights on the Concorde. He stepped down in 1992 in response to critical press coverage. A subsequent investigation revealed various financial improprieties and payments to his teenage girlfriend, resulting in Aramony's receiving a seven-year prison sentence in 1995 for fraud and filing illegal tax returns.[22]

Negative judgments about charities can prove especially harsh, as donors perceive any misbehavior as a violation of trust. In an experimental study, participants tolerated a small perk given to a corporate executive (such as expensive mineral water), but reacted negatively to a larger one (a chauffeured limousine).[23] Heads of a charity, however, enjoyed no such leeway; expensive mineral water elicited just as strongly negative evaluations as the limousine did, eroding trust in both the leader and the charity.

Scandals have terminated many political careers. Existing research has established the negative impact of political scandals on public opinion, reelection rates, ascension to higher office, and postretirement income in the private sector.[24] Sexual misconduct and corruption are the most common career killers, but more minor infractions can have a similar impact if they have particularly unusual or newsworthy features. The United Kingdom's parliamentary expenses scandal represents a recent example, in which members of Parliament had abused their permitted allowances. In one of the most notorious incidents, a former Conservative member of Parliament, Sir Peter John Viggers, claimed about £1,645 of public money in expenses to pay for a floating duck house. In another case, Labour Home Secretary Jacqui Smith charged taxpayers £10 for two pornographic movies viewed by her husband and inappropriately claimed a secondary home allowance. Smith later lost her seat in Parliament after many of her previous supporters abandoned her; Sir Peter Viggers did not seek reelection.[25]

While moral intuitions are strong and persistent, they are not immutable, as demonstrated by a field experiment in which researchers studied parent behavior in day-care centers. Their staffs were rankled by the chronic tardiness of parents arriving to collect their children, forcing them to stay after hours so as not to leave the children unattended. To reduce this unwanted behavior, the day-care centers introduced a monetary fine for late parents, only to find that the fine system substantially *increased* the number of late-arriving parents, a situation that continued even after removing the late arrival fee. Parents originally felt a sense of obligation—a moral norm not to be late—but the introduction of the fee reframed their belief from a sense of communal duty to an exchange orientation. The fine became a price paid for a service, a price that many busy parents decided they would gladly pay.[26]

We can summarize the main sources of outrage as follows:

- People are very sensitive to perceived norm violations. They excel at recognizing them and willingly participate in punishing the violators, even if participation is costly.

- Moral outrage tends to be derived from intuitive judgments driven by emotions rather than from deliberate, conscious reasoning. This shapes not only our own judgments but also our evaluation of the judgments of others.

- Moral outrage leads to a desire for punishment. This desire is primarily based not on conscious reasoning to avoid future harm, but on a deep-seated desire for retribution.

- Moral outrage will be particularly pronounced when the objectionable behavior occurs in the context of violated trust.

- Perception frames can be malleable. Agents can switch between exchange orientations and normative frameworks.

These processes can be particularly dangerous for executives and boards, as they may conceptualize a transaction in purely economic terms, whereas the public sees it as occurring in a normative framework based on trust, triggering a moral mindset that leads to moral outrage and the desire to punish the perceived evildoer.

THE ULTIMATUM GAME

Consider a simple choice problem in which two negotiators have a fixed amount of money to split, say $100. Now consider the following scenario. One of the negotiators (the proposer) makes an offer to the other negotiator (the replier), who can either accept or reject it, with rejection resulting in a zero payoff for both. The proposer can make only a single offer; however, there is no opportunity for counteroffers. Now, put yourself in the shoes of a replier who has been offered $1, leaving $99 for the other player to keep for himself. How would you react?

Most people would grow angry and reject the offer, leaving both parties with nothing. Notice that there is something puzzling about this reaction. Shouldn't the replier be reasonable and accept the $1? After all, it's better than nothing! While $1 is in fact greater than zero, people rarely behave in a manner that reflects this; instead, they will consistently reject offers that are below a certain threshold. That threshold varies by culture, but it generally ranges from 30 to 50 percent of the total amount. Moreover, proposers seem to anticipate this reaction and tend to offer proposals that are close to the acceptable amount, knowing that lowball offers face likely rejection.

> Norm violations, whether perceived or real, frequently trigger moral outrage. Moral outrage tends to be based on intuitive judgments, accompanied by strong emotions and a desire for punishment. Moral outrage will be particularly pronounced when the objectionable behavior occurs in the context of violated trust.

Known as the Ultimatum Game, this choice situation is one of the most studied decision problems in modern experimental economics. Upon its discovery in 1982 by a team of German economists, it created a sensation, as it seemed to violate a fundamental principle of economics: that rational actors always prefer something to nothing.[27]

Economists have offered many explanations for this anomaly, but the findings proved robust. One suggestion centered on the replier's ability to identify the proposer, but it became clear that negotiators leave substantial amounts of money on the table even if it is impossible to establish the identity of the other party. Demographic factors such as race and gender play little role, but children become more fair-minded in Ultimatum Games as they grow older, which suggests that fairness norms are learned in a cultural context.[28]

The Ultimatum Game offers one of the most powerful pieces of evidence for the existence of universal fairness norms. Proposals that the replier perceives as unfair trigger a form of outrage similar to that triggered by norm violations, including the willingness to engage in costly punishment, even by unaffected third parties.[29] While the existence of such norms appears to be universal, their exact content varies by culture. Some cultures are more tolerant of less equitable distributions than others. Japan and Israel, for example, have lower offer thresholds than the United States or Europe. In some cultures, proposers even offer *more* than half the pie.[30]

In a reputational context, companies must concern themselves not only with respondents (those who are party to an agreement), but also with third parties that observe a transaction. Issues of fairness arise with particular intensity in the context of pricing, especially for goods and services that people deem necessary. Bread riots are a familiar example throughout history, but similar issues occur for electricity and gas rates, oil prices, credit cards, and consumer loans. In their own defense, companies invariably point out that they have entered into legal, voluntary transactions between consenting parties, but these arguments rarely outweigh strong fairness intuitions triggered by situations reminiscent of the Ultimatum Game. Let us consider how these issues become germane in two examples.

> Recent research supports the existence of universal fairness norms. Violation of fairness norms triggers moral outrage and a desire for retribution. The exact content of fairness norms varies by culture.

CHARGING POOR PEOPLE MORE

Since the great financial crisis of 2007–2008, much of the criticism of the financial sector has focused on the subprime mortgage industry and its role in the financial meltdown. Hindsight on the ultimate outcome can cloud one's memory, but politicians and industry observers once lauded subprime mortgages as a desirable vehicle to expand homeownership to segments of the society that had previously lacked access to traditional "prime" loans.[31]

Countrywide Financial was one of the largest independent mortgage lenders in the United States until its 2008 acquisition by Bank of America. Former Countrywide CEO Angelo Mozilo stated that the company's subprime strategy was not solely financially motivated, but also tried to create "multicultural market communities" for borrowers. "The gap between low-income and minority homeownership, and what is classified as white homeownership, remains intolerably too wide," he said. Not coincidentally, minority owners represented the fastest-growing group seeking subprime mortgages. Whether genuine or not, these sentiments reflected a fairly complex public policy argument that many people shared. Both Democratic and Republican administrations pushed for increased access to mortgages for low-income borrowers, especially through the giant lenders, government-sponsored enterprises Fannie Mae and Freddie Mac. Fannie Mae pledged $2 trillion over a decade to expand access to credit to aid "minorities, families headed by women, new immigrants and other underserved consumers." "Many Americans have enjoyed substantial financial gains in our current era of prosperity," Fannie Mae CEO Franklin D. Raines said. "But in home-ownership, there remains a significant divide between the 'haves' and 'haven't yets.'"[32]

These positions reflect a focus on desirable social consequences based on economic principles. The idea is that financial innovations such as a data-driven understanding of default risk or the creation of mortgage-based securities allow lenders to tolerate greater variations of risks among borrowers, permitting access to credit for population segments that were previously excluded. This phenomenon became known as the "democratization" of the consumer credit and mortgage markets.[33]

Regardless of the validity of such arguments, the subprime lending model is prone to cause moral outrage. First, the very nature of the typical customer segments (minorities, immigrants, the elderly, and the poor) triggers concerns about exploitation, discrimination, and predatory lending practices. Second, the subprime business model *charges poor people higher rates.* Of course, the effective rate may be largely driven by financial markets and reflect higher average default rates, but it looks unfair to people who are unfamiliar with concepts of risk-weighted return. The high profit margins of subprime lending companies only fueled this suspicion of unfair pricing. Finally, subprime lenders faced not only the risk of default, but also the risk of losing their customers because of refinancing. In fact, a subprime customer who manages to make payments on time will see her credit rating improve to the point where she may qualify for a much lower prime rate. This erodes the subprime lender's margins, which in turn creates incentives for lock-in mechanisms such as significant prepayment penalties. Such terms may look acceptable to a borrower who is entering a subprime loan, given the lack of viable alternatives and the excitement of first-time home-ownership, but it can come to feel like financial handcuffs later.

The ensuing public outrage can trigger severe regulatory and legal problems. On June 7, 2010, Bank of America, Countrywide's new owner, agreed to pay $108 million to settle charges brought against the company by the Federal Trade Commission (FTC).[34] The FTC had accused Countrywide of predatory lending practices, saying that it had charged more than 200,000 customers highly inflated prices to service

> Pricing can lead to outrage driven by fairness concerns. Reference to market prices will be ineffective if the disadvantaged party can count on public sympathy and has few options. Typical pricing models ignore these factors.

their mortgages and had failed to inform customers when new fees were added to their loans. Earlier, Bank of America also agreed to provide assistance to delinquent or near-delinquent borrowers who became so as a consequence of predatory loan practices. The initiative amounted to $8.4 billion in interest rate and principal reductions, affecting as many as 400,000 eligible customers.[35] A few months later, Angelo Mozilo, Countrywide's CEO, settled civil fraud charges brought by the SEC for $67.5 million. Because of a prior indemnification agreement, Bank of America agreed to cover $45 million of the fine.[36]

Countrywide Financial Corporation may or may not be representative of the industry, but it is far from the only subprime lending company that has faced hostile media coverage, intense activist pressure, and lawsuits by regulators and attorneys general. A decade earlier, Citigroup had faced similar problems in its acquisition of the subprime lender The Associates in the fall of 2000. Three months after the merger closed, the Federal Trade Commission filed a complaint in federal court charging The Associates with "systematic and widespread abusive lending practices," as well as violating the "Truth in Lending Act, Fair Credit Reporting Act, and Equal Credit Opportunity Act" through "unfair tactics."[37] Citigroup subsequently paid $215 million in redress to customers and changed its lending practices.[38]

Lending and financial services are particularly at risk for moral outrage, but other industries can be affected as well as the recent history of the pharmaceutical industry demonstrates.

SUING NELSON MANDELA

Since its discovery in 1981, HIV/AIDS has infected 60 million people worldwide, with 95 percent of those individuals coming from developing countries. Although a cure has not been found, pharmaceutical companies have developed antiretroviral (ARV) drugs that inhibit the virus's ability to replicate or enter host cells. Since the introduction of drugs such as Retrovir by pharmaceutical company GlaxoSmithKline, the number of deaths from AIDS-related diseases in the United States has decreased substantially, from 50,000 annually in 1995 to 10,000 in 2001. Sub-Saharan Africa, however, had nearly 30 million cases of HIV in 2002, an infection rate of about 9 percent of the population that caused more than 9 million deaths. These dramatic disparities put the issue of access to lifesaving medications on the top of the global health agenda. During the early 1990s, for example, World Health Organization (WHO) representatives estimated that treatment of HIV cost $10,000 or more per year. At that time, the average annual income for South Africans was approximately $2,600, while the per capita income for Tanzania in 2004 was $280.[39]

Developing new drug treatments is expensive and highly unpredictable. GlaxoSmithKline's initial investment in AZT—an early ARV drug—was estimated at $80 million to $180 million, with the company spending $30 million annually on research and development of new drugs. Since generic drug producers do not have to expend additional resources on research and development, their drugs—which are similar to the large pharmaceutical companies' products in quality and efficacy—cost little to manufacture. For example, GlaxoSmithKline sells the AIDS drug Combivir for $7,000, but the active ingredient can be purchased for only $240 on the international generic market.[40]

These price differences have made pharmaceutical companies such as GlaxoSmithKline targets of choice in the drug-pricing debate. Activist groups like AIDS Coalition to Unleash Power (ACT-UP) and Doctors without Borders have led protests against pharmaceutical companies with slogans such as "GlaxoSmithKline! GlobalSerialKiller." They also created opportunities for generic manufacturers like the Indian generic drug maker Cipla, which offered to sell ARV drug cocktails to the humanitarian agency Doctors without Borders at only $350 annually for each patient, well below the typical price of $10,000 to $15,000 per patient per year.[41]

Drug companies argued that these actions blatantly violated their intellectual property rights. In 1998, 39 drug companies, through the Pharmaceutical Research and Manufacturers of America (PhRMA), launched a lawsuit against the South African government to challenge a patent law allowing the importation of inexpensive, generic AIDS medication. The companies asserted that the law breached international trade agreements and gave the health minister the unconstitutional power to ignore patent rights. After a massive global media backlash—Nobel Peace laureate Nelson Mandela was president of South Africa at the time—and sustained activist pressure, all 39 companies eventually dropped their legal action against South Africa. Industry experts argued that this defeat for the drug industry would also lower its incentives to invest in the exploration for other lifesaving drugs.[42]

In an effort to counteract the reputational damage, pharmaceutical companies began a series of price reductions on their drug products. Bristol-Myers Squibb and Merck both announced significant discounts on their AIDS drug cocktails, with Bristol-Myers charging patients $1 per day and Merck $600 per year. GlaxoSmithKline extended its preferential pricing system beyond governments to NGOs, aid groups, churches, and charities and eased access to various drugs like malarial pills. For example, Trizivir, a combination drug pill costing $27.92 in the United States, sold for only $6.60 in developing countries under the new pricing system.[43]

The cost of prescription drugs has also become an issue in developed countries. In the United States, for instance, drug expenditures rose from $12 billion (4.9 percent of health-care costs) in 1980 to $184.1 billion (11 percent) in 2003. Consequently, despite lingering safety concerns, some Americans have resorted to reimporting drugs from the Canadian and Mexican markets, where individuals can save an estimated 20 to 80 percent on pharmaceutical products. For example, the drug Ritonavir, which is part of many HIV/AIDS treatments, costs as little as $700 per year in Canada instead of $7,800 per year in the United States.[44]

The ongoing debates over pricing and access have severely eroded the reputation of the pharmaceutical industry. In a 2007 survey of customer and stakeholder perception of the industry conducted by PricewaterhouseCoopers, 45 percent of consumers believed that drug companies' R&D strategies were largely driven by sales considerations, while 62 percent of stakeholders agreed that pharmaceutical companies suppress negative clinical trials in order to boost sales and 73 percent of stakeholders agreed that pharmaceutical companies spent excessive amounts of money attempting to prevent competition from generic drug companies.[45]

Let us take a closer look at the underlying principles. Notice first that drug companies routinely justify high retail prices by citing the substantial cost of investing in new drug research. They estimate that it costs nearly $800 million to bring a new drug to market.[46] They must then recoup these development costs over the lifetime of the drug through prices above the marginal cost to produce them. R&D-driven drug companies therefore need to charge higher prices than those charged by generic manufacturers, who do not need to amortize these same costs of development.

The R&D incentive argument rests on the need for incentives to create value by investing in unproven drugs. This argument may persuade a trained economist, but it remains implausible to a layperson. First, untrained members of the public tend to focus on the distribution of value, not its production.[47] Contrary to economic principles, the public typically assumes that the amount of wealth is fixed. This so-called zero-sum fallacy naturally leads observers to focus on how this fixed pie should be distributed. Once distribution concerns become central, people's attention shifts from issues of efficiency and wealth creation to issues of fairness, as captured by the Ultimatum Game.

> Economic intuitions by untrained members of the public focus on the distribution of value, not its production. Arguments that rely on creating incentives for value creation are frequently greeted with skepticism. The focus on distribution triggers fairness concerns.

Once the focus is on questions of fairness in distribution, it becomes plainly obvious to many that everything should be done to save innocent victims from certain death. If they are given the choice between allocating benefits to patients or to companies, most neutral observers will not hesitate to choose the former. The general public's tendency to overestimate the average rate of corporate profit exacerbates this feeling of unfairness; what, after all, is a few more dollars to an already wildly profitable drug company? According to the Survey of Americans and Economists on the Economy (SAEE), the average respondent estimated corporate profit rates at 46.7 percent, while the true number is closer to 3 percent.[48] All of this leads to a perception of the rich exploiting the poor who are fighting for their lives and have no choice—a surefire recipe for a reputational disaster.

WHEN ACTIONS SPEAK VOLUMES

Moral judgments can apply both to actions and to persons. The importance of person-based judgments is not just idle philosophical speculation, but figures prominently in everyday judgments. For this reason, even perks that are of modest economic value can trigger sufficient outrage to bring down a politician or a CEO. The mechanism at work is that in addition to harboring distaste for an act, observers use the behavior as a cue to make inferences about the agent who performs that act. Acts that are generally considered to be of little consequence can therefore severely damage an agent's reputation when they are interpreted as a proxy for that agent's basic moral dispositions.[49]

Humans' ability to evaluate an agent's moral character represents one of the most basic dimensions of social cognition. Such evaluations occur automatically, quickly and effortlessly, develop remarkably early in life, and, despite some variability, occur across cultures. Assessments of an agent's moral character help us decide whether to trust that person, and whether to rely on him in situations of vulnerability. Psychological research indicates that when people evaluate another person's moral character, certain core elements such as empathy and competence are particularly important. A lack of empathy, for example, may signal selfish behavior in joint endeavors when mutual trust is critical. The involuntary nature of many cues for demonstrating empathy makes it difficult to fake, which in turn makes it particularly informative in personal interactions.[50]

These mechanisms lie at the root of the outrage over executive compensation. In 2005, the former CEO of Tyco, Dennis Kozlowski, was convicted on 22 counts of defrauding shareholders of more than $100 million, tax evasion, and other charges. What people remembered most, however, were revelations that he had spent $6,000 of corporate funds on a shower curtain and had had Tyco pay half of the $2.1 million for a birthday party for his wife in Sardinia, Italy, which included such extravagances as a vodka-urinating ice sculpture in the shape of Michelangelo's statue *David*.[51]

> A person's actions are frequently interpreted as signals about that person's moral character. Actions that are strange or bizarre lead to particularly harsh judgments, even if the material impact is limited. The outrage over executive perks is one of the principal examples of this phenomenon.

Upon hearing such details, people cannot help but make inferences about the kind of person that would ask for and accept such perks. The bizarre nature of some of the details—$15,000 for a dog umbrella stand, for example—further increases suspicions about the leader's basic moral disposition, which then trigger doubts as to his general trustworthiness.

Experimental evidence supports such intuitions. Suppose you have to hire a promising executive for a new position, and you must choose between one candidate who asks for a $2,000,000 salary and another who requests a $1,000,000 salary plus a $40,000 marble table engraved with her portrait. The overwhelming majority of subjects prefer the more expensive candidate.[52] However, replacing the marble table with a $40,000 signing bonus sways most subjects to select the cheaper candidate. Moreover, the marble-loving candidate received significantly lower ratings on integrity and expectations of future responsible behavior. Executive corporate governance expert and compensation critic Nell Minow has repeatedly argued that investors should use eyebrow-raising perks as red flags when evaluating a company's governance performance.[53]

This has important consequences for boards and compensation committees. Imagine the following scenario in a negotiation between a board of directors and a prospective CEO on her compensation package.

The chairman proposes a standard package consisting of a base salary, a bonus structure, and stock options. During negotiations, the CEO requests perquisites, including a private dining room and a private elevator to her office. Fulfilling these requests would cost the company only a modest sum, as it could easily and inexpensively remodel an adjacent meeting room as a dining room and redirect one of the existing elevators so that it would go directly to the CEO's office. In total, such a request might add no more than 1 percent to the first-year overall compensation, and the CEO clearly cares a great deal about this particular aspect of her compensation package.

At a superficial level, this looks like a good deal for everybody, as the shareholders need not make a significant outlay of cash to make the CEO feel wanted. After all, this is an agreement between private parties for their mutual benefit and is clearly within the boundaries of the law.

This chapter should have shown that this simple transaction is loaded with booby traps. The company is making a mistake if it ignores the symbolic nature of the request, as it sends a message to everyone in the company and beyond that the CEO is special and does not live by the same standards that apply to others. Second, such perks will be interpreted as signals about the CEO's integrity and responsibility, irrespective of whether these signals are valid. Boards need to evaluate such demands carefully, even if they seem trivial in the grand scheme of a larger compensation package. They will not seem trivial in retrospect if the CEO underperforms; in fact, they will look indefensible. Board members need to defend their company's reputation and also their own, and corporate scandals are reputation killers.

THINGS TO REMEMBER

Successful reputation management is proactive. It requires the ability to anticipate reputational risks and opportunities. Developing such a mindset is not easy, as it requires the ability to consistently see business decisions from multiple points of view. It is thus essential to understand what to look for. What are the drivers that have the most reputational impact? In this chapter, we discussed the first factor: moral outrage. Let us summarize some of the key findings.

- Moral outrage is derived from perceived norm violations. The deeper the attachment to moral norms, the greater the outrage. Trust violations are particularly serious.

- Outrage is accompanied by strong emotions and a desire for punishment rather than deliberate reasoning.

- Fairness is one of the most widely held moral norms. It can be observed universally, although its exact content is affected by culture.

- Many business decisions are based on efficiency calculations and ignore fairness. They focus on incentives and the creation of wealth. Laypeople tend to focus on fairness and the distribution of wealth.

- Issues of pricing and compensation are particularly prone to trigger outrage. In many cases, they are also interpreted as signals about a person's or an organization's "moral character."

Executives and board members need to take these drivers of reputational risk into consideration when making seemingly standard business decisions. If they do not, the risk of corporate scandals looms large.

CHAPTER 5

THE KATRINA CHRONICLES

Doing the Right Thing and Getting Credit for It

"This was one of the few times at Wal-Mart when we did the right things and actually got credit for it. Everywhere I go, everybody wants to talk about what [we] did."

—**Lee Scott,** former CEO, Wal-Mart,
September 10, 2005[1]

I mproving reputational equity is not easy. It frequently requires an integrated approach and changes in business practices, but sometimes opportunities present themselves. One such opportunity caused *Fortune* magazine to give three companies a rare hero treatment. On October 3, 2005, under the front-page headline "When Government Broke Down, Business Stepped Up," *Fortune* featured the responses of three companies to the Katrina crisis: Wal-Mart, FedEx, and Home Depot.

This positive coverage was particularly uncommon for Wal-Mart. As we saw in Chapter 3, the company had received constant criticism of its business practices, ranging from its impact on the environment to its provision of inadequate health care for its employees to community resistance to the opening of new Wal-Mart stores. This time, things were different. After years of criticism, the company finally felt appreciated for what it does best: bring goods to people, efficiently and fast. Katrina not only represented a remarkable relief effort, but also marked the beginning of one of the most remarkable reputation rebuilding efforts in the history of modern business.

Wal-Mart's swift response was no accident; it was the result of meticulous preparation and execution based on the company's decades of experience in dealing with stores that had been affected by hurricanes and other natural disasters and its strength in logistics and supply chain management. When Hurricane Katrina hit the coast of Louisiana on August 29, 2005, Wal-Mart was ready. While its primary focus was on helping Wal-Mart's associates cope personally with the immediate disaster, as well as protecting the affected stores and reopening them as soon as possible, the company's Emergency Operations Center also worked to fill gaps in the relief efforts that were underway. According to Jason Jackson, director of business continuity and global security at Wal-Mart:

> We worked hand in hand with communities, non-governmental organizations, other private sector companies, and governmental officials at all levels on a variety of topics, ranging from provision of supplies, to information, communications, energy support, fuel, and sheltering. . . . We provided generator support to non–Wal-Mart facilities . . . brought basic needs to communities that had nothing and . . . delivered approximately 2,500 trailers of emergency supplies.[2]

Disaster relief provides one of the clearest examples of companies trying to do the right thing. In recent years, this topic has been looked at in the context of "strategic corporate social responsibility (CSR)."[3] Such efforts often spring from genuine humanitarian motives, but they can also benefit the companies.

> Opportunities to improve reputational equity are rare. Civic engagement and corporate social responsibility offer such opportunities. This is particularly true in the context of disaster relief.

The claim is that companies can better achieve their business objectives by engaging in socially beneficial actions; in effect, they can do well by doing good. In this chapter, we will investigate strategies for improving a company's reputation by doing the right thing and getting credit for it.[4]

CORPORATE SOCIAL RESPONSIBILITY— THE STRATEGIC PERSPECTIVE

The last decade has seen a surge of interest in corporate social responsibility. The number of annual sustainability and corporate citizenship reports has skyrocketed, and CEOs increasingly rank CSR as a "central" or "important" concern for senior managers.[5] This increasing interest in corporate social responsibility is not idle talk, as companies have also made significant changes in their business practices. Examples range from improved global labor standards (Nike, Adidas, and Ikea), sustainable supply chains (Home Depot's and Lowe's decision not to sell wood from old-growth forests), and animal welfare measures (McDonald's and Yum! Brands poultry policies) to general public policy issues such as measures to ease global warming and protect human rights (Exelon and The Gap). Particularly striking have been recent attempts by major global corporations to rebrand themselves as ecologically responsible, such as BP's "Beyond Petroleum" and carbon footprint campaign and GE's "Ecoimagination" initiative.

Emphasis on corporate social responsibility is not a new phenomenon. Procter & Gamble established a profit-sharing program in the 1880s and promoted an eight-hour workday long before the policy became statutorily mandated in 1916. Henry Ford paid his workers twice the market rate, and companies such as Heinz, IBM, and Hershey subsidized education and other community benefits.

What *is* new is an emerging consensus that promoting corporate social responsibility is no longer a task for only a few prosperous companies, but a necessary business practice for all. Companies are increasingly judged by standards beyond shareholder value maximization, and therefore they must develop strategies and policies to meet those heightened standards.

Ian Davis, a former worldwide managing director of McKinsey & Co., recently listed the need for companies to gain sustained social acceptance as one of the key emerging global trends in business:

> The role and behavior of big business will come under increasingly sharp scrutiny. As businesses expand their global reach, and as the economic demands on the environment intensify, the level of societal suspicion about big business is likely to increase. The tenets of current global business ideology—for example, shareholder value, free trade, intellectual-property rights, and profit repatriation—are not understood, let alone accepted, in many parts of the world. . . . Business, particularly big business, will never be loved. It can, however, be more appreciated. Business leaders need to argue and demonstrate more forcefully the intellectual, social, and economic case for business in society and the massive contributions business makes to social welfare.[6]

This argument is a question not of morality—what companies *should* do—but of strategy, which centers instead on what they *need* to do if they are to succeed in today's environment, whether they are motivated purely by profits or by other goals beyond increasing shareholder value. In other words, the debate is less about business ethics and more about management practice.

The question, then, is under what circumstances and to what extent CSR is a successful *strategy*. The issues are whether and when CSR improves the performance of a business unit, which companies should adopt it, and how CSR strategies should be implemented. From this perspective, the issue of whether a company should engage in CSR activities is not fundamentally different from whether it should pursue a high-quality or low-cost strategy. It also suggests that significant variations in both patterns of CSR activities and their impact on business performance should be expected.

The first question about CSR as a strategy is whether it works. In the management literature, this question has been expressed as whether it "pays to be green" or whether companies are "doing well by doing good." A large body of literature has tried to establish whether firms that engage in CSR activities exhibit better financial performance than companies that do not. The debate rages among management scholars on this issue, but the evidence for a positive association between CSR and financial performance is at best mixed. Some studies find a small positive effect, some find no effect, and others find a negative effect.[7] Serious challenges arise regarding identifying and measuring CSR (what exactly counts as a CSR activity?) and the direction of causation (are firms more profitable because they engage in CSR, or can they afford to engage in CSR because they are more profitable?).

Irrespective of the validity of the existing findings, from a strategy perspective, this line of research is not very fruitful, because we would expect the effect of CSR activities to depend heavily on the market or the product, just like that of any other business strategy. The existing literature has tried to establish whether, *on average*, socially responsible companies perform better than their counterparts. However, markets are frequently characterized by product differentiation. Some firms in an industry may rely on a high-quality/high-price strategy, while others adopt a low-quality/low-price strategy. In many markets, ranging from consumer goods to financial services, such differentiated strategies are highly stable.

For example, if we ask whether *on average* high quality pays off, we might find no relationship whatsoever. *Both* Tiffany and Wal-Mart may be highly profitable in their respective retailing segments, one by adopting a high-quality/high-cost strategy and the other by adopting a strategy of low-quality/low-cost. Similarly, in a market that is differentiated by CSR activities, it is entirely possible that both socially responsible *and* "regular" firms can be profitable. In other words, there may be one "ecological niche" for socially responsible firms and another one for companies that do not care at all for CSR. Empirical studies that correlate social and financial performance are useful only if they can address the question of why and under what circumstances firms can benefit from adopting socially responsible business practices.

Proponents of the business case for CSR have pointed to various benefits of CSR activities. Some of these benefits are mainly operational. Here CSR (especially environmental CSR) is used as a heuristic to improve process performance. BP's adoption of a firmwide cap on greenhouse emissions combined with a corporate emissions trading system in 1997 is one well-known example. That decision proved highly successful, as BP not only reduced its emissions significantly, but also reported that the trading system increased net income by more than $600 million.[8] In this case, CSR helped to improve operational efficiency. BP had been flaring natural gas from some of its wells, but the cost of doing so was difficult to identify; it did not show up as a cash cost on a balance sheet, but rather constituted a hidden opportunity cost. CSR played the role of a heuristic that made it more likely that management would identify such cost savings.

These forms of CSR should be utterly uncontroversial and should be adopted by any company that is interested in improving its operations. To put it differently, even if Exxon Mobil fundamentally disagreed with BP on the importance of climate change, imitating BP's trading scheme would be advisable, as long as the system indeed led to the stated cost savings. What may vary across companies is the extent to which such heuristics are fruitful and which CSR domain will be most important.

The other proposed advantages are mainly reputational, whether they involve relationships with customers, investors, regulators, politicians, or the general public. The company wants these stakeholders to hold beliefs and attitudes about the company that will give it an edge in the marketplace, but these attitudes now have a very specific content. They are not about safety, quality, or reliability, but about ethical and social concerns.

Corporate social responsibility can have operational benefits, for example, in reducing costs. When it is advocated as a strategy, it needs to be able to generate and capture value or reduce risks. This will vary from company to company.

Notice that the fundamental premise of CSR as a reputational strategy is that some significant segment of the stakeholders in the company's business environment has moral values and is willing and able to act on them. As we discussed in Chapter 4, there is significant evidence that this is the case. These morally motivated agents may be part of the value chain (customers, employees, or investors) or external stakeholders (NGOs, journalists, politicians, and so on). CSR strategies can then be constructed to generate and capture value or to minimize risk.

COMPETING IN THE MARKET FOR VIRTUE

To generate value, CSR needs to satisfy a possibly latent "demand for virtue." It provides value to the "moral self" of customers, employees, and investors, and therefore makes a company more competitive in the market for customers, talent, and capital. Therefore, CSR is frequently thought of as a benefit-focused competitive strategy; it provides a competitive advantage to a company based on satisfying this demand for virtue.

Note that this approach is conceptually distinct from the operational rationale discussed previously. The demand-for-virtue rationale works only if there are enough stakeholders with moral motivations. The operational rationale does not depend on such a premise; it would work even if the world were populated solely by actors straight out of an economics textbook.

Viewed from this perspective, CSR operates in the same way as a strategy that focuses on providing customers with high quality. In the context of customers, the strategy makes sense if there is a customer segment that is willing to pay enough for a high-quality product to compensate the company for more than the higher cost of providing the high-quality product. There are many examples of businesses putting such strategies in action; they are frequently small companies created by visionary entrepreneurs. Well-known examples include Ben & Jerry's, Patagonia, Seventh Generation, the Body Shop, Whole Foods, and British chocolate maker Green & Black's.

It is striking that these firms largely serve niche markets with high-end products and well-to-do customers. It is much less clear whether these strategies can be implemented by multinational companies, especially those that offer a wide range of products. To assess the prospects for such strategies in general, we need to understand their logic in more detail.

Competition for customers by using a CSR strategy usually occurs in the context of "socially responsible brands," which are based on the idea that customers prefer to buy products from companies that abide by certain moral principles. This may result in customers' willingness to pay more (a higher price point) or in a company's larger market share. In other words, socially responsible brands allow customers to express a demand for virtue. The existence of such a demand, however, is not enough for a sustainable business model. Companies must be able to capture this value by building sustainable competitive advantages.

To attain a competitive advantage through a product differentiation strategy, various conditions need to hold. First, there must be a segment of customers that is willing to pay enough for the socially responsible product to cover the additional costs of providing it. In other words, if the variable costs of providing a socially responsible brand are higher than those for a customary brand, the willingness of consumers to pay extra (or buy more) must be sufficiently high and the segment must be sufficiently big to cover fixed costs. Second, if social responsibility is to qualify as a competitive advantage, socially responsible brands must not be easily imitated. In contrast to other non-price attributes, such as quality, convenience, or location, consumers cannot directly verify whether a company or product makes good on its promise of social responsibility. We have encountered this phenomenon in Chapter 3 in the concept of "credence attributes," that is, attributes of goods that are relevant to consumers but that cannot be directly experienced in the act of consumption and thus must be believed. This means that companies that try to differentiate themselves along a social responsibility dimension need to invest in building their reputation. Since reputation building takes time, quick imitation of this strategy by other firms is difficult.

> Value creation strategies involving CSR require a sustained demand for virtuous products that is sufficient to cover the additional costs. Such strategies can be sustained in markets with differentiated products. At present, however, these markets are limited in scope.

In such markets, we will find product differentiation. All the examples listed previously meet these characteristics. For example, Ben & Jerry's differentiated itself from Häagen-Dazs on the social responsibility dimension, while both differentiate themselves from generic store brands on the quality dimension. Starbucks sells fair trade coffee next to conventional varietals. Modern competitive strategy focuses on how such differentiated outcomes may constitute stable outcomes in markets with various customer segments. That is, neither competitor has an incentive to imitate the other, and both can be profitable.[9]

In summary, for brand-based CSR strategies to work, they must play by the rules of competitive strategy. They must establish a sustainable competitive advantage and identify a market segment that is willing to pay for the extra value offered. At this point in time, the most successful examples of such strategies are "boutique" businesses serving high-end markets. Little evidence yet exists that this strategy is broadly applicable to other industry segments.

One can apply a similar line of reasoning to competition for talent and capital, with a similar rationale. As consumers, employees may be motivated by moral concerns, so a socially responsible firm may be better able to attract and retain more talented and productive employees. The underlying assumption is that employees value working for a company that has an ethical reputation. This may result in employees' willingness to work for a lower monetary compensation package, or in an equivalent compensation package attracting a greater number of more productive employees. In addition to helping to attract more productive employees, CSR may help to retain them and improve employee morale, which may increase overall productivity.

That said, at this point there is little quantitative support for a link between CSR policies and successful hiring, retention, or productivity. Many factors influence job decisions and productivity, including an employer's CSR activities. What needs to be established is whether, holding these other factors constant, companies recover the additional costs of engaging in CSR activities by achieving better success in the market for talent. At present, there is largely anecdotal evidence to support this assertion.

Similar caveats apply to competition for capital. For this strategy to work, one needs "virtue-driven investors," that is, investors who evaluate the returns on their investment based on not only a company's financial performance but also its impact on society. This phenomenon is also known as *socially responsible investing* (SRI). The SRI market share has grown rapidly over the last decade and currently accounts for about 12 percent of all U.S. assets under professional management.[10] As in the case of socially responsible brands, most research has focused on the question of whether SRI funds outperform typical portfolios. As with socially responsible brands, there is little empirical evidence for this.[11]

There is, however, growing evidence that CSR activities can have a positive effect in the special case of *environmental* performance.[12] One possible explanation for this finding is that capital markets treat good environmental performance as evidence for lower liability risks. This approach differs from any of the strategic approaches discussed so far, which relied on the idea that CSR policies serve as a competitive strategy that can satisfy the demand for virtue. The common thread in all demand-based approaches is that a CSR-driven institution is able to differentiate itself from its competitors so that it is more attractive to value-based business partners.

An explanation for CSR that focuses on minimizing *risks*, however, provides an entirely different rationale for companies to adopt CSR policies, based on the conflict between markets and their social and political environment. The key actors here are not customers or suppliers, but social activists, the media, pressure groups, politicians, and the courts, as discussed in Chapter 3. Companies that adopt CSR policies for that reason are not trying to differentiate themselves; they are trying to avoid being singled out for questionable business practices. The companies' objective is not to create a competitive advantage, but to avoid a competitive disadvantage caused by increased risk or reputational damage. In short, these strategies involve playing defense, not offense.

RISKS AND REGULATION

As we saw in Chapters 3 and 4, a main driver of both reputational and regulatory risk is the moral judgments of both customers *and* noncustomers that may take action against a company with the goal of forcing it to comply with their proclaimed moral stand. In other words, we can conceptualize these values and principles as constituting the formal and informal "rules of the game" of market competition. If they perceive a violation of the rules, external stakeholders may impose costs on companies to make them change their policies and practices.

Note that these rules of the game go beyond current legally binding rules and regulations. Some countries do not prohibit a company from employing 12-year-olds in its manufacturing plants or dumping toxic waste into a river. Still, such behavior violates widely held ethical standards. Also, the rules of the game usually vary significantly from country to country and from market to market. Again, this is true not only of legal rules, but especially of ethical norms and values. Finally, the rules of the game are contested and ever-changing. Only a decade ago, concerns about animal rights did not weigh heavily on American businesses; today, food companies have extensive animal welfare policies.

These three factors (informality, cross-country variation, and change) are largely responsible for the development of crises when companies are confronted by a hostile stakeholder environment. We saw this clearly in Wal-Mart's strategic shift in Chapter 3. Wal-Mart's subsequent change in business practices initially reflected not a desire to differentiate itself as the socially responsible retailer, but an attempt to minimize reputational damage. To lower the long-term expected costs from reputational damage, a company "invests" in socially responsible business practices. Such an investment will improve its competitive position if the costs of complying with these practices are on average smaller than the expected savings from the avoidance of reputational damage.

In addition, companies may try to decrease the likelihood of regulatory or legal action. In the case of self-regulation, companies may "voluntarily" adopt socially responsible business practices to preempt regulation by legislatures, agencies, or the courts. The rating systems used in the entertainment industry and advertising restrictions in the spirits industry are well-known examples.

At some point, firms will be held accountable if their actions violate the commonly accepted rules of the game, whether the negative consequences are legal, regulatory, or reputational. Investors recognize these risks and incorporate them into their valuation of companies. Good corporate social performance, then, can be interpreted as an "insurance policy" against such risks. Recent research suggests that such savings can be substantial. In the case of a product recall, for example, companies with highly rated CSR records lose on average $600 million less in firm market value than companies with low CSR activities.[13]

Note that this argument is very different from the one that relied on socially respon-

> CSR can also be viewed as a risk mitigation strategy. It then serves as "insurance" against reputational crises.

sible investors. Here investors are assumed to care *only* about financial rewards. Still, responsible companies are rewarded, not because investors care about their CSR activities per se, but because such companies are less likely to be penalized for having violated the implicit contract between companies and society concerning what is acceptable corporate behavior.

"THE ONLY LIFELINE WAS THE WAL-MART"

Disaster relief is CSR in action, a microcosm of how to build reputational capital through social engagement. It is the mirror image of the reputational crises discussed in Chapter 1—a moment when people are paying attention to a company's attempts to do the right thing. As with any other strategy, it must be executed well; it is *never* just the thought that counts.

Wal-Mart's response to Katrina was part of a wider effort by the company to improve its image in the eyes of the public.[14] Although Wal-Mart was not alone in its efforts to provide relief to the victims of Katrina—Amgen, Intel, GE, and McDonald's contributed millions of dollars to the effort—Wal-Mart came to be viewed as the "leader of the pack." According to CEO Lee Scott: "This was one of the few times at Wal-Mart when we did the right thing and actually got credit for it. Everywhere I go, everybody wants to talk about what [we] did."

Wal-Mart's effective response to Katrina was the result of careful planning and preparation. The company has an Emergency Operations Center (EOC) near its home office in Arkansas that monitors developments in the United States that might adversely affect the company—everything from customer and worker injuries to parking lot crimes and unusual vandalism, and, of course, natural disasters. Hurricanes are virtually par for the course at the EOC. Accessing its data warehouse, Wal-Mart could anticipate customer needs in hurricane-threatened areas with great accuracy and specificity. Among other things, customers typically stock up on bottled water, flashlights, portable generators of electricity, and light sheltering materials before a storm, and immediately following it, they seek out chain saws, cleaning materials, and certain foodstuffs, such as Strawberry Pop-Tarts. Why Pop-Tarts? "They are preserved until you open them, the whole family can eat them, and they taste good," said Dan Phillips, vice president of information systems.

As soon as the EOC noticed a tropical depression heading for Florida, the wheels of the massive supply chain were set in motion. The company's trucking network was contacted, and its warehouses began to prepare storm staples for shipment to threatened areas. Emergency supplies to keep stores open (e.g., generators and dry ice for maintaining refrigeration of perishable food) were also sent. Wal-Mart's director of business continuity and global security, Jason Jackson, explained it as follows: "When a district manager calls from the field to tell the operations manager in the center that he needs 10 trucks of water, the operations manager can turn to the person manning the replenishment systems. The replenishment manager then checks his supplies. He says, 'I can get you eight [trucks] today and two tomorrow.' He then tells the logistics guy. This all takes place in a matter of seconds."

On August 25, 2005, Hurricane Katrina passed through south Florida rather uneventfully. It appeared to be heading up to the panhandle, but on August 26, Wal-Mart meteorologists informed Jackson that Katrina had suddenly changed course toward New Orleans. Jackson issued an emergency alert for the area—12 hours before the official advisory from the National Weather Service—and began to reroute the materials that had been sent to the Florida panhandle, while mobilizing additional resources in dozens of Wal-Mart distribution centers in nearby states. Jackson called the mobilization "a giant game of chess."

When the storm ravaged New Orleans and the Gulf Coast on August 29, 2005, Wal-Mart was well positioned to make a difference. As the extent of the damage became clear, managers on the scene were allowed to help the needy and to provide temporary shelter and even operational bases for law-enforcement authorities. In the opinion of many observers, the company proved more nimble than the Federal Emergency Management Agency (FEMA) and other governmental authorities. According to Sheriff Harry Lee, "If the Federal Government would have responded as quickly as Wal-Mart, we could have saved more lives. . . . FEMA executives were there, but they didn't do anything for four or five days." In all, the company contributed $17 million to the relief effort and an additional $3 million in merchandise. Once they had unloaded their cargoes, truck drivers volunteered their services for the transport of additional food and aid necessities. After the immediate crisis had passed, Wal-Mart set up donation centers, missing-person "locator boards," and Internet communication facilities.

In addition to managing the operational aspects of the Katrina response, the company managed its communication strategy carefully. In messages repeated by Jackson and others, Wal-Mart emphasized that the company applied its particular "corporate strengths" in the management of the relief efforts. Wal-Mart stayed away from corporate announcements or advertisements, focusing instead on personal appearances. CEO Lee Scott, for example, joined former presidents Bill Clinton and George H. W. Bush at the Houston Astrodome to bolster the spirits of Katrina evacuees. Wal-Mart's public face consisted primarily of local employees, such as store managers or truck drivers, whom Wal-Mart made available to the media for interviews, an unusual but very effective decision. Local employees typically have more credibility than senior management in times of crisis, for they are seen as the less calculating "everyman." That allowed them to tell powerful stories about neighbors helping neighbors that reflected well on Wal-Mart.

For example, having weathered the storm, Mississippi comanager Jessica Lewis acted on her own initiative to gather goods and offer them to the needy. According to Jackson, "Jessica and her family gathered nonperishable items and placed them in the parking lot for the people of the community to come and get what they needed—at no charge, and she provided bottled water to the local emergency services. . . . Jessica was the lifeline for this community until other help arrived." Lewis later recalled: "It broke my heart to see [people] like this. These were my kids' teachers. Some of them were my teachers. They were the parents of the kids on my kids' sports teams. They were my neighbors. They were my customers." After setting up her own relief center, where she distributed everything salvageable from the store, whether it was water or medications from the pharmacy, she recalled thinking, "This is the right thing to do. I hope my bosses aren't going to have a problem with that."

A truck driver who had delivered relief supplies to the flood zone remembered: "When I arrived it sounded like someone scored a touchdown in a football game. . . . I could have sat there and shook hands all day, they were so happy to see me."

There were dozens of other examples, each portrayed as an illustration of the Wal-Mart culture of operational efficiency. Aaron F. Broussard, president of Jefferson Parish in the New Orleans suburbs, later told host Tim Russert in a *Meet the Press* interview that if "the American government would have responded like Wal-Mart has responded, we wouldn't be in this crisis."[15]

THE GOOD SAMARITAN PRINCIPLE

Wal-Mart's relief efforts were almost universally praised as having "stepped up" to the crisis. According to one industry analyst, "Short-term, you could think of all the media exposure as a promotional vehicle for Wal-Mart. But I see longer-term benefits, too. Most people who were dramatically affected were Wal-Mart consumers. They're going to remember Wal-Mart was there."[16]

This praise was no accident. Recent research suggests that companies need to follow certain principles to be viewed positively during a disaster. Natural disasters and reputational crises are best understood as mirror events. What makes external disasters particularly intriguing is that they constitute situations in which the corporation has neither a direct nor a tangential causal role in the victims' misfortune, and therefore has no direct responsibility to intervene. Such disasters stand in stark contrast to internal corporate crises, where the corporation has some (perceived) causal responsibility, and therefore there is an expectation that it will take action to ameliorate any negative effects.

In both cases, the critical issue is not the assignment of blame, but the resolution of the situation. That does not mean that there are no downsides; an incompetent or self-serving response to a disaster will not be easily forgiven or forgotten, even if the company had nothing to do with the disaster itself.

In the context of reputational crises, we developed the Trust Radar. The corresponding principle in the context of natural disasters is the Good Samaritan Principle, which refers to the famous parable from the Gospel of Luke (10:30–35). The New International Version translates the story as follows:

> A man was going down from Jerusalem to Jericho, when he was
> attacked by robbers. They stripped him of his clothes, beat him and
> went away, leaving him half dead. A priest happened to be going

down the same road, and when he saw the man, he passed by on the other side. So too, a Levite, when he came to the place and saw him, passed by on the other side. But a Samaritan, as he traveled, came where the man was; and when he saw him, he took pity on him. He went to him and bandaged his wounds, pouring on oil and wine. Then he put the man on his own donkey, brought him to an inn and took care of him. The next day he took out two denarii and gave them to the innkeeper. "Look after him," he said, "and when I return, I will reimburse you for any extra expense you may have."

The Good Samaritan has become a paradigm for the helper of those in need. Note a few details from the parable. First, the Samaritan's motives are portrayed as being purely altruistic and caring; he is not motivated by kinship or community. One important subtext of the story is that the Samaritan helps the victim despite the well-known enmity between Samaritans and Jews at the time. What makes the actions of the Samaritan so poignant is that he takes action after fellow Jews of high social and religious status (priests and Levites) have passed the victim by. Second, the Samaritan's help is not just well intended, but also competent. (Note the skillful treatment of the victim's wounds.) The Samaritan also donates money, but he does much more than that.

Recent research has suggested that these intuitions hold true in general. Task *competence* and *warmth* are the two critical components by which companies are judged during a disaster.[17] The deeper reason for these reactions is that disasters and terrorist attacks trigger a shift in orientation among customers and the general public; they come to view the company as a member of the community, not as an abstract provider of goods and services.

Individuals divide relationships into those with a communal orientation and those with an exchange orientation. The primary distinction between these two orientations is the norms that govern the giving and receiving of benefits. In exchange relationships, people provide benefits to others only to the extent that they expect to receive equivalent benefits in return. In communal relationships, one provides benefits to demonstrate care and concern for another. Whereas interactions with a company are typically exchange-oriented, characterized by tit-for-tat, reciprocal interactions and negotiations, external disasters shift this lens toward a more communal orientation, where responses are mainly judged on two dimensions: competence and warmth. Psychologists have shown that these two components can account for most of the variance in perceptions of general social behavior.[18]

Research in controlled laboratory experiments confirms this intuition.[19] When asked to evaluate fictitious news stories about companies providing assistance during a disaster, subjects respond more positively if the company provides competent help or if it shows genuine warmth. Donating money, for example, is viewed far less positively than sending executives to assist personally in relief efforts. Similarly, sending the company's skin moisturizers to a disaster site when what is needed is clean water will not be viewed positively.

> Disaster response is a paradigmatic example of CSR activities. To be successful, companies need to follow the Good Samaritan Principle: be competent and caring. Strategic fit is less relevant.

Importantly, the two factors of competence and warmth do not have an additive effect, but rather interact to determine individuals' perceptions of the company. The evidence suggests that corporations that demonstrate high interpersonal warmth but low competence are perceived in the most negative light. In turn, responses that are lower in warmth but higher in competence are perceived less negatively. What may be at work here is a suspicion that an incompetent response accompanied by expressions of empathy is hypocritical and self-serving. Our expectations of the competence of companies are so high that if they do not deliver, we suspect ulterior motives.

This paramount importance of competence also has some strategic consequences. In the debate on CSR, Michael Porter and others have argued for the importance of closely linking a company's CSR activities with its corporate strategy. That is, a pharmaceutical company should focus on topics such as expanding access to health care, while a technology company may want to engage in the issue of science education. The existing research suggests that in the context of disaster response, this connection may be less important, because by focusing too much on its core competency, the company may choose a response that is ineffective, convincing observers that the response was self-serving.

Finally, companies need to be careful how they talk about their good deeds. Philip Morris's "Working to Make a Difference" initiative demonstrates the risk of appearing overly self-congratulatory. In 2000, the company donated $115 million to charities such as battered women's shelters and homeless shelters, and spent $150 million on an advertising campaign touting its charitable contributions. In one of the ads, a woman named Laura tells viewers, "When I was nine months pregnant, my husband beat me. But thanks to Philip Morris, one of the largest supporters of battered women's shelters, women (like me) and children are starting new lives." After the ratio of dollars spent on actual contributions to those spent on touting the contributions became known, Philip Morris was widely attacked in the press and on the Internet.[20] Companies have low trust reservoirs. If they talk too much about their good works, the public suspects that they have ulterior motives.[21]

Wal-Mart's Katrina response was a textbook example of the Good Samaritan Principle, with superb preparation and execution. Naturally, Wal-Mart benefited from its existing strength in supply chain management and logistics. But it was the human dimension of the company's response that made the strategy work. The countless stories of individual store managers and truck drivers helping others, sometimes taking substantial personal risks to do so, made the merely effective personal, adding warmth to competence. Katrina became a powerful symbol for Wal-Mart, showing how the company could solve its reputational problems by leveraging its existing strengths for a new purpose.

THINGS TO REMEMBER

Improving reputational equity is not easy. But sometimes opportunities present themselves. Disaster response is one such opportunity where companies can act as heroes. Providing assistance after a terrorist attack or a natural disaster is a paradigmatic case of corporate social responsibility. Being a helper in times of need seems easy enough. But as in other instances of corporate social responsibility, there are effective and ineffective approaches.

We can summarize the general lessons as follows:

- In a disaster, act as if you are a member of the community. Focus on task competence and warmth.

- Good intentions alone are not sufficient. Help must be administered competently and effectively.

- When there is a conflict between your core competency and what is needed, go with what is needed.

Katrina showed that companies are increasingly being asked to assume responsibilities that are traditionally associated with governments (disaster relief, emergency transport, shelter, and rebuilding). The striking contrast with the ineptitude of the government's response in New Orleans certainly improved corporate images. That said, without a long-term strategy, such gains will be short-lived. Moreover, what was exceptional during Katrina will now be expected of companies; there will be no excuse for failing to deliver. This is just one example of a more general trend: companies are increasingly being evaluated by standards other than the maximization of shareholder value. CEOs and board members realize this shift, but are unsure of how to address it. Reputation management provides a framework. Investment in CSR activities can serve as reputation insurance, which can come in handy in times of need.

CHAPTER 6

THE TERMINATOR GENE

From Outrage to Fear

"The way Thomas Edison demonstrated how great electricity was was by providing lights for the first nighttime baseball game. People were in awe. What if he had decided to demonstrate the electric chair instead? And what if his second product had been the electric cattle prod? Would we have electricity today?"

—Dr. Virginia Walbot, Stanford University[1]

FEAR FACTORS

Reputational damage is drawn from two main sources: outrage and fear. We have encountered outrage in the context of many crises and scandals. It is usually based on moral judgments, a profound sense of unfairness, or a violation of fundamental laws and norms. Executive compensation and perks are among the most prominent examples, as in the cases of AIG, Merrill Lynch, and Tyco, among others. But examples can also be found in the context of predatory marketing and pricing, as in the case of payday loans, credit card fees, subprime mortgages, consumer lending, and access to lifesaving drugs.

> Fear is the second main driver of reputational damage. Fear is an emotional response that frequently does not reflect objective risk. Fear can be triggered by identifiable factors, such as:
>
> - Novelty
> - Powerlessness
> - Salience
> - Victims
> - Dread

The second source of reputational damage is fear. We have encountered fear in many different contexts, whether it be Thomas the Tank Engine or the Mercedes case. Sometimes fears are based on actual risk, but in many cases, there is a large gap between objective risk and risk perception.

Emotions and plausible heuristics play an important role.[2] This is particularly true when laypeople evaluate complex risks with which they are unfamiliar. If they significantly overestimate the risks, fear is the consequence.

The following five factors are particularly important in driving fear.

Novelty

Non-experts have a tendency to overrate the danger of some unfamiliar technologies (e.g., nuclear power) and underrate the danger of more familiar ones (e.g., X-rays). Lack of familiarity, however, does not imply lack of opinion. Affect-driven opinions are particularly common when individuals are first exposed to a new technology. Moreover, ambiguous future information is likely to be interpreted in light of the initially formed opinion. That is, people who are initially inclined to view a new technology negatively are more likely to seek out additional negative information and interpret ambiguous information in a negative light, thereby reinforcing their original attitude.[3]

Powerlessness

A sense of control lowers perceived risk; a sense of powerlessness increases it. Drivers, for example, underestimate the risks of accidents under the false assumption that they can avoid most accidents. These attitudes affect voluntary seat-belt use and the willingness to wear motorcycle helmets. Conversely, potentially harmful food ingredients, mold, or environmental chemicals can lead to widespread fears—even if their objective risk is fairly moderate.

Salience

Specific examples and other recent events affect risk perception, even if they are not statistically or causally related; triggering the relevant association is enough. The fear of dying in an airplane crash rather than, say, a car crash will increase after widespread coverage of an airplane crash. The salience of the imagery of plane wreckage is easier to access and therefore makes another crash seem more likely to happen in the future. Movies such as *Jaws* have made many people afraid of being killed in a shark attack, even though the risk is roughly the same as that of dying from falling in a sandcastle hole.[4] In the same vein, a toymaker may find it harder to sell Chinese-made toys after sweeping recalls by competitors, even if the company outsources to different plants and has tighter quality-assurance procedures.

Victims

Individuals tend to be more fearful of an event that may affect identifiable victims, such as vulnerable populations (for example, children) or comparable groups ("people like me"), or if the situation seems unfair. A mobile phone tower installed next to a kindergarten will create stronger fears of the dangers from radiation emissions.[5]

Dread

Feelings of dread refer to the visceral fear that "the worst" could happen; the more dreadful a possible consequence seems, the less tolerance there is for risk. Dread refers not just to bad consequences but to very bad consequences, such as death from cancer or from an atomic explosion.

Concern, fear, and the perception of risk can be mitigated. The greater the perceived benefit, for example, the greater the tolerance for risk. The importance of possible benefits results in part from the immediate positive feeling generated by imagining desired outcomes, which lowers risk perception. Research on risk tolerance has also shown that individuals are less willing to accept risk in the context of gains (e.g., a guaranteed small reward versus a gamble between a larger reward or nothing) but are very risk tolerant when the choices are framed as a loss (i.e., a guaranteed small loss versus a gamble between a larger loss or no loss at all).

But if such mitigating factors are absent, for example, in the case of a technology that promises obscure gains that are difficult to understand, observers will experience a heightened sense of fear and concern. In addition to the intrinsic characteristics of an issue given by fear factors and mitigators, cultural and ideological context, media coverage, or the trust bank account of the company can further increase or decrease their effect.[6]

Nuclear power is one of the paradigmatic examples of the power of fear factors amplified by activists and the media. When nuclear power plants were first built, they were novel and mysterious. Their potential consequences were dreadful, and their benefits (such as lower energy prices) were abstract and of small magnitude for any given individual. It seemed to local communities as if they had no control over these risks, and the Chernobyl accident dramatically increased their fears, despite different technologies and regulatory regimes.

THE CHALLENGE OF EMERGING TECHNOLOGIES

Nuclear power is not the only emerging technology that has run into heavy resistance from a fearful public.[7] The history of innovative technologies is full of examples of promising technologies that encountered not only indifference but also substantial resistance, and thus never reached their economic potential. Examples include genetically modified food, stem cell research, and many others. In some cases, carefully crafted market-entry campaigns were derailed by hostile media coverage, creating fear among customers. In other cases, companies were targeted by well-organized activist groups, and their opposition led to regulatory changes. In the most extreme cases, such as that of genetically modified food products in Europe, companies lost their license to operate in the marketplace.

The paradigmatic example of these difficulties is Monsanto's troubles with genetically modified organisms (GMOs) in food products.[8] Applications of biotech to industry fall into two categories. On the one hand, we have what's called "green biotech"—applications to food and agriculture. On the other hand, we have "red biotech"—applications to medicine. One of the best-known examples of green biotech is Monsanto's Roundup Ready soybean seeds, which were introduced for the 1996 planting season. Roundup Ready seeds are genetically modified so that they tolerate Monsanto's Roundup agricultural herbicides; this tolerance allows growers to spray Roundup herbicides on their fields during the growing season to kill weeds, while leaving the crops unharmed.[9] By reducing the need for broad herbicide use, Roundup Ready seeds may lead to higher crop yields.

> Promising technologies frequently encounter resistance and never reach their full potential. Fear based on opinion rather than experience is a main factor in these situations. Different applications of the same technology can differ dramatically in terms of their potential to create fear.

Although there were concerns about Monsanto's products in all markets, Europe became Monsanto's Waterloo. The company's aggressive, technology-focused approach did not play well with many of the nongovernmental organizations (NGOs) that are crucial in shaping European public opinion. Soon a major food retailer in Iceland was leading the charge against genetically modified (GM) food, and organic farmers in England led fierce protests, claiming that genetically modified crops could contaminate nearby organic farms. This culminated in activists pulling up test fields of GM crops, which further increased media coverage. Even Charles, Prince of Wales, came out strongly against genetically modified foods.[10]

The EU subsequently adopted a moratorium on GMOs (which is still largely in place more than a decade later), and Monsanto's share price dropped 35 percent. Monsanto's CEO, Robert Shapiro, retired in 2000 after engineering the merger of Monsanto with Pharmacia and Upjohn. Pharmacia later spun off Monsanto as a separate company in 2002. Yet at the same time, medical applications of biotechnology were adopted in Europe without much fanfare, including controversial treatments and diagnostics such as gene therapy and genetic testing.

Let us compare the two applications with respect to their fear factors. Both applications are novel and unfamiliar. This is a challenge that they both share. As to control, patients need to consent to any therapy, whereas consumers have no control over whether and to what extent biotech products enter the food supply. Lack of labeling will further increase this sense of powerlessness. Medical applications of biotechnology, such as gene therapy, can have substantial dread risks. This is also true of agricultural applications, although to a lesser degree. Examples include concerns about allergic reactions and the emergence of antibiotic-resistant bacteria, along with environmental concerns such as superweeds, loss of biodiversity, and so forth.

But the biggest differences are in the area of benefits. The health benefits of biotechnology—such as saving lives—are usually immediately evident. The economic benefits of agricultural biotech, such as increased crop yields and lower food costs, however, are spread over many products or have only a small impact on consumers, compared with nutritional or other health benefits.[11] Note also that in the case of saving lives, the focus is on preventing a loss, whereas agricultural benefits are naturally conceptualized as gains. In sum, the fear index of biotechnology for agricultural products far exceeds the comparable index for health applications.

All the amplifying factors were also present. The opposition to agricultural biotech followed essentially the same ideological battle lines as the fight against nuclear power, which had taken place a decade earlier and was the formative moment for the northern European environmental movement. As the U.S.-based chemical company that had made the infamous herbicide Agent Orange, used during the Vietnam War, Monsanto enjoyed little trust with a skeptical public.[12] Medical applications of biotech faced no such difficulties. Many of them were brought to market by European health-care companies that did not have that sort of baggage.

In addition, there was a specific difficulty in the respective media environments. The Reputational Terrain can help us understand these differences. In the case of genetically modified soybeans, the problem for biotech companies is as follows. As illustrated in Figure 6-1, the technology's benefits are fairly technical (improved efficiency, lower cost, and so on) and are likely to be discussed on the left-hand side of the media spectrum, whereas the risks (health concerns for humans and environmental impact) are likely to be located in the very top right-hand corner. Mass coverage of green biotech, therefore, is more likely to be highly critical of biotech products and to portray the company offering them as villainous.

Figure 6-1 **Risk Segments—Green Biotech**

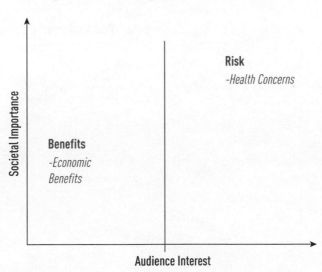

Activist strategies tend to increase this disparity further. For example, a particularly evocative designation that labeled genetically modified products as "Frankenstein foods" struck a chord with consumers, who feared manmade monstrosities gone awry, and was used quite effectively against the bioagriculture industry by critics such as Jeremy

Rifkin of the Pure Food Campaign. Moreover, researchers had started to voice concern over the potential harm to monarch butterfly larvae, giving somewhat abstract concerns over ecological impact a concrete and beloved victim.[13]

The biotech industry did not help its case by using some very unfortunate terminology. One such example was the term *terminator gene*, which was used to describe genetically modified seeds that grow into sterile plants to protect the intellectual property of seed companies. The use of terminator genes, also known as "genetic use restriction technologies," meant that farmers could not harvest seeds from one year for the next year's planting. Critics expressed concerns that such technologies could lead to decreased biodiversity and sustained economic dependence of small farmers.[14]

The situation for medical applications of biotech is very different (see Figure 6-2).

Figure 6-2 **Risk Segments—Red Biotech**

The key difference is that now the benefits (saving lives and curing diseases) are in the *same location* as the costs, giving companies a much better chance to position themselves favorably.

The point is not that red biotech does not carry risks. Indeed, the risks can be substantial, in terms of both ethical concerns and potential side effects for patients, and the benefits may be questionable.[15] The point is rather that medical benefits are typically located in a segment of the Reputational Terrain that gives the company or product the opportunity to tell a straightforward and credible story of saving lives.

Following this logic, location in the Reputational Terrain will vary according to the characteristics of the product. For example, Vitamin A–enriched so-called golden rice[16] might be viewed more favorably than genetically modified potatoes that contain insecticides, even though from a public policy point of view, a genetically modified potato that is protected from pests may have the same or even a more beneficial impact on global nutrition. The difference is the direct health benefit to vulnerable populations, such as malnourished children. Thus, not only was agricultural biotech likely to face substantial resistance because of its fear index, but these fears were also likely to be amplified by the media environment.

This has potentially profound consequences for product introduction strategies, such as deciding which products should be the lead applications of a new technology. Products that have clear benefits associated with them should be introduced first if gaining public acceptance is a major concern. (Recall the quote by Stanford's Dr. Walbot on Thomas Edison that opened this chapter.) It also implies that a sole focus on reducing the perceived risk may not always be the most effective strategy for a biotech company.

Even more worrisome, once members of the public have formed an initial opinion, often based on little more than a news report or an expressed opinion on a blog, they tend to search out information that confirms—rather than challenges—their initial attitudes. Research has shown that those who perceived greater benefits from GM foods spent more time gathering and reading favorable information about GMOs than those who had no prior opinion or negative opinions toward GM foods. Other empirical work on technology acceptance has noted the same confirmation-seeking behavior.[17]

In sum, GMOs were textbook examples of new technologies generating a strong sense of fear. So, how do we manage them? One answer is credibility transfer, a technique that we first encountered in Chapter 3. Third-party influence is particularly potent for new technologies, for which, by definition, only a very few experts can rely on deep knowledge or personal experience.[18] Working with third parties, of course, is not easy. But it can be done successfully, even with highly controversial products.

One such example was the introduction of the Flavr Savr tomato.[19] Developed by biotech pioneer Calgene, the Flavr Savr tomato contained a modified gene that was designed to inhibit the release of an enzyme that was the main cause of tomatoes softening as they ripen. Calgene's insight was that if the enzyme was turned off, Flavr Savr tomatoes could be picked vine-ripened. The company envisioned a tomato with improved color and taste that was easier to ship (because it remained firm) and had an extended shelf life in stores.

In addition, a marker gene was introduced at the site of the modified Flavr Savr gene to detect its location and placement. It was this marker gene that raised concerns among antibiotech-food advocates, who questioned its safety. Roger Salquist, Calgene's CEO, deftly used credible third parties to diffuse these fears. The key component of the strategy was to ask the Food and Drug Administration (FDA) for a ruling on the safety of the marker gene as a food additive, which Calgene applied for in 1992. In the eyes of many regulatory experts, getting the FDA to rule on the gene was not legally required, but if approval was granted, it could prove an inspired way to allay consumer fears about bioengineered food, given the FDA's high credibility with U.S. consumers.[20]

In addition, Calgene provided both the U.S. Department of Agriculture and the FDA with its test results even when it was not required to do so. The company also supplied information to store managers regarding genetically modified food, ran education campaigns for the public, and sent out numerous press releases to the media about the development of the new tomato even before it was ready for production. All this was done to help familiarize and educate the public about a genetically engineered tomato that was nowhere near ready for market. Salquist's view was that the more information that was made available to the public about this new tomato, the more comfortable the public would feel about it. When the Flavr Savr finally did hit stores in 1994, it was eagerly anticipated and arrived to little opposition—exactly the way Salquist had planned.[21]

Calgene's success during the launch can be explained by various factors. First, Calgene managed the issue of public trust proactively. It reached out to stakeholders and treated them as partners with legitimate concerns who could be engaged in a dialogue. Its relationship with government agencies and Congress was treated as a strategic alliance, with a keen understanding of the other side's incentives. Congressional staffers, for example, knew very little about this new technology, but they needed to develop at least some expertise quickly. Calgene made its research scientists available as sources of information—no talking points or prepared statements, just free-flowing discussions. By doing this, Calgene hit all four dimensions of the Trust Radar (transparency, expertise, commitment, and even some level of empathy), which created a genuine, mutually advantageous relationship.

Second, Calgene entered the public debate early and even advanced it. In this, Salquist exhibited a keen understanding of media coverage. For example, Calgene wanted all the stories of "Frankenfoods" out early, so that when the tomato finally hit the stores, the issue had become old news and the focus was on taste, not controversy. Also, Salquist intentionally made some provocative statements about some of the tomato's more radical critics. The idea was to make sure to be quoted, to be invited to media interviews and debates, to be heard when it mattered.

Third, the Flavr Savr tomato offered a direct benefit to customers: better flavor and longer shelf life, as well as the reduction of standard chemical treatments. Calgene emphasized this benefit through the name *Flavr Savr*, rather than using a technical or scary term such as *terminator gene*.

Fourth, Salquist served as the steward of the trust-building strategy. He realized early that obtaining a license to operate—that is, entering the market with this product—was by no means a given. This ensured alignment throughout the organization, even when difficult trade-offs had to be considered, as when the company voluntarily submitted to additional regulatory oversight. Calgene did all of this with a total workforce of fewer than 150 employees, most of whom were research scientists. Indeed, Calgene's small size may have been a blessing in disguise, as it required the CEO to lead the initiative.

Critics have attributed Monsanto's failure in Europe to arrogance and an exclusive focus on the scientific aspects of its product. But the story is more nuanced. Monsanto previously had successfully introduced synthetic milk hormones, also known as recombinant bovine growth hormones (rBGH), into the U.S. market.[22] The growth hormone boosted a cow's milk production by 10 to 20 percent, thereby increasing the farmer's profit from each cow. Although Monsanto won regulatory approval to sell its product in the United States, it did so with substantial opposition from both public and private advocates. Issues included the impact that Monsanto's product would have on small farmers and concerns about human and animal health. Even though Monsanto did not sell directly to end consumers, its product was part of a supply chain that eventually reached consumers in the form of milk products. Thus, concerns from these end consumers might raise an alarm among Monsanto's customers who sold directly to the public.

One of the key issues that both incited and mitigated the controversies surrounding rBGH was labeling. Advocacy groups such as Consumers Union and the Pure Food Campaign sought to label milk as "rBGH-free." Monsanto countered with an antilabeling campaign. It funded efforts by its dairy-farmer customers to protest such labeling, and it engaged the FDA directly on the issue in order to clarify legal and regulatory matters as well as to leverage the strong reputation of the FDA to alleviate consumer fears.

The FDA subsequently stated in a guidance document that labeling milk as "rBGH-free" was potentially misleading to customers, as it might suggest that the milk was safer than or superior to milk from treated cows.[23] The agency also noted that there is currently no way to verify a producer's claim that milk from treated cows was not used, since there was no measurable difference between the milk of treated and untreated cows. The FDA finally stated that producers could label their products "rBGH-free" as long as they printed a clarifying statement, such as "no significant difference has been shown between milk derived from rBGH-treated and non-rBGH-treated cows." The strategy was at least a partial success. It did reassure many customers, but it also led to a prolonged battle with producers such as ice cream company Ben & Jerry's over the right to label its ice creams as "rBGH-free."[24]

So why did Monsanto fail in Europe but succeed in the United States? The answer is that the credibility of third parties varies across countries and cultures. In other words, Monsanto essentially employed the same strategic approach in Europe as it did in the growth hormone case in the United States: the use of government regulators as trusted third parties. But this approach assumed that regulators enjoy similar levels of trust in other countries.

The credibility of particular third parties, in fact, varies dramatically from issue to issue and from country to country. For example, in northern Europe, nongovernmental organizations have some of the highest credibility scores with the public, while government agencies rank near the bottom, along with individual corporations. In the United Kingdom, in particular, trust in government agencies has yet to be restored after their bungled response to mad cow disease in the 1990s. So an endorsement by the U.K. Ministry of Health did not confer much added credibility. The situation is, however, quite the opposite in Japan and the United States, where government agencies such as the FDA still enjoy high credibility with consumers, indicating that a trust-building approach that works in one market may not work in another.[25]

> When new technologies encounter resistance, companies lack credibility with customers and stakeholders. The use of credible third parties can alleviate this problem. The credibility of particular third parties will vary by market and country, however. The use of credibility ladders can help in designing targeted strategies.

In such cases, it is useful to construct "credibility ladders." The goal is to collaborate with those parties that have the *highest credibility in the given market*. Credibility ladders can be constructed from surveys and focus groups, as well as from citation data. So by using government agencies, Monsanto inadvertently targeted the lower ranks of the ladder, which were no match for an attack by concerned scientists and NGOs.

NANOTECH

As we have seen, excitement about technological innovation can quickly turn to concern—with disastrous consequences for the industry. Such issues as product acceptance pertain not only to consumer-oriented products, as in the case of the Flavr Savr tomato, but also to business-to-business (B2B) products, as in the case of Monsanto's Roundup Ready soybeans, which are used as an ingredient in many processed food items. In both cases, the issue was triggered by worries by the general public about product safety, environmental impact, and the like.

In the case of consumer products, such worries may undermine consumer trust, resulting in lower sales. In the case of business-to-business products, the direct impact may be not on the supplier (e.g., Monsanto) but on the branded company that is using Roundup Ready soybeans as an ingredient in its products, say, candy bars. Concerned about loss of customers, consumer brand companies will then put pressure on their suppliers to ensure that products are "GMO-free," which in turn undermines the sales of the supplier, in this case Monsanto. In other words, if there are concerns about a product or technology, these concerns quickly move up the supply chain, undermining the business success of the technology.

Nanotechnology is facing a similar set of challenges. In a recent report on future technologies, including nanotechnology, Dr. Doug Parr, Greenpeace UK's chief scientist, did not mince words: "Any technology placed in the hands of those who care little about the possible environmental, health, or social impacts is potentially disastrous."[26]

In contrast to biotech, nuclear power, or stem cell research, however, concerns about nanotech products so far have not been a significant impediment. Indeed, existing public opinion survey research suggests a fairly broad acceptance of nanotechnology. As we now may suspect, not much trust should be placed in these data. Public support for nanotech products is shallow at best and can easily move toward fear and resistance.

Public knowledge of nanotechnology is very limited, with more than 80 percent of Americans reporting that they know either "just a little" or "nothing" about nanotechnology. Nevertheless, almost 90 percent of the participants polled had an opinion about the risks or benefits of nanotech. Respondents who held a negative attitude toward nanotechnology were more likely to report that the risks outweighed the benefits, whereas those who held a positive attitude typically believed the opposite. Strikingly, obtaining information about nanotechnology *prior* to reporting their judgment did not influence the respondents' expressed opinion. Providing additional information after an initial judgment was formed tended to reinforce the original attitude rather than change it.[27]

The evidence suggests that with the proper triggering event (similar to, for example, the potential harm to monarch butterfly larvae in the debate on GMOs) or a coordinated campaign (such as the anti-GMO campaign in the United Kingdom), individuals will form immediate affective responses based on little information that will fall along the same ideological lines as opinions on other controversial issues, such as global warming and nuclear power. Simply presenting additional information about nanotechnology could potentially be counterproductive, serving only to reinforce and harden existing attitudes.

Nanotech shares much of its risk profile with GMOs. One of the critical issues will be the benefits of nanotech. Medical applications, for example, are far more promising than cosmetic applications. Consider the example of sunscreen, one of the more prominent uses of nanotechnology in consumer products. There are direct benefits to consumers (nanotechnology makes the sunscreen less greasy), but they are limited.[28] In addition, some of the sunscreens are marketed to children.

Such products provide excellent targets for activists. As in the case of biotech, nanotech companies frequently are not good targets for activists, as they lack the brand recognition that will trigger significant media interest, a necessary component for the success of an activist campaign. Rather, the potential vulnerability of the nanotech industry rests with its customers, such as well-known consumer goods companies that worry about their brand and their reputation in a highly competitive market, as in the case of sunscreen makers. Once consumer goods companies sense a negative impact on their brands because of the reputational challenges of a key ingredient, they have an incentive to shift to suppliers that do not have similar problems. This may lead to labeling and standards and even to the emergence of premium products that are "nanotech-free."

Nanotech companies will need to win the battle for public opinion if they want to avoid the emergence of a market for nanotech-free products. The history of controversial technologies has shown that focusing on the technological and scientific aspects is not sufficient. Rather, public fears about safety or about the environmental or social impact of these products may lead to private regulation through the mechanisms of private politics. Previous technologies with similar impact (such as GMOs) have faced significant challenges in this regard, which has limited their broad adoption. The same process is to be expected for nanotechnology.

Nanotech companies should not be fooled by the comparative lack of activity up to this point. Their risk profiles are broadly similar to those in the biotech field. What is missing is a triggering event: the analogue to the monarch butterfly or the criticism by the Prince of Wales. Triggering events create the stage that turns risks into crises. The gasoline is already present; all that is missing is the match.

INNOVATION AND ITS CHALLENGES

As these examples illustrate, emerging technologies are prone to creating fears that may limit their adoption. Often, these fears are based on emotional responses triggered by activist campaigns or media coverage, rather than on a thorough understanding of the risks. The result can be limited acceptance in the marketplace. This can be the result of customer resistance, as in the case of GMOs and bovine growth hormone, or of regulatory action driven by public opinion, as in the case of the European Union's moratorium on genetically modified food products.

These risks are not limited to emerging technologies. New concerns about established technologies and products can have the same effect. One well-known example involved concerns about Alar, the trade name of an insecticide called daminozide, which was used in fruit and vegetable production. When Alar became linked to cancer in animals, the Natural Resource Defense Council successfully targeted the product and its maker, Uniroyal. The campaign featured news stories on *60 Minutes*, focused on apples in schools, and used celebrities such as the actress Meryl Streep. Four months after the campaign started, Uniroyal announced that it would no longer sell Alar in the United States.[29]

But innovative technologies are particularly at risk, as they cannot rely on a preexisting trust reservoir based on experience with the product or an established brand. Start-up companies backed by venture capital are one of the main drivers of innovation. It is here that the reputational risks are most pronounced.

Investors in innovative technologies need to be aware of technologies' fear factors. Fear factors may limit the effective market size. Addressing possible issues during the design phase is far preferable than waiting for a problem to arise.

Different industries have their typical risk factors. For biotech companies, safety, regulatory risks, and ethical issues (e.g., cloning and genetic testing) top the list. For Internet start-ups, data security and privacy are among the leading concerns. This has been an ongoing challenge for social networking sites such as Facebook.[30] But financial innovations, such as the development of exotic investment instruments, can face similar obstacles. A good example is the early history of derivatives triggered by the 1994 Orange County bankruptcy.[31] As in the case of biotech, concerns can vary tremendously across countries. Recently, Google's Street View feature caused an unexpected uproar in privacy-conscious Germany.[32]

THINGS TO REMEMBER

Outrage is one of the main drivers of reputational challenges. The other is fear. The public will tend to perceive risks in very different ways from experts. In this chapter, we have identified some of the main factors that drive fear and how they affect various businesses, especially in the context of emerging technologies, where direct customer experience is limited or nonexistent.

- Fear is an emotional response that frequently does not reflect objective risks but is triggered by identifiable attributes of a product or issue.

- Some of the most potent factors are:

  - Novelty

  - Powerlessness

  - Salience

  - Victims

  - Dread

- Cultural context, lack of mitigating factors, media coverage, or a company's low trust reservoir can amplify these effects.

- When a company finds itself in a low-trust environment, it should consider strategies that lead to credibility transfer from third parties with higher trust. Who has higher levels of trust will depend on the market and its social and cultural environment. The same institution that is highly trusted in one country may have low trust levels in another. Credibility ladders are a useful tool in selecting the right partner.

All too often, these risks are ignored, especially by investors, who may pay a heavy price in return. Once such risks are identified, they can be mitigated in various ways. The value or terms of the deal can be adjusted. An investor can ask for additional guarantees during the due-diligence process. An active investor may also bring about some changes in the business model. This requires a detailed understanding of how to integrate reputation management with a company's market strategy. It is to this task that we turn next.

CHAPTER 7

BEAT THE GRIM REAPER

Strategic Anticipation and the Management of Reputational Risk

It's an interesting asset class because it's less correlated to the rest of the market than other asset classes.

—**Andrew Terrell,** former co-head of Bear Stearns's longevity and mortality desk, on the trading of life insurance–based securities, also known as "death bonds"[1]

LIVING BENEFITS

Du...uring the early years of the AIDS crisis, a curious industry made up of small start-up companies like Beat the Grim Reaper International, Inc., emerged.[2] Founded by a high school English teacher who operated it out of his home, Beat the Grim Reaper was one of the pioneers of viatical settlements.[3]

A viatical settlement is a contract between the owner of a life insurance policy and a company like Beat the Grim Reaper, in which the company effectively purchases the beneficiary rights from the policyholder for some discounted percentage of the policy amount. The selling policyholder may then use the funds at her discretion, to fund anything from medical expenses to housing payments. Controversy arose because this contract was available only to policyholders with terminal illnesses, such as AIDS or late-stage cancer.

For example, viatical settlement companies would offer a terminally ill holder of a $100,000 policy an up-front cash payment of $60,000 in exchange for being named as the life insurance policy's new sole beneficiary. The company would continue to pay the policy's premiums until the patient's death, at which point it would collect the full $100,000 face value of the life insurance policy. The purchase discount varied widely based on the policyholder's health and implied life expectancy, the remaining necessary premium payments, and the prevailing market rates. The discount that companies deducted could be as high as 50 percent, but typically lay somewhere between 20 and 40 percent. As part of the approval process, settlement companies required an examination by an independent physician to estimate the policyholder's life expectancy.

Many patients used the proceeds to cover the costs of their illness, including the use of experimental treatments that were not covered by health insurers. Others used the proceeds to settle personal affairs or fulfill last wishes. While some companies provided their services exclusively to patients who were facing severe financial hardship, others placed no restrictions on their payout policies. Some companies continued to hold the purchased policies to maturity, while others acted as brokers, eventually reselling the life insurance policies to investors and keeping the spread between the two prices.

However, it did not take long for unscrupulous individuals to recognize the opportunities to exploit this unregulated market. Fraudsters falsified medical records to make the insured patients seem closer to their demise than they really were, and overaggressive intermediaries that were attempting to resell the purchased policies enticed unsophisticated investors—in some cases retirees—with sales pitches asking, "What are the two most certain things in life? Death and taxes!"[4]

In 1988, Ron Barbaro, the president of Canadian operations for Prudential Financial, Inc., at the time, toured Casey House, a Toronto hospice for advanced-stage AIDS patients.[5] Following the visit, Barbaro envisioned making an accelerated payment program available to any terminally ill Prudential policyholder. In effect, the program would offer patients the option of selling their policy back to Prudential directly, rather than dealing with the intermediary of a viatical settlement company. Barbaro explained that his original motivation was humanitarian in nature. "I was convinced that there had to be some way to ease the financial stress of dying," he said, even while acknowledging the potential pitfalls of this approach. "I was scared stiff. I did not know whether we were doing the right thing. . . . You're dealing with the final stages of someone's life. It's not something you advertise." To address these concerns, Barbaro assembled an ad hoc group that met for two days to discuss the viability of the accelerated benefits program.

Prudential faced substantial reputational risk by offering the program. One of the world's leading financial services companies, with $690 billion of assets under management, the company had a long history in the insurance business. Founded in New Jersey in 1875, the company had grown out of the Prudential Friendly Society, which made life insurance accessible to the working class by offering premiums as low as three cents per week. Renaming itself the Prudential Insurance Company of America, the company later adopted the Rock of Gibraltar as its logo, symbolizing the strength and security that it promised to its customers. Today, the company offers a wide range of financial services, including life insurance, annuities, mutual funds, investment management, and retirement-related services.[6]

In determining how the task force should address this issue, let us consider the nature of the decision that Prudential faced. Although the motivation for the proposal to offer accelerated benefits, tentatively named the "Living Benefits" program, may have been humanitarian, it needed to work within the context of Prudential's business in order to be sustainable. While Prudential may have viewed the Living Benefits project purely as a charitable endeavor, let us set aside this motivation for a moment and, for the sake of the argument, analyze the business case for moving ahead with the project.

We have seen repeatedly that the ability to rely on the other party when one is vulnerable is one of the key features of a trust-based relationship. By helping out its current customers in their time of need, Prudential could send a strong signal to future customers that it can be relied upon. Such a halo effect might sway potential customers toward selecting Prudential products.

Essentially, this is the same process that we saw in Chapter 2 in the context of the Mercedes and the Moose Test case, but with a focus on creating an opportunity. In both cases, the company's reputation—as shaped not only by advertisements and brand touch points, but also by newspaper articles, advice from friends, or recommendations by third parties—will influence customers' decisions. The pivotal point of this approach is Prudential's improved reputation because of the Living Benefits program; if Prudential launches it properly, it will have done the right thing and received credit for it.

This is not the only rationale for entering the market. Alternatively, Prudential might focus less on using the Living Benefits product to improve its brand and focus instead on the transactional aspects of the product. The rationale here would be to make money on each contract. Prudential has a competitive advantage over smaller start-ups like Beat the Grim Reaper, given its strong existing customer base, established sales structure, sophisticated financial modeling capacity, and proprietary mortality data from its life insurance business. This infrastructure creates a sustainable competitive advantage that Prudential could monetize, either by charging a price premium or by taking on a lower level of effective risk at pricing parity.

These two approaches are not incompatible. However, clarity about the company's strategic direction is critically important, as it will shape the way the product is offered. For example, Prudential faces competition from other established life insurance companies, such as Northwestern Mutual and MetLife. Therefore, a reputational approach would mean that Prudential would have to offer the Living Benefits program under the Prudential brand umbrella and restrict access to the program to Prudential customers, in order to prove that Prudential goes the extra mile to care for *its* customers, not just anybody.

The transactional approach would suggest a very different strategy. Here the competition is not existing life insurance companies (unless those incumbents also decided to enter the viatical settlement market) but start-ups like Beat the Grim Reaper. Prudential could then consider offering the option to holders of any life insurance policy, not just Prudential customers. In fact, Prudential could consider creating a subsidiary—possibly under a different brand name—that would have access to its financial models and marketing infrastructure, but would otherwise operate like an independent viatical settlement company. Whether maintaining the Prudential name for this entity makes sense then becomes a secondary decision based on tactical considerations.

The decision as to which strategy to pursue becomes clear when we look at the big picture. With a volume of approximately $250 million in revenues, the market for viatical settlements pales in comparison to the U.S. market for life insurance, which at the time was estimated at about $12 trillion in active life insurance policies.[7] As a result, the long-term benefits for the much larger life insurance business from even a very small halo effect would be likely to dwarf any short-term benefits from a transactional approach. Additionally, a reputation-based strategy arguably provides a better fit with Prudential's overall strategic positioning, which emphasizes reliability and stability, as demonstrated by its choice of logo.

The strategy, however, is not without its potential downside, as its success pivots on the company's ability to improve its reputation by generating goodwill through the Living Benefits program. Efforts to improve the company's reputation could always backfire and instead damage it, damage that could spill over to Prudential's reputation not only in life insurance products, but also in its other business lines like investment and retirement products and advice, all of which rely upon the maintenance of customer trust. In other words, Prudential needs to anticipate and assess the reputational risks carefully in launching the Living Benefits program.

ANTICIPATION

This allows us to take an important next step in the development of our reputation management toolbox. Up to now, we have dealt with

> Most reputational challenges do not happen because of some external event or misfortune, but rather arise as the direct consequence of company actions. Companies make decisions without considering the reputational impact of those decisions, so decision makers fail to act as the stewards of the company's reputation.

reputational issues as they arise. We have examined reputational crises, considered recovery strategies, and analyzed specific types of reputational challenges, from dealing with activists to disaster relief to corporate scandals. Along the way, we have also developed various tools to assist in the management of these issues, such as the Trust Radar and Reputational Terrain.

Underneath these topics lurks a hard truth: *most reputational challenges do not happen because of some external event or misfortune, but rather arise as the direct consequence of company actions.* In other words, companies usually bear at least some responsibility for finding themselves in trouble. Why? *Companies make decisions without considering the reputational impact of those decisions, so decision makers fail to act as the stewards of the company's reputation.*

The graph in Figure 7-1 is helpful in illustrating this point.[8]

Figure 7-1 **Reputation Dynamics**

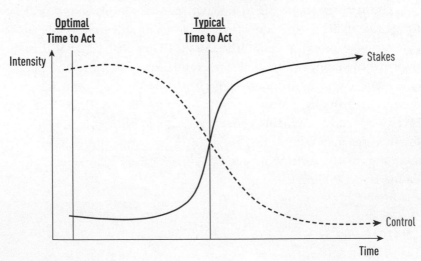

Figure 7-1 captures the difficulties that are inherent in reputation management, because it shows how control and impact move in opposite directions. During a reputational crisis, the stakes get higher as the company loses control. Customers and other stakeholders are paying attention, but the company must make decisions under extreme time pressure and with limited access to critical information. It is far better to manage one's reputation well in advance of a crisis, while the stakes are still low, the company retains substantial control, and time pressure is limited. In the case of Prudential, management could still decide to walk away from its accelerated benefits program before launching it. This might mean the loss of a business opportunity, but missed opportunities are preferable to facing major reputational crises with uncertain results.

Companies must therefore recognize the reputational impact of *any* business decision before it is made. The importance of this point cannot be overstated. Recall that our decision maker at Prudential is not its "chief reputation officer"—no such position existed at the time. Instead, it is an executive who is charged with making day-to-day decisions— here, whether to provide an added service to an existing product. Such a business decision can have a massive reputational impact, as illustrated by examples of executive compensation (such as AIG, Merrill Lynch, and Tyco in Chapter 4), new product launches (such as Mercedes in Chapter 2), supply chain management (such as RC2 in Chapter 1 or Wal-Mart in Chapter 3), disposal of old equipment (such as Shell in Chapter 3), and product design (such as Goldman Sachs in Chapters 1 and 2).

In all these cases, managers in departments ranging from HR to Engineering made decisions that had massive reputational consequences. Were these managers aware of these potential consequences? Did they act as guardians of the company's reputation, or did they merely focus on their narrow expertise and incentives?

> The reputational impact of a business decision can and must be assessed before the decision is made. This is the time when the stakes are low and control is high. Assessing reputational risk requires anticipating what a reputational crisis would look like and then taking proactive steps to prevent and prepare for it. Take the *Wall Street Journal* test: imagine how you would feel about a decision if it were accurately reported on the front page of the *Wall Street Journal*.

For most companies, the answer is the latter. Managers make decisions using all sorts of criteria, but the protection and enhancement of the company's reputation rarely receives more than lip service.

An easy way to improve decision-making processes is the *Wall Street Journal* test, which suggests that decision makers should ask themselves whether they would be proud if the decision were *accurately* reported on the front page of the *Wall Street Journal*. This test evocatively captures the idea that a decision may look different once it comes under public scrutiny. Strategic anticipation of reputational risk, however, goes beyond this simple approach by understanding the trade-offs between reputational risk and business opportunity.

These considerations also address the misconception that reputation management can be left to specialists from the communication, legal, or compliance function. The key to successful reputation management is that *all decision makers in the organization view themselves as stewards of the company's reputation*. To achieve this focus, companies need to have three components: strategy, process, and culture. This chapter will deal with strategy, while the next two chapters will discuss process and culture.

The concept of reputation dynamics is the key to integrating reputational stewardship with everyday business decisions. It emphasizes the fact that a company's environment during a reputational crisis will look very different from its environment in normal times. In the case of AIG's retention agreements, for example, a confidential contract between two parties faced sudden scrutiny in the glaring spotlight of 24-hour news coverage, simplified for a mass audience, with an emphasis on emotional impact and moral outrage. Advocacy groups that typically lie dormant or unorganized may jump on the stage, followed by politicians, regulators, and other officials.

The spotlight will focus not only on the company's *current* actions, such as how the CEO answers questions and what the company will do to fix the problem, but also on its *past* actions. Reporters will ask when the company first knew about the problem, or why management didn't do more to fix it. The thought process behind each past decision can be brought out into the public arena and questioned. These past actions and decisions are now part of the record and cannot be changed. Even those actions that looked reasonable at the time may wither under scrutiny from a hostile audience in a crisis context after their negative consequences come to light.

After the Gulf of Mexico oil spill, every minute decision that BP made concerning its safety processes took on disproportionate significance, leading to severe criticism of the company. After the failed Moose Test, Mercedes's use of computer-simulated safety testing rather than "real testing" drew the ire of journalists, who suggested that the company might have sacrificed safety to lower development costs. And when Toyota had to recall its cars, commentators quickly alleged that its aggressive growth strategy had sacrificed quality and safety.[9]

To avoid these situations, *proactive* reputation management needs to anticipate the possibility of such developments and incorporate them into decision making. Any issue that is likely to end

> Once a company faces a reputational crisis, the public will pay attention not only to what is happening now, but to what was done before to prevent it. This perspective needs to be incorporated into today's decisions. Through our business decisions today, we are creating the facts that will be the basis for our story tomorrow.

up in the top right quadrant of our Reputational Terrain from Chapter 2—one that is likely to be discussed as a story, with villains, victims, and heroes—requires a proactive mindset that reflects an awareness that *through our business decision today, we are creating the facts that will be the basis for our story tomorrow.*

This approach constitutes the critical switch from a crisis management to a risk management mindset. Taking reputational risk seriously does not necessarily mean refraining from giving the green light to decisions that carry some reputational risk. Rather, the goal of proactive reputation management is to identify possible risks and mitigate them through *current* actions to reach an acceptable balance level of risk and control (see Figure 7-2). Future reputational risk can be managed today only if it is identified and weighed during the decision-making process.

Figure 7-2 **Reputation Dynamics—The Strategy Connection**

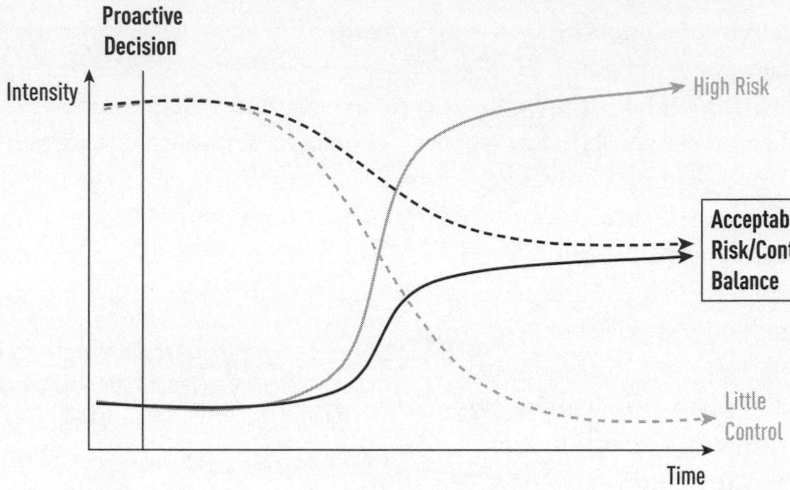

Once we have assessed an issue's reputational risk, we need to move to the next step and take appropriate action. The effective mitigation of reputational risk has two critical components: prevention and preparation (see Figure 7-3).

Figure 7-3 **Reputation Dynamics—Strategies**

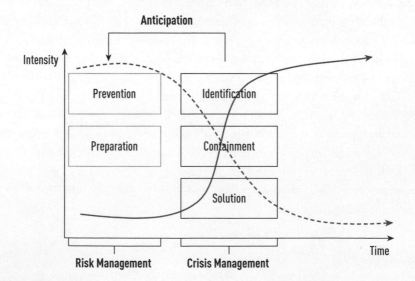

Prevention consists of steps to reduce or eliminate a particular risk. In a quality management context, it may result in additional quality controls; in a marketing context, it may demand the elimination of problematic sales practices. In an M&A context, it may mean that a company walks away from an acquisition or renegotiates its terms when the target's questionable business practices come to light during due diligence. In general, prevention strategies aim to *reduce the likelihood* that an adverse event will occur.

Granted, one cannot prevent all risks, which brings *preparation* strategies into play. Should an adverse event materialize, these strategies attempt to *mitigate its impact*. For example, prudent reputational risk management involves a company's awareness that it may lose control over customer perceptions during a reputational crisis, as Mercedes experienced during the Moose Test episode.

In an activist-rich environment, outreach and collaboration with moderate advocacy groups may create a credible ally that can prove invaluable during a future confrontation. This works, however, only if outreach occurs before the company is targeted. Once the company is assigned the role of villain, moderate advocates and other credible third parties will not touch it with a 10-foot pole. A preparation strategy therefore involves establishing relationships with trusted third parties in advance, so that the company can call upon them in a crisis. As discussed in Chapter 3, McDonald's collaboration with renowned animal welfare expert Dr. Temple Grandin represents such a relationship. When PETA targeted McDonald's over its suppliers' chicken-slaughtering practices, McDonald's turned to Dr. Grandin for support. Building such relationships takes time, mutual trust, and, most of all, anticipation; by the time a crisis strikes, it is too late.

Preparation and prevention strategies allow us to integrate proactive reputation management into a standard risk management framework, as shown in Figure 7-4.[10]

These strategies are not necessarily independent, as they can mutually reinforce each other. For example, an insurance company could be concerned about the improper sales practices of its agents, knowing that even if the agents are independent contractors, the company will take the heat if a problem occurs. Policing each and every agent is impossible. But a prevention strategy, such as a strict compliance program, also demonstrates the company's commitment to address the problem. The message is simple: "We have been aware of the problem, and we have taken the following steps to address it long

Figure 7-4 **Reputational Risk Management**

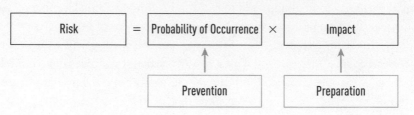

before it became a media story." Accompanying the policy by audits, secret shopper programs, and similar efforts will further enhance the effectiveness of this approach. This may not solve the issue entirely, but it positions the company as proactive, thoughtful, and concerned about its customers, while reinforcing its operational competence by demonstrating that the problem did not catch the company off guard.

To get the maximal impact from a preparation strategy, companies need to design proactive steps that work within the proper risk segment. If the analysis suggests a high degree of advocacy potential, the policies must be easy to understand and communicate so that they can serve as the basis for tomorrow's story. A situation with low advocacy potential might justify a more technical approach. Similarly, a company will need to invest more in prevention and preparation strategies in situations where an issue is at the core of the business model.

> Prevention and preparation are the two main components of reputational risk management strategies. Prevention strategies are intended to reduce the likelihood of an event occurring; preparation strategies are designed to limit its impact.

Crisis plans can be an important component of a preparation strategy, but companies must use them with caution. First, crisis plans should not be treated as algorithms, recipes, or black boxes, to be followed blindly. Crisis preparation should instead allow for unforeseen contingencies, as particular incidents almost always have some peculiar feature that the crisis plan could not have anticipated.

Recall the Southwest Airlines crash discussed in Chapter 1. Many crisis plans are structured around escalation levels. In the case of an airline, Level 1 may consist of a crash with no passenger injuries, with Level 2 being triggered by an injury to a passenger, Level 3 by a passenger fatality, and Level 4 by mass fatalities. Depending on the escalation level, an airline may have local management handle a Level 1 incident, while Level 4 may require the involvement of the CEO and the board.

What might such a plan have prescribed for the Southwest Airlines crash in Chicago? Sticking to the letter of the crisis plan, the answer would be Level 1. A six-year-old boy was killed, but no *passenger* was gravely injured. Of course, this conclusion is absurd, and Southwest's actions were based on the seriousness of the situation. But things are not always that obvious.

A crisis plan is therefore best understood as a process that prepares the mind. Conducting assessments hypothetically rather than in the midst of a crisis-induced pressure cooker frees the mind to think strategically and to find creative solutions. By forcing management to anticipate possible scenarios and to design solutions, companies become more adept at identifying problems and developing the tactical steps that would need to be undertaken in a crisis.

And there is another important reason for having a plan. For known, inherent business risks—such as crashes for airlines or product recalls for consumer goods manufacturers—companies must develop crisis plans because the public will expect them to have done so. The media and the public are unlikely to understand or forgive companies that are unprepared for a crisis.

An important aspect of crisis preparation is the ability to draw on the relevant talent within the organization. Managing a crisis effectively almost always requires finding innovative solutions to unexpected problems. This is best accomplished by a dedicated team with diverse viewpoints and experiences. In the Mercedes case, for example, a brand perception problem was resolved by a new technology that was intended for a different purpose. Neither engineers nor marketers were likely to spot this solution on their own. It required the engagement of both viewpoints as well as the ability to quickly locate and engage the necessary skills in a rapidly changing situation.

ANTICIPATION IN ACTION

Let us now apply these principles to Prudential's decision problem. The company is in the early part of the Reputation Dynamics, so it can still focus on prevention and preparation. To design these proactive strategies effectively, we should first list the possible reputational risks, assess their magnitude, and design mitigation strategies.

Let us illustrate this approach with a few examples.

RISK: "Bad Reputation" of the Viatical Settlement Industry

Description: The existing industry has a somewhat unsavory, even seedy reputation. Names such as "Beat the Grim Reaper" do not help.

Assessment: This is a moderate risk that can easily be mitigated.

Mitigation: The key to mitigating this risk has two components:

1. Prudential needs to leverage its existing reputation as a trusted provider of financial and insurance products, thereby differentiating it from less trustworthy start-up companies.

2. Prudential needs to focus its messages on its ability to help a specific family that is in need. By helping these victims, Prudential naturally assumes the role of hero. The company should consider direct-to-consumer advertising, which poses little additional risk because the Living Benefits program is eminently newsworthy anyway. In other words, if management has any residual concerns about advertising the initiative, the Living Benefits program is probably not ready for launch in the first place.

RISK: The Bereft Family

Description: Once a viatical settlement is completed, the original beneficiary—usually the patient's family—no longer will receive the full value of the policy. At best, the family will inherit a discounted amount, while at worst, the patient's significant medical and personal expenses will leave the family with nothing.

Assessment: This issue has very high advocacy potential, with the grieving family as an easily identifiable victim, but straightforward mitigation strategies exist.

Mitigation:

1. Prudential can decide to offer the program only in cases of financial hardship, which limits the possibility of frivolous spending (the "going to Vegas" scenario), to the detriment of the family.

2. The company may require the consent of beneficiaries.

3. Prudential may purchase only some portion of the face value, such as 50 percent, insisting that the beneficiaries retain the remaining 50 percent.

These mitigation strategies will serve as preventive measures (by reducing the likelihood of severe problems), but their real value may come from a preparation strategy. It will take only one or two cases of outraged families to trigger potentially devastating media coverage. If that should happen, Prudential will need to tell a convincing story. That story needs to be based on facts, which need to be created today. The mitigation strategy allows a simple but high-impact response: "We have been aware of this concern and have taken steps to make sure that it does not occur. Our solution is not perfect, but it is an important step in the right direction."

RISK: Patient Competence

Description: The decision to enter into a viatical settlement may have significant long-term consequences for patients and their families, but terminally ill patients may not be in a position to assess the consequences competently. After all, they are under tremendous psychological stress and may suffer from chronic pain, requiring ongoing treatment and medication that can compromise their decision-making ability.

Assessment: This issue has very high advocacy potential, as patients present a ready-made victim storyline. Additionally, failure to manage this risk may reignite issues related to the original beneficiaries or the industry's poor reputation, as it may lead to charges of unscrupulous sales tactics taking advantage of terminally ill patients.

Mitigation: This issue is more difficult to manage because it undercuts any argument that a viatical settlement is merely a consensual contract; the very possibility of a competent decision is questioned. A psychological evaluation might represent a good first step, but given the explosive nature of this concern, Prudential should consider further measures. One possibility is to borrow an idea from the mortgage business. In many U.S. states, buyers are granted a "cooling-off period" of three working days after the signing of the contract.[11] The idea is to protect the buyer from predatory sales practices by allowing him to annul the contract within the cooling-off period. Prudential could use a similar approach here by offering, say, a two-week waiting period, during which the patient could reverse her decision to accept an accelerated benefit agreement without any adverse consequences. Prudential may also want to reach out to various patient advocacy groups (such as HIV/AIDS and cancer victims groups, as well as religious and charitable organizations) to provide counseling services during this two-week period. It could sponsor toll-free hotlines staffed by volunteer counselors from these groups, who could provide independent advice to patients and their families and general assistance during the decision-making process.

As in the case of bereft families, the mitigation strategy can serve as both a prevention and a preparation measure. It will not eliminate all possible cases, but it creates a coherent approach to an anticipated problem that the company can easily communicate, even on a high-pressure stage like *60 Minutes*. Most important, the possibility of collaboration with patient advocates—who may generally be critical of insurance companies—adds much-needed credibility to the approach. Advocacy groups and charitable organizations may be inclined to participate in such an initiative because it provides important assistance to their constituents, provided the program is offered responsibly. Such outreach efforts, however, need to be put in place well before the product is launched. During a crisis, patient advocates will not want to associate with a company that is being portrayed as preying on their constituents.

This is just a partial list of the risks to be considered; other issues include regulatory issues[12] and the perception that the holder of a viatical settlement has a stake in the patient's early death. This last issue applies primarily to companies that offer only viatical settlements, but Prudential needs to have an answer ready should the issue arise.

These solutions show how to manage reputational risks. They involve proactive communication strategies, contingency plans, and stakeholder outreach—the consequence of a strategic mindset that is the focus of this chapter. (Reputation management processes will be discussed in Chapter 8.) In some cases, we had to modify the company's policies (as in the case of waiting periods), but by carefully designing prevention and preparation strategies, Prudential can significantly mitigate its reputational risk. However, one last issue lurks below the surface, requiring a more thorough approach.

The standard view of contracts would suggest that a viatical settlement constitutes an agreement between two consenting parties who are both better off because of the agreement—the basis of any business relationship. However, we must remember the Ultimatum Game and the role of fairness norms from Chapter 4. In that situation, both parties also needed to agree, and an agreement was valuable for both parties. Still, highly inequitable situations as portrayed in the Ultimatum Game trigger strong, emotionally charged fairness intuitions, prompting the kind of moral outrage that we saw in Chapter 4. People naturally feel that the proposer is taking unfair advantage of the other party and should be held accountable.

Of course, Prudential is in precisely this situation, as it is acting as the proposer, with the patient in the powerless position of the responder. The offer will be based on a standard policy, with little room for negotiation; effectively, the patient can only accept or reject it. If Prudential fails to manage the issue of fairness carefully, it will cause widespread outrage, not only among patients and their families, but among third parties, including the media, advocates, and public officials.

Prudential needs to address these concerns as part of its pricing strategy. Let us review how prices for the Living Benefits program would be determined. After a patient has completed the medical exam, Prudential will estimate a life expectancy. Holding premiums, interest rates, and other financial factors constant, the payout to the patient will depend on this life expectancy, as in Figure 7-5.

The schedule that payouts will follow can be illustrated by a steeply downward-sloping curve that reflects the substantial financial risk of

Figure 7-5 **Living Benefits—Pricing Schedule**

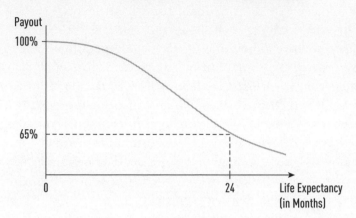

viatical settlements: the longer the estimated life expectancy, the higher the residual uncertainty. In addition to general financial risk, a medical breakthrough, for example, could dramatically increase the patient's life expectancy. For a viatical settlement company, this would decrease the value of the corresponding pool of life insurance policies, and could even cause the company to lose money, as it needs to continue paying the policies' premiums. To manage this high-risk environment, companies heavily discounted payments for patients with a high life expectancy and capped eligibility at approximately 24 months of expected survival.[13]

A viatical settlement company must naturally build some profit margin into its pricing schedule. For example, a 24-month contract that is profitable at a payout of 55 percent may break even at 65 percent. Prudential decided early in the process that the policy would be "revenue neutral." In other words, zero profit was acceptable, but the project also could not lose money. Thus, a policy with an expected survival time of 24 months could not justify a payment of more than 65 percent.

Looking at the pricing schedule in Figure 7-5, we can see where the land mine is buried. A patient's life expectancy is derived from a distribution of mortality data, so it holds only on average. Some individuals with a life expectancy of 24 months will indeed die after 24 months, but some may live 60 months, while others may survive for only a few weeks. Patients with a life expectancy of 24 months could therefore receive only 65 cents on the dollar, only to pass away a month later.

According to the payment schedule, this makes perfect sense, until you consider a scenario in which Prudential's Living Benefits program faces heavy media scrutiny. Given the characteristics of the issue—a highly sympathetic, identifiable victim facing a large and powerful insurance company in a situation with substantial societal importance and audience interest—we would expect a very high level of media advocacy.

We must recognize that in this environment, a shift of perspective will occur. Journalists and commentators will focus not on the details of the payment schedule, but on the implied price difference. The lay-people—who are unfamiliar with the pricing of risky assets—will focus solely on the difference between 100 percent and 65 percent (see Figure 7-6). Based on their experience and their sense of fairness, they will invariably conclude that Prudential has acted in a predatory fashion by taking advantage of the terminally ill. The public will view this price difference in the same way as they view lowball offers in the Ultimatum Game, and they will feel the same resultant outrage.

Figure 7-6 **Living Benefits—Pricing and Fairness**

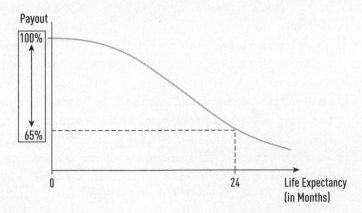

How did this go wrong? The key problem occurred when the perspective shifted from that of an actuary to that of a layperson. An expert will focus on the curve and conclude that this pricing schedule is reasonable, while a layperson will focus on the price difference and conclude that it is outrageously unfair. Why the difference? First, laypeople will not understand the logic behind the curve. It takes some level of mathematical education to follow the pricing model in sufficient detail. Second, in all likelihood, Prudential would not disclose its pricing schedule, as it is a trade secret, to be guarded from competitors and customers. As a result, journalists and the public would have only one thing to observe: the difference between 100 percent and 65 percent. Third, laypeople will naively compare this difference to other forms of financial products with which they are more familiar, such as the interest on their mortgage, car loan, or credit cards. Even compared to credit card fees, the discount *seems* excessive, even predatory.

The most damaging scenario here is the case of a patient who had a 24-month life expectancy, receives 65 cents on the dollar for his life insurance policy, and dies after a few weeks. The public will naturally compare this to the full value of the life insurance policy and consider the patient to have been cheated. The family's suffering from a tragic and unexpected loss will cause it to be viewed with additional sympathy. Given that life expectancy is merely an estimate based on some sort of life-span distribution, there *will* be at least a small number of cases that fall into this category, and an aggressive journalist who is looking for a compelling story will need no more than a few such cases; one case is a fact, two a trend.

Even if Prudential is only just breaking even by purchasing at 65 percent, it will struggle to communicate this in a credible fashion under the glare of media scrutiny. The press will suspect accounting tricks and misrepresentations of what constitutes a profit. The public will also discount the fact that this is a contract between consenting parties, because they will perceive that Prudential has unfairly taken advantage of a very unequal situation. As in the Ultimatum Game in Chapter 4, all the conditions for outrage are present.

What about the carefully cultivated support from patient advocacy groups? Like any other strategic alliance, this collaboration between the company and the advocates needs to be based on common interests. There is a common interest in marketing the Living Benefits program responsibly, but those common interests diverge when it comes to pric-ing, *even if Prudential is willing to make zero profit.* A patient advocacy group will care little about Prudential's profitability or economic pros-pects; in fact, it would prefer that Prudential subsidize the program.

As for other players in the industry, Prudential knows that none of its insurance company competitors are offering the service. Prudential is the first, and therefore will be the one that is targeted by journalists. Any misstep by Prudential that damages its brand only helps its compet-itors. Viatical settlement companies, on the other hand, have a question-able reputation to begin with, and therefore have little to offer in terms of "vouching" for Prudential or verifying that it has acted honorably.

If it pursues its original pricing model, Prudential will be perceived as predatory, and no one will come to its defense. The reputational impact is likely to be very negative, given the advocacy environment. It is here that strategic thinking matters the most. From an internal operational perspective, the pricing strategy makes sense, but from an external, unsophisticated, and partially informed perspective, it looks monstrous. Strategic thinking requires the ability to assume this outside perspective and integrate it into decision making.

Now that we know where the problem lies, how do we resolve it? Our analysis revealed that public opinion will turn on the perception of unfair pricing, as in the Ultimatum Game. This raises the question of what the public would consider to be a fair price. If we stick to the standard logic of supply and demand, this may sound meaningless, but it is precisely those judgments that generate the problem. I would expect that most people would consider something in the range of 90 to 95 percent to be fair (and if you disagree, run an experiment!). Starting at a reference point of 100 percent, we may grant Prudential some form of compensation, based on our assessment of what is fair, which may be derived from what we pay in mortgage or credit card interest.

That means that Prudential could never pay out less than, say, 90 percent. However, that does not mean that the company has to subsidize the program; remember that there were multiple levers that determined pricing, among them life expectancy. All Prudential would have to do is shorten the eligibility period. In other words, start with a payout rate of 90 percent, and then draw a horizontal line from the vertical axis to where it crosses the payout curve. That intersection point will occur at some much shorter life expectancy; in Figure 7-7, it crosses at six months. In other words, to make sure that Prudential breaks even *and* never pays out less than 90 percent, the program would be offered only to patients with a life expectancy of less than six months.

Figure 7-7 **Living Benefits—Segmenting by Reputational Risk**

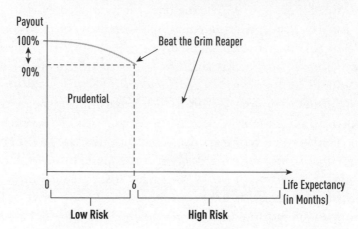

In this situation, Prudential would be operating *only* in an area of low reputational risk. Note that viatical settlement companies like Beat the Grim Reaper do not face the same reputational risk as Prudential—they have no reputation to lose, and thus are likely to stay in the high-risk market. They are small and unknown, have little brand equity, and operate only in this market, so their reputational risk is very limited.

This means that Prudential is ceding some of its potential market to these smaller competitors, but only in the region of the market that has high reputational risk. Now we can see why it was so important to be clear about the strategic objective of the Living Benefits program; had we pursued a transactional approach, this loss of market share would constitute a serious problem, but our decision to focus on a reputational strategy means that the positive reputational impact more than makes up for a few lost transactions.

In effect, this constitutes a reputational risk segmentation strategy, as Prudential will contest only the low-risk market, which fits with its overall position in the marketplace. This reflects a shrewd alignment of reputational risk with Prudential's market strategy, and an acknowledgment that the risk landscape that Prudential faces is very different from that faced by Beat the Grim Reaper.

This example should also put to rest any residual support for the idea that reputational risk management can be delegated to functional experts. By the time a chief reputational risk officer or the head of communications could get involved, the product would already have been launched with the original pricing strategy, the crisis would have occurred, and the damage would be done. That said, the input of Communication, Legal, and Regulatory Management when the product decision is made would be highly beneficial.

FROM DEATH BENEFITS TO LIVING BENEFITS

After testing the approach first in a "live-and-learn" experimental program, Prudential became the first life insurance company to offer the newly named Living Benefits to any policyholder with a terminal condition. To qualify for the program, a Prudential policyholder had to provide certification from a physician that he had less than six months to live. The insurer would pay these policyholders the face amount of the policy, minus a $150 administrative fee and six months of interest, which Prudential calculated at 8 percent annually between 1990 and 1993. This typically meant that the policyholder would receive approximately 95 percent of the policy's face value.

Prudential's Living Benefits program quickly received front-page coverage, first in Canada and then globally. Amidst a wave of largely positive coverage, personal finances expert Sylvia Porter characterized the initiative as "an overdue change in the concept of life insurance that may revolutionize the industry." The program's payouts were rather modest; by October 1993, Prudential had awarded $47 million in early payouts to 572 policyholders, and other companies began following Prudential's lead. But Prudential enjoyed a substantial reputational halo effect, highlighted by positive news coverage like the *New York Times* profile of patient Patricia North, a sculptor who had relied on a Prudential early payout program to finance a lifesaving bone-marrow transplant procedure.[14] The article mentioned Prudential by name 10 times, portrayed it as a pioneer in the industry, and praised it for its compassionate approach.

For the first half of 1990, Prudential's life insurance sales rose 25 percent, which the company attributed largely to the new Living Benefits addition. Employees within the company also responded positively to the new product. Having led a parallel U.S. task force on the Living Benefits product, Prudential's top product development actuary explained that "employees throughout Prudential felt good about the company that would offer this kind of benefit . . . and show compassion to people that really are in need." In 1990, Ron Barbaro was promoted to the position of president, due in large part to the success of his experimental Canadian program, and received multiple ethics and leadership awards. I leave it to your imagination how the public would have responded had Prudential paid out as little as 65 cents on the dollar.

DEATH BONDS

The story of viatical settlements does not end with Prudential. In 1995, the publicly traded viatical settlement firm Dignity Partners bundled 300 life insurance policies totaling $35 million and sold the securities to investors. The policies came primarily from AIDS patients, although some were purchased from terminal cancer patients. This packaged deal was the first time life insurance policies had followed the path of car and credit card loans and mortgages, which had long been bundled and securitized to large investors in the secondary market. At the time, Dignity Partners's founder and chairman, Bradley Rotter, told the *San Francisco Chronicle* that the capital markets offered unlimited financing for companies like Dignity Partners to purchase life insurance policies from terminally ill patients.[15]

A year later, the viatical settlement industry was virtually wiped out when several reports presented at the 11th International Conference on AIDS in Vancouver showed that powerful combinations of drugs featuring so-called protease inhibitors could dramatically reduce the amount of virus in AIDS sufferers, increasing the possibility of long-term survival for patients. The development suggested that AIDS would change from a death sentence to a "medically managed chronic condition." It also devastated the fledgling viatical settlement industry.[16]

Dignity Partners's share price fell nearly 80 percent in just two days, ultimately forcing it to leave the business.[17]

The most recent chapter of this saga started about a decade later. Using their expertise in creating ever more complex subprime mortgage-backed securities, Wall Street investment bankers seeking to develop other fixed-income investment vehicles with a similar structure rediscovered life settlement securitization. Like earlier viatical settlements, these new life settlement securities relied on elderly or terminally ill individuals selling their life insurance policies for cash. However, bankers now packaged hundreds or thousands of these policies into bonds (nicknamed "death bonds"), which were then sold to investors, who would receive payouts from the policies when the policyholders died.[18] As before, investors continued paying for the policy premiums until the holders' deaths, and therefore stood to profit from the early deaths of the individuals who had sold their policies.

As in the case of mortgage-based securities, credit rating agencies rated the life settlement bonds by running background checks on issuers. Banks like Goldman Sachs also developed tradable indexes of life settlements (a "death index"), allowing investors to effectively place bets on whether policyholders would live longer or die sooner than expected.

Modern finance theory implies that because of the large number of policies, these life settlement securities should be more predictable—and therefore safer—than earlier viatical settlements. In order to reduce risk further, life settlement securities combined life settlements from people with a range of diseases, such as leukemia, heart disease, and Alzheimer's. This diversification prevented a breakthrough treatment in one disease from affecting an entire pool of patients, as when the development of antiretroviral drug cocktails significantly extended the life expectancy of AIDS patients and made the viatical financial model unprofitable.

The life settlement market still presents a potentially lucrative investment opportunity, with $26 trillion in life insurance policies across the country. Although only a small fraction of policyholders is both interested in and eligible for entering into a life settlement contract, market experts predict that the industry could reach as much as $500 billion. More important, death rates are effectively uncorrelated with market indexes, which would make life settlement–based securities attractive as diversification vehicles. "These assets do not have risks that are difficult to estimate, and they are not, for the most part, exposed to broader economic risks," said Joshua Coval, a professor of finance at the Harvard Business School. "By pooling and tranching, you are not amplifying systemic risks in the underlying assets." Consequently, the eligibility requirements for life settlements have been loosened, and now also include some chronic diseases, such as severe diabetes.

Just as with the subprime market, however, critics question the regulatory powers—or lack thereof—in life settlement securities. "The securitization of life settlements adds another element of possible risk to an industry that is already in need of enhanced regulations, more transparency, and consumer safeguards," said Senator Herb Kohl, chairman of the Special Committee on Aging. In 2007, CNN interviewer and talk-show host Larry King brought public attention to the lax regulation of the industry when he sued an insurance brokerage for allegedly conning him out of millions of dollars in a life insurance settlement. In 2004, King purchased two life insurance policies worth $10 million and $5 million, respectively, then sold the policies for a combined total of $1.4 million. King accused the insurer broker—Meltzer Group—of failing to inform him of the commissions, fees, and payments collected by the group, as well as not actively searching for prospective purchasers who would pay a higher price for his policies.[19] King also blamed the group for not warning him that entering into a life settlement would substantially increase the difficulty of purchasing life insurance in the future.[20] Stay tuned.

"PROTECT OUR HOUSE"

If the history of the viatical industry, from humble beginnings to life settlement–backed death bonds, eerily reminds you of the subprime mortgage industry, you are not alone. Subprime lending and life settlements share not only the same financial wizardry but also a long history of concerns about their business practices.

As we have seen in Chapter 4, the outrage potential of the subprime lending industry is high and has led to ongoing pressure by the media, activists, regulators, and politicians. Navigating these treacherous waters is difficult at the best of times and can lead to strong emotional reactions. When attacked for its mortgage lending and financial lending practices in 2007, Countrywide Financial, one of the largest subprime mortgage lenders, developed the "protect our house" campaign, which asked employees to wear green plastic wristbands, reminiscent of the yellow wristbands issued by former cycling great Lance Armstrong's LIVESTRONG cancer support and research foundation. Employees were also asked to sign an online pledge with the words "I pledge my support to Countrywide and will help Protect Our House."[21] These reactions reflect anger and defensiveness. Effective reputation management requires strategic sophistication and the ability to see one's own business from another perspective, even if one does not agree with that perspective—a challenge that the industry never fully mastered.

THINGS TO REMEMBER

Our goal in this chapter was to develop a strategic mindset. We used the problem of entry into a highly controversial market as our main example. Prudential's strategy to address these challenges was imaginative and required a high degree of strategic sophistication. Management showed the ability to maintain an external perspective throughout the decision-making processes and incorporated this perspective into the design of the new product and its market-entry strategy. Let us recall some of the general lessons derived from this example.

- Most reputational challenges do not happen because of some external event, but rather are the consequence of an earlier business decision.

- Reputational challenges can arise from any area of day-to-day decision making, but executives tend to make decisions without considering the reputational impact.

- The reputational impact of a business decision must be assessed before the decision is made. In contrast to a crisis, this is the time when the stakes are low and control is high.

- Through their decisions today, companies create the facts that will serve as the basis for a story tomorrow. Once a record has been created, it cannot be changed.

- Assessing reputational risk requires anticipating what a reputational crisis would look like and taking proactive steps to prevent and prepare for that crisis.

- A good heuristic to help imagine what a crisis would look like is the *Wall Street Journal* test: how would you feel about a decision if it were accurately reported on the front page of the *Wall Street Journal*?

Once a company is on stage, the spotlight will focus not just on current but on past actions as well. When did executives know about a problem, and what did they do to fix it? Even decisions that may have looked reasonable at the time may look highly problematic under the glaring media spotlight.

Successfully managing these issues can be difficult, as the Prudential case demonstrated, but at least Prudential had one advantage: it knew that it was contemplating entry into a very controversial market. Many companies do not enjoy that luxury. Instead, they must anticipate what issues may arise and how serious they are. This requires processes—the topic of our next chapter.

CHAPTER 8

THE AIM TEAM

How to Build a Sixth Sense

"We believe the 9/11 attacks revealed four kinds of failures: in imagination, policy, capabilities, and management."

—The National Commission on Terrorist Attacks
upon the United States, 2004[1]

O n April 10, 2006, the U.S. Centers for Disease Control and Prevention (CDC) linked a surge in potentially blinding fungal infections
with Bausch & Lomb's ReNu with MoistureLoc contact lens solution.
As a result, Bausch & Lomb's stock price dropped by about 17 percent
in a day,[2] a loss that was sustained for roughly a year and amounted to
the destruction of around $630 million in shareholder value. Bausch
& Lomb subsequently experienced accounting restatements and was
acquired by the private equity firm Warburg Pincus.[3]

So far, there is nothing remarkable about this story. Concerns over
quality led to a reputational crisis; the company was unable to manage it
and was punished by investors. But there is another side to this tale. The
U.S. Centers for Disease Control and Prevention announced their findings on April 10, 2006. Yet the link between the infections and ReNu
had been revealed *months* earlier, on February 22, in a public announcement by Singapore's Ministry of Health. (Bausch & Lomb subsequently
withdrew the ReNu solution from its markets in Singapore and Hong
Kong.) The Singapore announcement had been reported in the region's
major newspapers, but had received little coverage in the United States.

Now, consider the snapshot of Bausch & Lomb's stock price in
Figure 8-1.

Figure 8-1 **Bausch & Lomb**

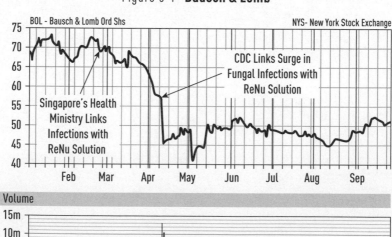

Note that the impact of the warning from Singapore's Ministry of Health on the stock was only a 3 percent loss, from $71.51 at the close of February 21 to $69.40 at the close of February 23, on very low trading volume—a very different reaction from that to the CDC announcement two months later.

The media viewed Bausch & Lomb's response as sluggish and unprepared, considering that the company had known about reports of the eye infection as early as November and had failed to use the two months after the announcement in Singapore more effectively.[4] After all, companies rarely have the luxury of receiving such a clear warning. This lack of anticipation may have been a consequence of underestimating the crisis or not realizing its full reputational impact, but given the particular characteristics of the issue (a quality issue, possible blindness, and a clear connection to the company's core competency), this is hard to believe. What more could have gone wrong?

In many cases, the answer is processes. Successful reputation management requires the ability to execute fast and effectively. This is critical both during a reputational crisis, when time is of the essence and information is extremely precious, and in calmer periods, when companies are designing proactive strategies.

GOVERNANCE

Who should own reputation management? Many executives answer: everyone. That sounds reasonable enough, but it is easy for things that are owned by everybody to actually be owned by nobody. Questions about decision rights, reporting, and accountability still need to be answered. Locating reputation management in the organizational structure of a company can be tricky, even for companies that "get it." What we typically observe are feast-to-famine cycles.

Phase 1: A crisis occurs—with massive losses for the company.

Phase 2: Management realizes that it would not be prepared should a similar event occur in the future.

Phase 3: Management develops contingency plans and designates responsible personnel.

Phase 4: Nothing happens. The event fades from memory. Crisis plans gather dust.

Phase 5: Management is looking for cost-cutting opportunities and eliminates the capability or starves it of funds.

If this reminds you of dieting or exercise regimens, you are not mistaken. There is a striking similarity here. Both have tremendous preventive benefits, and both are easily undermined by short-term incentives.

One good solution, therefore, is to locate the ultimate accountability for reputation management processes at a level of the organization whose job description is the long-term viability of the company: the board. One reason why the board is a good choice is that it can keep management's incentives for short-term solutions in check. By setting clear guidelines and emphasizing the need to safeguard reputational equity, the board can help management avoid shortsighted cost-cutting mistakes.

Within the board, there are various options. Ultimately, the optimal location depends on the sources of value and the types of risk. For example, companies with a very active and important stakeholder environment that may spill over into new regulations or legislation might choose to have the policy committee oversee reputation management. But for most companies, a good location is the place where enterprise risk management resides, which is typically the audit committee. This location enables better integration with other risk dimensions (that is, financial, brand, and operational risk) and facilitates trade-offs, planning, process evaluation, and strategy reviews.

Recent surveys of board members demonstrate that this view is gaining ground. Board members routinely list risk management as one of their main responsibilities. Among the main risk types, regulatory compliance tops the list, immediately followed by reputational risk.[5]

But the board's role is to oversee and supervise; it is not to manage the company. So, where should reputation management reside within a company's decision-making structure? I have argued throughout this book that it belongs squarely on the agenda of senior management, including the CEO. Indeed, you may recall that it was the emphasis that CEOs put on reputation that was one of the reasons that led to this book.

But it is worth pondering the role of the CEO in more detail. After all, there are many problems and issues that demand the CEO's attention. Does reputation deserve this prominence? The previous chapters gave a partial answer. To be successful, reputation management needs to be inextricably linked with a company's business strategy. But couldn't that still be accomplished at a lower level of management?

The reason why reputation management belongs on the CEO's agenda is that not only is reputational risk one of the main risks facing the company, but the company's reputation is also one of the few sources of sustained competitive advantage. Companies with stellar reputations can charge premiums and are difficult to imitate.[6]

One of the CEO's main tasks is to integrate reputation management into the operational processes of the business. One approach to accomplishing this task has been to create a separate corporate function: a chief reputation officer (CRO) or chief reputational risk officer (CRRO). This approach works only if the position carries weight and if the company can avoid creating yet another corporate officer with little budget and less influence. The danger in this approach is that it could create additional barriers to an integration of reputation management and business strategy and actually hurt the process rather than help it. An instructive analogy is the role of the head of human resources (HR). In some companies, the HR process is isolated from the rest of the business; in other companies, the CEO owns the people process, which, perhaps counterintuitively, enhances the effectiveness of the head of HR rather than diminishes it.[7]

An alternative is the creation of a corporate reputation council (CRC). This is a cross-functional unit composed of senior executives with actual decision-making authority. The actual composition of the council needs to mirror the organizational structure of the company. For example, a matrix organization based on global territory and product line would have representatives from both the major territories and the business lines. In addition, the main corporate functions (marketing, finance, supply chain, HR, communication, legal, government relations, and so on) need to be represented, as reputational problems are almost always multidimensional. The decision structure must be designed to handle the complexity of such issues.

In my experience, a good structure is to have the deputy head of each function represented on an ongoing basis, with the head executive present at critical times. Corporate reputation councils ideally report to the chief operating officer (COO), if the company has that function, or its closest analogue if it does not. Other than during times of crisis, it is sufficient to have the council meet for half a day a month. This time allocation forces prioritization and prompt decision making. The CRC needs to be supported by a tactical team to assist in the decision-making process and the execution phase.

As an example of a CRC in action, recall the Brent Spar case from Chapter 3. As we saw in the discussion of this incident, at the time Shell lacked the appropriate decision-making structure and handled the issue as a U.K. regulatory matter. The existence of a CRC would have made such a lack of perspective unlikely, as representatives from other regions (such as northern Europe) would probably have pointed to a potential public backlash. In the case of an integrated oil company, the upstream exploration business would have a seat at the table and provide the much-needed engineering perspective, with detailed input on cost, risk, and legal context. Internal communication could prepare strategies for Shell's employees and business partners, such as contractors, gas stations, and distributors, while Legal and Government Affairs could help navigate the treacherous waters of European politics.

It is critical that the CRC mirrors the actual operating structure of the business. Shell's reputational risk was global, yet its strategy focused only on the United Kingdom. One of the reasons that Toyota was slow in responding to the 2010 sudden acceleration crisis was the lack of a truly global decision-making structure. While Toyota's economic fortunes were heavily dependent on robust U.S. sales, decision making was largely centered in Japan, with little input from the United States. Similarly, BP lacked a strong presence in the U.S. regulatory and political environment, despite the fact that BP's U.S. oil and gas assets represented more than one-quarter of the group's total annual production.[8]

Good governance and decision-making structures are necessary for effective reputation management, but even these alone are not sufficient. To see why, recall some of the core insights that we have developed so far:

- Reputation consists of the perceptions of customers and other constituencies.

- In many cases, these perceptions are derived not from actual experience with the company or a deep knowledge of any given issue, but from an ever-changing mixture of opinion and information driven by the media, peer-to-peer Web sites, and various influencers ranging from experts to advocacy groups.

- Proactive reputation management requires companies to identify issues early, connect them with the business strategy, develop prevention and preparation strategies, and implement possible changes in business practices in advance of an issue's gaining momentum.

This sequence can break down at various points. Executives may not realize the importance of reputation management for business success, governance structures may be lacking, or incentive structures may reward short-term vision. But companies may also fail to adopt effective strategies simply because they are unaware of the imminent danger. In other words, even perfectly designed governance and decision-making structures will be ineffective if they lack critical intelligence: decisions are then made in the dark.

This is the business case for investing in intelligence capabilities. Because reputation is driven by many ever-changing actors, the strategic landscape is frequently diffuse and unclear. Because successful reputational strategies need to be designed before a crisis occurs, simply surveying customers, investors, or other business partners will not do. Once customers or investors start to worry, it is too late—the deck is already stacked against the company.

> Effective reputation management is supported by proper processes. The two key components are decision making and intelligence structures. Reputational governance structures need to mirror the company's organization. A separate chief reputation officer is frequently not the best solution.

Therefore, in many cases, traditional business research tools such as surveys and focus groups can only measure the damage rather than prevent it in the first place. Proactive reputation management is impossible without good intelligence.

INTELLIGENCE

In my advisory work, I spend about 60 percent of my time on reputational crisis situations. During the initial conversations, executives will frequently make statements like, "We never saw this coming," or, "This came out of the blue." These statements express a sense of surprise and, perhaps, may also be intended to excuse or diminish the responsibility of the executive (or executives) who failed to anticipate the incident. But strategically these statements constitute something else: evidence of an intelligence failure.

In contexts such as national security, the importance of intelligence is self-evident. But the business application of frameworks from the field of intelligence has so far been quite limited to specialized areas such as competitive intelligence, personnel background checks, due diligence, and so forth.[9] While useful, these applications are not typically central to corporate functions.

This is not the case for proactive reputation management. Successful anticipation of reputational issues and the design of a strategy to deal with them is impossible without adequate intelligence. We can see this by noticing that in our development of reputation management tools, we moved backward along the time axis. We started with reputational crises and saw the critical importance of the media, both traditional and user-generated, in shaping customer and stakeholder perception. We then developed tools to manage these challenges: the Trust Radar and the Reputational Terrain. In Chapter 3, we discussed the critical role of influencers in triggering or magnifying reputational crises. We discussed the concept of the Second Circle and various approaches for anticipating the strategies of influencers. Next we discussed the two dimensions of issues that are critical for reputational crises: outrage and fear. We discussed how these dimensions can be used to anticipate reputational concerns before they materialize. Finally, we showed how reputation management can be integrated with a company's market strategy, and we used the Reputation Dynamics chart to design proactive strategies.

Figure 8-2 captures this progression. Issues with high outrage or fear potential lead to the activation of influencers and the formation of new advocacy groups and coalitions. Such issues also either directly

Figure 8-2 **Issues—Influencers—Impact**

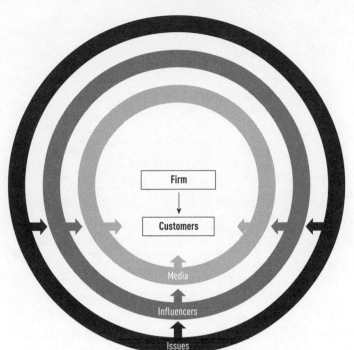

or indirectly lead to media scrutiny, triggered by advocacy strategies, which then generates business impact by shaping the perceptions of customers, investors, employees, regulators, and the like.

The chain of events typically progresses in this fashion. That is, issues activate influencers, and both trigger media engagement, which leads to business impact. As seen in Figure 8-3, using our Reputation Dynamics framework, we can locate this development from early to later along the time axis. But to do this, we need to add a crucial insight: *low stakes also mean low awareness.* In other words, if an issue has little or no impact on a business, it is easily overlooked. It does not demand immediate attention. After all, nothing has happened—yet. Of course, the low-impact/low-awareness period is exactly the time when action is required and success is most likely because of relatively high levels of control.

Figure 8-3 **The Awareness-Control Trade-Off**

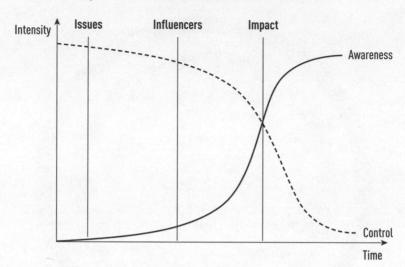

This constitutes a genuine conundrum. As we saw, in many cases, companies can completely avoid or at least mitigate reputational crises by changing their business practices, engaging in stakeholder outreach, or preparing detailed communication plans. But developing such responses takes time—the one thing that companies do not have once an issue has reached crisis proportions. In many cases, reputational challenges have their origin in areas that companies do not monitor frequently. In retrospect, the warning signs could have been identified, but they never reached the key decision makers. Issues that turned out to be enterprise-critical were not even identified as potential risks; they never made it onto the radar screen. As "unknown unknowns," they could never be integrated into a proper risk management framework.

This is the value proposition for investing in intelligence capabilities. Reputational intelligence systems essentially have three components:

- Issue identification

- Issue evaluation

- Issue monitoring

Issue Identification

The purpose of the *issue identification* function is to create awareness. The goal is simply to list all issues that may affect a company's reputation or other related risks. In some cases, this is easy. In the Living Benefits scenario, Prudential was always aware of the potential for public outrage; it was obvious and right in your face. In the example of Citigroup's acquisition of subprime lender The Associates, discussed in Chapter 4, however, the acquiring company was surprised by the amount of public scrutiny.

Although issue identification may sound like an easy task, it is not. Indeed, it may be one of the most difficult problems in areas where good intelligence is critical for survival: national security and counterterrorism. One function of intelligence is to obtain access to secrets. This is the best-known function of intelligence services. The appropriate solution is spying; it is the domain of James Bond and colleagues. The structure works as follows: an intelligence agency knows of the existence of, say, a secret document that is well hidden and well protected. The task is to obtain this secret information.

But many of today's intelligence challenges have less to do with secrets and more to do with surprises.[10] Former U.S. Defense Secretary Donald Rumsfeld underscored this when he said:

> Reports that say that something hasn't happened are always interesting to me, because as we know, there are known knowns; there are things we know we know. We also know there are known unknowns; that is to say we know there are some things we do not know. But there are also unknown unknowns—the ones we don't know we don't know.[11]

Rumsfeld's tenure as secretary of defense has been heavily criticized, and this statement has been much ridiculed. Indeed, it received the Plain English Campaign's premier "Foot in Mouth" trophy for least comprehensible statement by a public official in December 2003.[12] But it points out a crucial insight: not every risk is known, and not every unknown is a risk.

As difficult as it is to manage risks, once we engage in risk management, we know what *can* happen; we just don't know whether it *will* happen. Indeed, in some cases, we may even have estimates of the likelihood that a particular occurrence will happen. Consider the case of managing health. When people are diagnosed with high blood pressure, they know that they need to manage that risk through changes in lifestyle, diet, and so forth. Their doctors may tell them that high blood pressure may increase their risk of stroke four to six times and may lead to heart failure and other serious heart problems. Based on these data, the physician may discuss treatment options as well as risks and side effects leading to a treatment regime that balances expected risks and benefits.

Now compare this to, say, Wilson's disease, a genetic disorder that affects approximately 30 people out of 1 million. The disease is brought on by dysfunction in a liver enzyme that is crucial in eliminating copper from the body.[13] The resultant buildup of copper can cause acute hepatitis, neurologic disturbances (tremors, difficulty swallowing, difficulty speaking), and psychiatric abnormalities (depression, paranoia). Diagnosis can be accomplished by correctly identifying these symptoms or through copper analysis of a liver biopsy. Untreated, Wilson's disease is frequently fatal by the age of 30 or requires a liver transplant, but simple drug treatments that facilitate copper excretion can result in a normal lifespan for patients who are diagnosed early.

I suspect that you have never heard of this disease. I certainly had not before writing this book. But if affected people remain unaware of it, they may lose their lives. Note that this is a very different scenario from the hypertension case discussed above: we are aware of what the treatment options are and even their respective success rates. We can therefore make an informed decision, weighing the risks. But if we are unaware of a risk, this evaluation is impossible.

Of course, now that you are aware of the risk of Wilson's disease, you may decide that the cost of undergoing the test for you or your children is worthwhile, given the risks involved. Health awareness campaigns have exactly this purpose. Their goal is to reduce unknown unknowns.

This idea applies to far more than just health care and national security. It has gained some recent prominence in Nassim Taleb's notion of a "black swan," an unexpected high-impact event that has been left out of standard models of financial risk management.[14]

It is not possible to resolve these issues in principle, but they can be alleviated in practice. Intelligence organizations can help to reduce unknown unknowns and increase situational awareness.

Consider the example of the 9/11 attacks. Much of the subsequent investigation of possible intelligence failures focused on the fact that this was an entirely new type of attack that had never been used before and therefore could not have been foreseen. But this was not the position of the 9/11 Commission, which identified four areas of systemic intelligence failures—those of imagination, policy, capabilities, and management—and discussed them in detail in its report.[15]

Upon greater reflection, there is nothing fundamentally new about the use of aircraft as weapons. Crashing planes into buildings combines two very old terrorist tactics: suicide bombings and the hijacking of airplanes.[16] Once this relationship is stated, the possibility of the 9/11 attacks seems obvious, but imagining it was not. That said, there are processes that facilitate the likelihood of anticipating unexpected events, or, in the words of the 9/11 Commission, of "institutionalizing imagination."

There are two approaches to institutionalizing imagination: people and technology. One important lesson of many postdisaster assessments of intelligence failures is that the critical pieces were present, but the dots were not connected to generate actionable intelligence. For a company like McDonald's, intelligence may reside in the vast network of its franchisees, its owner-operators. For the insurance giant State Farm, it may be in its agents. Similarly, customers and employees can be invaluable sources of intelligence.

But the mere aggregation of information is not intelligence. Intelligence is the art of applying imperfect and partial knowledge to create actionable insights. It is based on imagination, analysis, and judgment. But imagination requires some creativity.[17] This can be nicely observed in crisis teams. Very often the solution to a crisis requires a new approach—a strategy that the company has never used before. For example, Mercedes used a new technology to solve a market perception problem, and Prudential needed to change a pricing model that triggered moral outrage despite being revenue-neutral.

NASA's rescue of the moon mission *Apollo 13* provided a memorable example of the ability to imagine new solutions under pressure.

During the crisis, a team of engineers at NASA had to create a CO_2 filter that essentially put a square peg into a round hole, using nothing but what was available to the astronauts on the spacecraft.[18] Small teams with diverse perspectives can be innovation engines if they are put into one room without interruptions and removed from all other responsibilities.[19] This is one of the main rationales for creating diverse, dedicated crisis teams.

But crisis teams are a major commitment; they are appropriate for managing a crisis, but, in all likelihood, they are too costly for day-to-day responsibilities. The question, then, is how to integrate the need for ongoing intelligence into an existing corporate structure. Such an intelligence capability is ideally organized as a tactical team that provides intelligence assessment, develops strategy options, and assists in the execution of reputation management strategies. The intelligence capability should support the corporate reputation council and connect with the rest of the organization.

In reference to former Procter & Gamble executive Deborah Anderson, one of the pioneers of this approach, we will refer to this tactical team as the anticipatory issues management team, or simply the AIM team.[20] AIM teams do not have to be large, provided they are closely connected with other business functions. Even a team of only a few members can be highly effective.

Rapidly changing issue dynamics require monitoring of the external environment. Stakeholder outreach and ongoing, collaborative relationships can be invaluable in getting an early reading on emerging issues, but even that is not enough. Many issues emerge in fringe groups, on obscure Web sites, in research papers, and so forth. In retrospect, many issues could have been identified, but nobody knew where to look, or even that attempting to search for them would have been a good idea.

> The purpose of issue identification is to create awareness. It consists of human and open-source intelligence. The main goal is to reduce unknown unknowns.

Generally speaking, the challenge is not that critical information is missing or kept secret—it's that there is just too much of it. Information about reputational risk is usually not available in a structured or numerical format the way financial information is; rather, it is buried in a sea of sources, such as news articles, Web sites, and blogs. The difficulty is finding the proverbial needle in the haystack without knowing what the needle looks like and where the haystack is. Under these conditions, information extraction and evaluation are daunting tasks.

Certainly the rise of user-generated media and the Internet presents a monitoring challenge, but it also offers tremendous opportunity for catching concerns early, since issues are frequently first mentioned on the Web. In other words, issues can be found and mitigated before they reach the mainstream media and begin to generate the business impact.[21] But one has to know where to look. Fortunately, recent technical breakthroughs in the automatic processing of unstructured data permit organizations to identify emerging issues more easily. Technology can help to tame the monster that it created.

Algorithms developed by linguists and computer scientists are increasingly able to sort documents by topic, even if these topics are not predefined.[22] Here is how it works. Suppose you had to sort thousands of recipes by cuisine. When you see a recipe, even if you have never tried it, you will probably be able to classify it correctly by cuisine. For example, a recipe with pasta, tomato, olive oil, and garlic is likely to be Italian. Of course, you will be wrong sometimes, but most of the time you will get it right. Why is that? There are some key words (pasta, tomato, olive oil, garlic) that you associate with Italian cuisine. Similarly, bamboo shoots and bean sprouts would be associated with Chinese food, curry and coriander with Indian food, and so forth. Computer algorithms can learn these key characteristics and sort them accordingly. Now suppose such an algorithm analyzes a recipe that requires rice, curry, and bamboo shoots. No existing category can accommodate this case, and so the algorithm starts a new category. You have just discovered a cuisine that you might never have been aware of: Nepalese.

More generally, by learning what is regular and typical, such computer programs can also identify what is unusual. This can be a previously unknown cuisine or an issue that a company is unfamiliar with.

This approach and its associated methods were developed in the context of national security and counterterrorism. The goal there was to help analysts to identify previously unimagined terrorist attacks and security risks. We can neither search for nor manage what we are unaware of. Companies have started to experiment with such approaches, but existing technologies are not perfect. They generate too many false positives that need to be screened out and are best deployed to support human analysts rather than as a stand-alone solution. However, when they are properly deployed, they dramatically increase the performance of issue identification systems.

Issue Evaluation

Next, companies need to determine which issues are *enterprise-critical* and which are mere irritations. This requires defining and assessing risk profiles that are specific to an issue, a product, or a company. We need to know which issues are just minor nuisances and which may become catastrophic. The ability to make such distinctions is predicated on a proper risk segmentation tool. Figure 8-4 illustrates the two dimensions of reputational risk.

Figure 8-4 **Segmenting Reputational Risk**

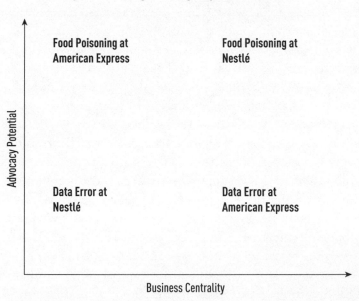

The *business centrality* dimension captures how closely an issue is connected to a company's core value proposition. Compare a case of severe food poisoning in the executive dining room leading to the hospitalization of the company's chairman with an IT error resulting in a

2 percent overpayment of a large number of suppliers. In this example, portrayed in Figure 8-4, issues of data management are of much greater concern to a financial services company than to a food company; the reverse will be true of food safety. In both cases (food safety for Nestlé, a technical data error for American Express), the issue directly touches upon a core competency that the company needs to demonstrate consistently in order to maintain the trust of its customers.

Advocacy potential refers to a different risk dimension. It is a summary measure of the tools developed in Chapters 2 through 5. Here we use them not to manage a reputational problem, but to assess the reputational magnitude of an emerging issue. With respect to the media, it captures the potential of an issue to generate more hostile media attention (move toward the upper right corner in the Reputational Terrain). With respect to advocacy groups, it captures the presence of well-organized, highly motivated activists. Similarly, high outrage or fear potential or connection to a broader issues environment, such as manufacturing quality in China, will increase an issue's advocacy potential. It is important to remember that some of these factors may seem trivial or unimportant from an operational perspective. But recall the importance of the name *Moose Test*, the case of celebrity investors, or the involvement of identifiable sympathetic victims.

Notice that all of these assessments need to take place *before* an issue has led to a reputational problem. The necessary skill is to identify their potential for trouble. Increased advocacy potential of an issue makes it more likely that customers and stakeholders (including regulators) will pay attention to that issue and take an adversarial stance. This will usually lead to a more serious management challenge.

One would think that identifying the business centrality of an issue would not be a difficult task once companies are apprised of a concern. Anything that affects a company's value proposition, core competencies, competitive advantage, or core values should trigger a greater response. But surprisingly, even otherwise well-managed companies can struggle with this challenge.

This can be seen in the cases of Toyota, Goldman Sachs, and BP. The Toyota brand stands for quality, durability, and safety. Each one of these core values was under attack during the recent recalls. Yet, Toyota originally conceptualized the problem as an engineering issue. Similarly, Goldman Sachs is distinguished by two brand attributes: "smartest guys in the room" and "clients first." During the recent hearings on Goldman's synthetic collateralized debt obligations (CDOs), Goldman's reputation for cleverness survived intact, but its reputation for client focus took a serious beating. The tricky balance for Goldman was how to avoid a legal standard of fiduciary duty while maintaining a client-first perception in the marketplace. Goldman's legalistic responses, however, may have undermined client trust. Finally, BP's brand position as an environmentally responsible company was inconsistent with the lack of sufficient internal processes to guarantee environmental safety during the Deepwater Horizon oil spill in the Gulf of Mexico.

> Issue evaluation requires a ranking of issues according to their potential severity. Business centrality and advocacy potential are the two main dimensions on which to assess the importance of an issue.

In sum, companies that have a clear understanding of their identity and culture not only have a better record when they have to manage a reputational crisis, but are also more successful in evaluating the potential business impact of emerging issues.

Issue Monitoring

The last task consists of monitoring when issues move from latency to having a serious impact. We discussed such dynamics extensively using the Reputational Terrain. Recall, for example, the case of Internet gambling, where concerns about protection for children or reports about the use of Internet gambling for money laundering by terrorists can dramatically increase the advocacy potential of this issue. It is important to realize that the importance of an issue may also be shaped by factors that are external to the company or even the industry. A meat contamination scandal in one grocery chain will have an impact on sales of fresh meat by competing chains as well. A quality issue of lead in toys manufactured in China should also trigger an increased alert for companies in other industries if they have a significant manufacturing presence in China.

As in the case of issue identification, modern information technology can help with these tasks. Simple automatic counting of stories can provide a sense of the growth or disappearance of an issue. More advanced approaches can track changes in the popularity of general topics. Finally, modern algorithms from the field of "sentiment analysis" can be used to classify newspaper stories, blog postings, and other such material into positive, neutral, or negative categories.[23] This can be used to create sentiment indexes that can be tracked over time. Sentiment analysis should include user-generated media, where issues stay alive much longer than they do on broadcast media. A video posted on You-Tube may stay there forever. Done right, this type of monitoring can be used very effectively.

When creating such indexes, it is important to be clear that they should follow psychological principles as closely as possible. For example, it is known from psychological experiments that positive stories have far less impact than negative stories. A good rule of thumb is:

One negative = Five positives

Thus, in constructing an index, a negative story should be weighted five times more heavily than a positive story.[24] More advanced indexes can alter weights based on the credibility of the source (e.g., a negative *New York Times* story would count more than a negative remark from an average blogger), position in the paper (front page versus page 18), and so forth. Once such metrics are constructed, they can be used not only to monitor ongoing issues, but also to provide real-time feedback. In other words, company strategies can be evaluated based on whether they have moved the needle. This allows a quick adjustment of ineffective approaches.

THE REPUTATION MANAGEMENT SYSTEM

Governance structure and intelligence capabilities need to be integrated. We call this integration the Reputation Management System. Figure 8-5 illustrates this integration.

The corporate reputation council (CRC) governs the Reputation Management System. It needs to represent the various business segments and critical corporate functions. Ideally, it should mirror the organizational structure of the company. In some businesses, it makes sense to extend the jurisdiction of the CRC to include regulatory and political developments as well as macroeconomic ones. In that case, it effectively becomes the corporate relations council.

Figure 8-5 **The Reputation Management System**

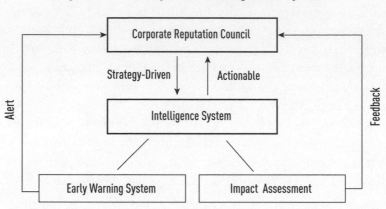

The governance structure needs to be closely connected with the intelligence function. This means that the CRC provides strategic direction to the intelligence function and receives actionable intelligence that is directly connected to the corporate strategy. The intelligence function provides the core capabilities of issue identification, evaluation, and monitoring. The goal is both to function as an early warning system and to be able to assess the impact of corporate actions through a feedback mechanism. Without an intelligence function, the CRC will be operating in the dark and making decisions based on intuition rather than data. A company's intelligence function may range from informal monitoring of various media sources and proactive stakeholder outreach to the creation of a fully developed internal intelligence capability with its own staff and budget: an AIM team.

Intelligence functions are not just important for management. Given the critical role of the board as a guardian of the company's reputation, it is surprising and worrisome that most corporate boards are not supported by a separate intelligence function. Such a function is ideally provided by a third party, not by company staff. Much of the critical reputational intelligence is external to the company, and it may lead board members to ask more probing questions of management.

Board members may be concerned that such an approach may be too adversarial and may undermine trust with management. A candid, transparent, and structured approach can mitigate these interpersonal risks. For example, it is preferable for the intelligence function to provide the board with ongoing intelligence on a routine basis rather than having the board request it only when the situation looks more dangerous. And boards, of course, frequently are required to seek independent counsel on legal, regulatory, and financial matters. Overall, irritating management slightly seems a small price to pay to avoid acting in ignorance of looming dangers.

THINGS TO REMEMBER

If reputation management is a capability, it requires processes. First, companies must develop a proper governance structure, which should mirror the company's organizational structure. A cross-functional council is preferable to a separate corporate function unless that function is endowed with sufficient influence and resources. Second, companies need an intelligence capability. In contrast to other corporate capabilities, an intelligence system is essential, not optional. Reputational challenges can emerge from anywhere in the company's operations or from the external business environment. The lack of intelligence capabilities means that the company either acts in the dark or loses its ability to manage such issues proactively.

A well-designed intelligence process has three components:

- Issue identification

- Issue evaluation

- Issue monitoring

A small but dedicated task force supported by technology and integrated with a corporate reputation council is highly recommended. Its goal is to identify the next threat and propose strategic options for management. Once the council makes a decision, the tactical team will help in its execution and impact assessment.

Corporate boards should consider obtaining a separate intelligence capability. This will provide not only much-needed early warning signs, but also an independent source of trusted information in times of crisis, when there may be a conflict between the board and management—exactly the moment when it is most valuable.

CHAPTER 9

ANDERSEN BEFORE THE FALL

Values, Culture, and the Teachable Moment

*"The '90s were a go-go period in which the mentality was
if you weren't getting rich, you were stupid."*

—**Duane Kullberg,** Former CEO,
Arthur Andersen[1]

n February 1998, Steve Miller, the interim CEO of Waste Management, released his in-depth review of the company's audit practices.[2]
His findings stunned Wall Street: Waste Management had "overstated"
its pretax earnings by $1.43 billion between 1992 and 1996. Further-
more, the company would make a $1.7 billion restatement of its earn-
ings—at that time, the largest in U.S. corporate history. At this news,
the stock price imploded, costing shareholders more than $6 billion vir-
tually overnight.[3]

This ensured that the U.S. Securities and Exchange Commission
(SEC) would investigate not only Waste Management, but also its long-
time accounting firm, Arthur Andersen, which had signed off on all of
the revenue statements that were now being revised. For years, the SEC
had criticized the practice of major accounting firms serving as both
auditors and consultants for their client companies, worrying that it
would create persistent conflicts of interest. Now the SEC took action.

Waste Management had been a very important client for Andersen,
which had served as the firm's external audit company since before it
even went public in 1971. Moreover, until 1997, every chief financial
officer and chief accounting officer in the company's public history had
been an Andersen alumnus. From 1991 to 1997, Andersen had earned
approximately $7.5 million in audit fees at Waste Management and
nearly $12 million from consulting.[4]

As the SEC investigation proceeded, relying heavily on subpoenaed
e-mails and memos written by Andersen employees, it appeared that
Andersen auditors had uncovered a number of questionable practices
at Waste Management as early as 1988. For example, Waste Management had apparently attempted to inflate its value by overestimating
the salvage value of its older garbage trucks, in effect claiming that they
were worth $30,000 each when the actual figure was closer to $12,000.[5]
Documents subpoenaed by the SEC suggested that Andersen auditors
had brought many of these issues to the attention of Waste Management executives. When Waste Management ignored Andersen's recommendations, however, the auditors seemed to have yielded. Andersen's
lawyers argued to the SEC that the auditors and the responsible partners
had followed "accepted standards" and defended some of the suggested
abuses as judgment calls on local issues that accounting norms had not
yet clearly addressed.

But the SEC disagreed. At the conclusion of the investigation in February 2001, the SEC determined that Arthur Andersen's audit reports on Waste Management were "materially false and misleading."[6] Lead partner Robert Allgyer, who had already resigned, was suspended from practicing for five years and was required to pay a $50,000 fine. Edward G. Maier and Walter Cercavschi, partners on the Waste Management engagement, were suspended for three years and required to pay fines of $40,000 and $30,000, respectively. Robert Kutsenda, who had served as the Central Region audit director at the time, was suspended for one year for conduct "in violation of applicable professional standards." In addition, Andersen agreed to pay a $7 million fine (at the time, the largest ever levied against an accounting firm) with no admission or denial of guilt regarding the violation of professional standards. As part of the deal, however, Andersen also agreed to an injunction requiring it to adhere to generally accepted accounting practices (GAAP) and generally accepted auditing standards (GAAS)—in effect, placing it on probation.[7]

Just over a year later, as a consequence of the Enron accounting scandal, its auditor, Arthur Andersen, collapsed as a functioning entity and announced that it would cease all auditing of public companies, 89 years after Arthur E. Andersen had taken over a small accounting firm in Chicago.

THE RISE AND FALL OF ANDROID CULTURE

The fall of Arthur Andersen is one of the great tragedies of modern business. Andersen had long set the industry standard for professionalism in external accounting. In its own eyes, the firm stood for public service and independent integrity, protecting shareholders' interests and the financial system. Andersen employees often spent their entire careers at the firm, whose corporate culture was strong and consistent, supported by a rigorous system of education and acculturation into the firm's values.

But cultures need to be tended to; otherwise they slowly wither away. Andersen is a classic example of how, through external pressure and internal neglect, norms cease to be binding and values lose their force. A company's reputation needs to be guarded by more than just strategies, processes, and policies—it needs to be protected by its people in their daily decisions.

Born in 1885 to a family of Norwegian immigrants, Arthur E. Andersen went on to become an accounting professor at Northwestern University. In 1913, together with a partner, Andersen decided to take over the company that came to bear his name. In an era in which accounting standards were in flux, the firm distinguished itself early on for its willingness to tell the unvarnished truth. Rather than bend to a client's demands, Arthur E. Andersen was prepared to lose an account in order to avoid compromising his firm's standards.

In one famous incident that became a staple in company lore, the president of a large client company barged into Andersen headquarters and demanded an audit certification on his own terms—flatly contradicting the findings of an accountant there. Without hesitation, Arthur E. Andersen answered: "There is not enough money in the city of Chicago to induce me to change the report." While he lost the client, his company's reputation for unyielding integrity was confirmed. In addition, with the establishment of the "Blueback" policy in 1939, partners would write a project wrap-up memo (in a blue cover) regarding anything that they had observed that might be of use to their client, from management practices to strategy. These memos distinguished the company from other accounting firms, which concentrated almost exclusively on the certification of their clients' numbers.

As the firm grew, its partners formed an elite corps; they all knew and respected one another as professionals. Under the strong leadership of Arthur E. Andersen, who owned the majority of shares in the partnership, an intimate and highly uniform culture developed, and his voice spoke for everyone on matters of policy. He wanted the firm to remain small, seeking outstanding talent just out of college—preferably from a modest background with a "Midwestern work ethic," and ideally from a family farm—who would be molded through an apprenticeship under a senior certified public accountant (CPA).

In 1940, the apprenticeship system was expanded into a formal training program that all new employees were required to attend. The training indoctrinated new recruits in the "Andersen Way." The Andersen Way was based on (1) honesty and integrity, (2) a one-firm, one-voice partnership model, and (3) a training in methodology that was uniformly applied and obeyed. Andersen employees were supposed to appear homogeneous and act predictably, and to be "trusted to do as they were taught." Their goal was to represent a venerable profession with pride, and to be the auditors that investors could trust.

In 1947, Arthur E. Andersen died without having named a successor. After a leadership crisis, the 25 remaining partners eventually elected Leonard Spacek to serve as managing partner and the leader of the firm. Spacek resembled Arthur E. Andersen in his midwestern background, his staunch support of the Andersen Way, and his fiercely independent thinking and uncompromising reputation. Spacek quickly proved himself a domineering and forceful leader; he had a strong vision for the accounting profession that he shared regardless of its popularity in the industry.

To back up his beliefs, Spacek increased Andersen's investment in its training programs, which consumed 15 to 20 percent of the firm's net revenue. His goal was to create an educational system that would produce "androids"—professionals with similar background, training, and demeanor—who would maintain the highest and most consistent professional accounting standards, understood as a public service. Andersen employees studied not only technical audit procedures, but also a personal code of conduct—a code so detailed that it included everything from the company dress code to required daily appearances in the "correct" business-lunch restaurants. In the profession, Andersen employees became famed as members of a culture with the strictest conformity in their appearance and behavior. The implication was that they were interchangeable and equally reliable as professionals of the highest degree. Their appearance and demeanor was so uniform that the limo drivers at O'Hare Airport claimed that they could recognize the "Arthur Androids" simply by their "grooming, clothes, stance, luggage, and briefcase."

Under Spacek's leadership, Andersen grew rapidly, though cautiously, entering international markets and offering new services. Rather than seeking growth through acquisitions of similar accounting firms, Spacek chose to develop new offices, using its recruiting and training system. Furthermore, the company began to greatly expand its consulting business in the early 1950s when it established itself as the leader among big accounting firms in computer technology consulting services. The company began hiring computer consultants, but the new hires introduced a different type of employee into the firm—the consultants were not part of the accounting culture, although in the beginning they received the same training as accountants.

To a degree, the Andersen culture remained cohesive, held together by the centralized training system and the authority and expertise of the partners. But there were tensions brewing; the partners were chafing under Spacek's rule. When Spacek retired in 1973, the partners voted to ensure that no single partner would ever again wield the kind of influence that Spacek and Andersen had; it became the era of "one partner, one vote." There had also been a huge increase in the partnership ranks, expanding from 25 members to 826 members during Spacek's tenure, and international offices had proliferated. As a result, partners no longer knew one another well, and they could no longer govern in person ("face-to-face") as they had previously. Moreover, the rise of Andersen consultants introduced a new mentality into the company—salesmanship in search of discretionary funds from clients—that differed fundamentally from the legally required services that external auditors provided year after year. As a result, cooperation and cultural cohesion began to weaken, as did the ability of the firm's managing partner to lead.

After Spacek's departure, the firm continued its rapid growth. To govern it more effectively, the new managing partner, Harvey Kapnick, broke the firm into service divisions of consulting, tax, and audit in the mid-1970s. While this move was adopted to create manageable units, it effectively split the firm into competing fiefdoms, of which consulting was experiencing the most rapid growth. By 1979, 42 percent of Andersen's $645 million in worldwide fees came from consulting and tax work, as opposed to accounting and auditing.

In addition, the consultants fought for, and won, the right to bypass the accountants' training regimen, and this further undermined the uniformity of Andersen's culture. According to some observers, at this moment, the "common good" ceased to be the basis of company loyalty, and division and geographic location became the ties that bound people together. The stage was set for a culture clash between old guard accountants and their consulting counterparts.

In addition to internal factors, external factors were having an impact on the firm as well. First, while audit revenues were dependable, since the audits were legally required for public companies, their profitability was stagnating. On the one hand, the U.S. government was pursuing efforts to inject more competition into the industry. Prior to a 1973 legal challenge for violation of antitrust laws, industry associations had prohibited competitive bidding between accounting firms; four years later, similar industry bans on advertising were lifted. On the other hand, a wave of consolidation was adding to the competition between firms. Increasingly, clients were being offered packages of audit services that resembled commodities, complete with advertising campaigns. Second, in the wake of the merger-and-acquisition trend that began in the 1960s, disappointed investors began to seek legal compensation for failed deals—often from accounting firms. To respond to the explosion of audit-related litigation, Andersen, on the advice of lawyers, adopted a damage-control policy. In addition, the firm joined the other big accounting companies to pool resources in an insurance fund to pay shareholder settlements. Third, to oppose regulatory oversight by the SEC and other agencies and political pressure from the U.S. Congress, the big accounting companies began to work as a cohesive industry coalition.[8]

As their profits skyrocketed, the consultants began to resent what they perceived as their subsidization of the accountants, and they called for greater freedom. On a per-partner basis, consultants were bringing in $2.3 million by 1989, while accountants achieved only $1.4 million, and yet, of the 2,134 partners, only 586 were consultants. As a result, Andersen created two separate business units: Arthur Andersen and Andersen Consulting. This split allowed the units to track all their accounts separately, including income and profits; they began to operate on their own floors of the same office building, entirely separate.

In 1992, the company initiated a purge of low-performance partners. Overall, 10 percent of all partners were forced out; in many cases, those who departed represented the traditional values of the firm and had functioned as mentors to younger accountants. As a result, the oversight of younger partners was sharply curtailed, while the local independence of Andersen offices grew.

The Professional Standards Group (PSG), an oversight office that had once been a plum assignment for the future accounting elite, visibly diminished in importance. While the PSG would continue to make rulings and pronouncements, local offices had gained a new independence to overrule voices that dissented from their judgment calls onsite.[9]

By the end of 1997, the tensions had become too great, and the Andersen Consulting partners voted unanimously to secede from

Andersen. The divorce was acrimonious, leading to an arbitration process at the International Chamber of Commerce in Paris. The decision was a major disappointment for the remainder of Arthur Andersen. To become a separate corporate entity, Andersen Consulting was required to pay $1 billion, far below the $14.6 billion that many Arthur Andersen partners had demanded—and expected. In January 2001, Andersen Consulting changed its name to Accenture, on its road to becoming one of the world's leading consulting firms.

Meanwhile, the issue of independence between the auditing and consulting functions across the industry was of increasing concern to SEC commissioner Arthur Levitt.[10] In June 2000, Levitt proposed tough new rules that would bar accounting firms from consulting for their clients.[11]

A bitter political battle followed, in which the big accounting firms lobbied Congress and the SEC.[12] In the end, a compromise was reached. While Levitt had to abandon the strict separation that he had proposed, the biggest accounting firms agreed to (1) disclose what they earned from auditing and consulting fees and (2) have the audit committees of company boards certify that their nonaudit services were compatible with their independence as auditors.[13]

With the prospect of reduced revenues in a stagnant market for traditional accounting services, and being extremely bitter about the unexpectedly "low" settlement from the divorce, the leaders of the accounting unit felt renewed pressure to find additional sources of revenue. According to former partner Barbara Ley Toffler, the firm felt "rudderless." This was the stage on which the drama of the Enron scandal played out.

DEER HUNTERS

The accounting industry is a perfect example of the difficulties of safeguarding a company's reputation. External auditors essentially sell one thing: their signature. It is their assurance to the investing public that the company's financial statements have been carefully examined and can be trusted. It is a business in which reputation is everything. As a result, the Big Four accounting firms need to rely on their partners and associates to be the guardians of this reputation each and every day, and to exercise judgment in a manner that preserves the auditor's quality standards without upsetting the client.

In an environment in which public companies are under intense pressure to deliver quarterly results, conflicts of interest abound. On the one hand, the client needs to be satisfied; on the other hand, the client may need to be told no. No individual process can remove this tension fully or predict and prescribe the appropriate action for every situation that might arise. The company must depend upon the judgment, experience, and integrity of the partners to guide their decisions. In other words, the company's reputation depends on its people. During its long and distinguished history, Andersen understood this as well as any other company. In an environment in which a decision by any partner can bring down the company, nothing is more important than selecting the right people and ensuring that they uphold the core values and embrace the collective consciousness of an unambiguous corporate culture. Corporate cultures are delicate equilibria, and some companies go to extremes to maintain them.[14]

> Reputation management strategies need to be implemented by people. Culture plays a major role in implementing effective reputation management processes. Cultures can be fragile. They need to be constantly reinforced. Otherwise they atrophy.

In his treatise *A Discourse on Inequality*, the Swiss philosopher Jean-Jacques Rousseau tells the following story about deer hunting to describe the dilemma of social cooperation:

> If a deer was to be taken, everyone saw that, in order to succeed, he must abide faithfully by his post: but if a hare happened to come within the reach of any one of them, it is not to be doubted that he pursued it without scruple, and, having seized his prey, cared very little, if by so doing he caused his companions to miss theirs.[15]

Let us clarify this story a little. Suppose there are two hunters, Bill and Bob. It takes two hunters to hunt a deer, but each hunter on his own can catch a rabbit. Of course, a deer is a far more successful prey than a rabbit, but pursuing it carries the risk of the hunters' being left with nothing. What should Bill do? As long as Bill is sure that Bob will participate in the hunt for the deer, Bill should too. Similarly, if Bill is sure that Bob will hunt rabbit, then that is what Bill should do as well.

So, hunting deer and hunting rabbits are both equilibria; they reinforce each other.

Things get interesting if Bill is not sure what Bob is doing. In this scenario, their individual decisions on how to proceed may depend on how bad it is for a hunter to go home with nothing. If it is catastrophic, then even a small degree of uncertainty as to whether Bob will be hunting for deer may lead Bill to hunt rabbits. If both of them hunt for rabbits, the deer will live another day.[16]

At a more abstract level, this little story provides some interesting insights. On the one hand, catching the deer is in both hunters' interest; they are each better off if they do so. On the other hand, relying on the other hunter to search for deer is risky. For either hunter, hunting for deer while the other hunts rabbits leads to the worst possible outcome. Hence, perhaps it is better to take the safe route and hunt rabbits instead.

Now let us change our story. Suppose, we replace "hunting deer" with "protecting the company's reputation" and "hunting rabbits" with "focusing only on one's own interest." As long as others are protecting the company's reputation, I have an incentive to do the same; after all, all of us (me included) will be better off if the company's reputation remains strong. As long as the company's reputation is strong, taking the chance of damaging it is not worth it. But if I suspect that others are cutting corners, wouldn't I be a fool if I did not do the same? In other words, unless I can observe your actions, I need to trust that you will do the right thing. As long as I trust you, I will do the right thing as well.

Telling a client no, refusing to sell a product to a dodgy customer, and not giving a loan to a borrower who is likely to default are all actions that people are more likely to take if they are confident that others are doing the same and that failure to do so is likely to have bad consequences. We like to think that these issues come down to ethics and integrity, and, of course, these matter a great deal. But there is something else at work here: individuals live in social environments. Behavior is reinforced by observing others. Culture matters.

The influence of others can be terrifying. Two famous experiments illustrate this. The first is the Zimbardo experiment.[17] In this study, conducted at Stanford University, undergraduate students were assigned to one of two roles, prisoners or guards, for a two-week period. Upon the adoption of these roles, prisoners quickly became submissive to guards, while at the same time guards became brutal enforcers. As the experiment progressed, guards treated prisoners with increasing cruelty and indecency, to the point where the lead experimenter described a third of the guards as having sadistic tendencies. None of the "friendly guards" voiced their concern about their fellow guards' behavior; instead, they passively allowed the abuse to continue. Near the conclusion of the experiment, the prisoners had pleaded for "parole" and had been willing to forgo the monetary compensation that they were to receive for participating in the study in exchange for being released. Even after relinquishing the motivation for participation (payment), the prisoners returned to their cells when their parole was denied. Guards had adapted perfectly to a role of abuser, prisoners to a role of victims. After six days, the researchers had to terminate the experiment.

In the so-called Milgram experiment[18] conducted at Yale University, participants (referred to as "teachers") were asked to administer electric shocks to another participant—the "learner"—when the learner answered questions incorrectly. In reality, all of the participants were teachers, and the learner was an actor whose responses were taped. As the experiment progressed, the level of shocks became increasingly painful, or so it seemed. Participants could hear cries of pain at lower levels, begging and pleading to stop at higher levels, and ultimately silence, as if the person had passed out. If at any point the participant who was administering shocks questioned the procedure, an experimenter simply replied with the prompts, "Please continue. The experiment requires you to continue. It is absolutely essential that you continue. You have no other choice; you must go on." This reinforcement was enough to prompt 65 percent of participants to continue administering shocks at an ostensibly dangerous level, even after cries of pain could no longer be heard.

The lessons portrayed in these experiments are clear: people will adjust to their environments and to the behavior of others—sometimes to an astonishing degree. It is a misleading oversimplification to say that only bad people will do bad things. "Good" people may do bad things as well, if the circumstances demand it. Selecting good people is not enough. Institutions, incentives, values, and culture need to be set up to lead people to serve as stewards of the company's reputation.

Back to our story. Clearly, a company wants to be in the trusted "deer" equilibrium. But, as we have seen, this trust equilibrium is not robust. Things can easily shift to an equilibrium in which people are looking out only for themselves. Here are a few things that are involved:

- People can be unsure of what is expected of them. Lack of clarity creates uncertainty, and uncertainty undermines trust.

- People need to be clear on what the consequences of their actions are. Nothing undermines a culture more than saying one thing and doing another.

- Hurting the company's reputation must have severe consequences. Also, the more that depends on the decision of each actor, the better.

- The company's standards need to be public. Public events create common understanding, and common understanding breeds trust.

Perhaps we can now appreciate Arthur E. Andersen's fanatical focus on culture and values. When he was in charge, there was never any doubt as to what the right action was and that taking the wrong action (even by a single individual) could be catastrophic for the firm as a whole. These lessons were reinforced by a common training experience and by company lore. Every new Andersen associate was told the anecdote about Arthur E. Andersen's refusing to yield to a client. It became public knowledge and was a yardstick for the company's values. Partners were evaluated, promoted, and disciplined based on these standards, and decisions were public.

THE TEACHABLE MOMENT

The crux of any corporate culture is how it handles violations of standards by otherwise top performers. Not enforcing one's own standards clearly when things get tough can have devastating consequences. In addition to creating a sense of cynicism, these failures confuse the workforce. Employees are no longer sure exactly what the rules are. Recall from the deer hunt example that all it takes for me to leave the trusted equilibrium is doubt as to whether you may do the same. Doubt is the destroyer of cultures.

This is particularly true of reputational crises that the company has barely survived. These near-death experiences put the company on stage; they create a public space that gathers attention. As we discussed in Chapter 1, there will be attention from customers, interest groups, regulators, and the like. But there is another group that will be paying close attention to the company's leaders—its own people.

Leadership will never send a stronger signal to its own people than through how it handles a reputational crisis; the experience teaches everyone what really matters. It is for this reason that reputational crises are tremendous learning opportunities. They can determine what the company's real future culture will be.

Recall from Chapter 7 that stakes and control are inversely related. Before a reputational crisis, the stakes are low and control is high; the opposite is true during the crisis. But there is another time when the stakes are low and control is high: after the crisis, when things "return to normal." This is portrayed in Figure 9-1.

> Reputational crises can be teachable moments. How the company reacts to a near-death experience will signal its true values and culture to its people. Leaders need to seize these opportunities rather than go back to business as usual.

It is a critical leadership mistake to quickly return to business as usual and miss this teachable moment: the opportunity to reinforce and strengthen the company's values and culture at a time when everybody is paying attention (and thus will remember!).[19]

A TALE OF TWO COMPANIES

General Electric (GE) and Siemens are in many respects twin companies. Both are highly diversified, globally operating companies with a strong engineering focus. Both GE and Siemens operate in industries that span financial services, energy, industrial manufacturing, and health care. Although GE is substantially larger, Siemens is the only other company that competes effectively in nearly all GE's main industries, except television broadcasting. That said, the companies' performance and histories contrast significantly. Between 1995 and 2004, for example, GE's operating margin was 14.2 percent, almost quadruple Siemens's 4 percent.[20]

Figure 9-1 **Reputation Dynamics—The Teachable Moment**

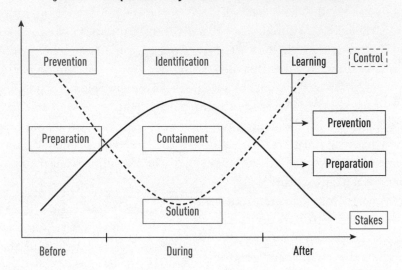

In November 2006, Siemens was accused of bribing foreign officials to secure contracts abroad. The incident was the first of a wave of scandals to hit the press. German officials raided offices and private homes, searching for evidence of bribery and embezzlement. Reinhard Siekaczek, a former accountant for Siemens and head of the telecommunications group, was one of five executives who were arrested in connection with the scandal. In an interview, Siekaczek stated that from 2002 to 2006, he had overseen an annual bribery budget of about $40 million to $50 million: "Company managers and sales staff used the slush fund to cozy up to corrupt government officials worldwide." Bribes were as high as 40 percent of the total cost of the contract. The most common method involved hiring an outside consultant, usually a local resident with ties to the ruling leaders, to help the company "win" a contract, then paying the fee to the consultant, who delivered the cash to the ultimate recipient. Siekaczek called the payments "vital to maintaining the competitiveness of Siemens overseas" and said that the bribes were "about keeping the business unit alive and not jeopardizing thousands of jobs overnight." His division accounted for more than $800 million of the $1.4 billion in illegal payments that Siemens made between 2001 and 2007. He was eventually sentenced to two years probation and received a $150,000 fine.[21]

Similar cases from around the world followed. In Italy in May 2007, Andreas Kley, a former finance chief at Siemens, and Horst Vigener, a consultant, were convicted of bribing employees of the Italian energy company Enel to secure contracts for power generators. Payments were made through a web of bank accounts in Liechtenstein and Switzerland to executives in Dubai, Abu Dhabi, and Monaco to secure €450 million ($609 million) of equipment supply contracts from 1999 to 2002.

"Bribery was Siemens's business model," said Uwe Dolata, the spokesman for the association of federal criminal investigators in Germany. "Siemens had institutionalized corruption." In a settlement with the U.S. Department of Justice and the SEC in December 2008, Siemens pleaded guilty to having violated accounting provisions of the Foreign Corrupt Practices Act (FCPA).[22] Ultimately, Siemens was to pay more than $2.6 billion: $1.6 billion in fines and fees to regulators in the United States and Germany, and more than $1 billion for internal investigations and reforms. The company was also shut out from projects financed by the World Bank for two years. In efforts to clean up its structures and personnel, the firm made dramatic changes. Under pressure from the company's supervisory board, its chairman, Heinrich von Pierer, announced his resignation in April 2007.[23] Shortly thereafter, CEO Klaus Kleinfeld announced that he would not renew his contract. Peter Löscher was then hired from Merck & Co. as CEO and proceeded to replace half of the company's top 100 executives.

In his efforts to bring about a change in practices, Löscher implemented a "zero tolerance policy" for the whole company. He considered the lack of ethics among managers to be the cause of the failure. He also implemented a compliance program centered on the concepts "prevent, detect, and respond."[24] Members of the supervisory and management board were sued individually and settled for seven-figure amounts.[25]

Siemens has since invested heavily to strengthen its compliance program. In 2007, the company increased the number of staff members working on compliance from 6 to almost 600 and provided training to 120,000 of its employees.[26] It hired GE veteran Peter Y. Solmssen as the new head of Corporate Legal and Compliance and started collaborating with the World Bank Institute to develop an anticorruption toolkit.

The pervasive use of bribery at Siemens was astonishing. However, in light of the shaky legal systems and rampant corruption in countries where the company was competing for large infrastructure contracts, the temptation to use bribery and other unsavory means was not entirely unexpected. Legal rules such as the FCPA provide some deterrent, but given the pressure for sales and earnings growth, the desire to find ways around the rules and regulations, especially in developing markets, can become very strong indeed. Is this just an unavoidable fact of doing business? Former Siemens executive Reinhard Siekaczek clearly thought so when he told the *New York Times*: "People will only say about Siemens that they were unlucky and that they broke the 11th Commandment. The 11th Commandment is: 'Don't get caught.'"

Here a comparison with GE is helpful. Its business environment is the same as Siemens's, and the pressure to deliver results is at least as intense. But over the years GE has developed a culture to address the same challenges that brought Siemens down. Its core concepts are integrity and accountability, or, in the words of former CEO Jack Welch:

> Nothing is more important than a company's integrity. It is the first and most important value in any organization. It not only means that people must abide by the letter and spirit of the law, it also means doing the right thing and fighting for what you believe is right.[27]

Let us see how this works in practice. In August 1991, the Department of Justice accused Herbert Steindler, an employee of GE's aircraft business, of conspiring with a former Israeli Air Force general, Rami Dotan, to defraud the U.S. government of $30 million for work that was never done.[28] Dotan set up a fake New Jersey subcontractor owned by a close friend of Steindler's. They then diverted U.S. military aid from a GE contract to unauthorized Israeli military projects. The funds were funneled into secret Swiss bank accounts set up by an Israeli intelligence operative between 1985 and 1988. The story broke when an American employee of GE, Chester L. Walsh, blew the whistle in 1990. After the two were found guilty, Walsh, along with his co-plaintiff, Taxpayers Against Fraud, a nonprofit public-interest organization dedicated to combating fraud against the federal government, were awarded $13.4 million, the largest amount ever awarded to a whistle-blower under the Federal False Claims Act at that time.[29]

In his autobiography, CEO Welch describes his reaction as follows. "I couldn't believe my ears. If there was one thing I preached every day at GE, it was integrity. It was our No. 1 value. Nothing came before it. We never had a corporate meeting where I didn't emphasize integrity in my closing remarks."[30]

Brian Rowe, who led GE Aviation from 1979 to 1993 as division president and CEO, recalls:

> Our people were naïve enough to believe the work was being done, and clearly we did not have good checks and balances in place. In addition, our main technical representative in Israel, rather than letting us know what was going on, had been collecting evidence on his own behalf so that he could file a government-backed qui tam (whistle-blower) suit against GE. This could make a very exciting novel or a movie, but when it involves your own people who thought they were doing a good job for the customer, it was nothing short of a disaster. It showed all of us that you must *check, check, check* even when it involves a customer.[31]

After the event was reported in Israeli newspapers, GE spent more than 19 months remedying the situation. Management hired a group of lawyers to help the GE audit team conduct a formal investigation. The team traced back every process involved in each associated contract and talked to each participant. Over a period of nine months, they reviewed 350,000 pages of documents and interviewed 100 witnesses.

The investigation concluded that Steindler was the only employee who knowingly had violated policies for direct financial gain. He was suspended immediately and fired after he refused to cooperate with the internal investigation. Another 20 employees were involved in the approval and execution of the contract, but were unaware of the scheme. In his autobiography, Welch explained, "They were outsmarted, or just sloppy, or they ignored warning signals."[32] Ultimately 10 of the 20 employees were fired or asked for their resignations, 6 were demoted, and 4 were reprimanded.[33]

Welch stated the significance of these consequences:

> It sent a clear message through the company: Sergeants were not going to be shot while generals and colonels could continue on as if nothing had happened. We wanted our managers to know that if an integrity violation occurred on their watch, it was their responsibil-

ity. That chiefs got shot for being indifferent to integrity was a huge event in GE.[34]

The crisis offered a teachable moment, and Welch clearly seized the opportunity to send a signal about the company's values and culture. What is particularly noteworthy is the emphasis on accountability. By publicly disciplining 20 executives who had failed to live up to GE's standards, the company's leadership wanted everybody in the company to understand what was expected of them: GE will not stop at individual culpability. In addition, a leader who fails to be vigilant or who ignores warning signals will be held accountable. Leaders are responsible not only for their own behavior, but for the behavior of their reports; they are the stewards of the company's processes and culture, and will be treated as such.

The consequence of this approach is a proactive compliance culture—the opposite of checking boxes and then looking for a way around them. That said, upholding these standards can be a brutal, gut-wrenching process. Brian Rowe, who executed several of the layoffs, reflected on the experience in his autobiography:

> I do not think I was any more devastated in my career than when I had to be the one who informed some of my key people of their fate. For once in my life, I really regretted that I was close to these men, as it was very difficult to take an action against them that I really did not believe in. Within a short time, we lost the management of the best military engine business in the world. I know I will never completely get over this incident. I am sure the people who suffered job actions will not either.[35]

Not all companies need a process as tough as the one that GE used, but companies with substantial reputational risk should consider it. If the action of any employee can bring down a company, developing a healthy obsession with integrity and accountability is a very good idea. Siemens CEO Peter Löscher echoed this sentiment when he said:

> It's completely clear that the management culture [at Siemens] failed. Managers broke the law. But this has nothing to do with a lack of rules. Siemens had and still has an outstanding set of rules. The only

problem is that they were apparently being violated on an ongoing basis. The management culture was simply not practiced consistently and uniformly. This is why my job now is to install a new culture. And I can guarantee you that senior management will practice what it preaches—to a T.[36]

A TEACHABLE MOMENT MISSED

How did Arthur Andersen react to the Waste Management incident? Of the partners who were implicated, only Robert Allgyer left the firm. In spite of his being investigated by the SEC and his subsequent one-year suspension, Robert Kutsenda was promoted to managing partner of global risk management. Because Andersen had suffered penalties in shareholder lawsuits based on its internal documents, one of Kutsenda's most important new tasks was to formulate a policy that would limit Andersen's exposure to such problems in the future. In February 2000, he submitted a policy regarding "organization, retention and destruction" of client engagement information. "Information gathered or considered in connection with performing client engagements should be evaluated by the engagement partner and manager," the policy stated, "and only essential information to support our conclusions should be retained."[37] In May of that year, that policy was sent to every Andersen employee by e-mail. Ironically, it was precisely Andersen's document retention policy that played a major role in its downfall over Enron.

During the Waste Management investigation, a rapid succession of similar crises came to light. While many Andersen representatives argued that these kinds of problems were inevitable and that they by no means indicated that there was any systemic problem at work, the new cases bore striking similarities to the Waste Management situation. In the case of the Baptist Foundation of Arizona (BFA), which declared bankruptcy in 1999, Andersen settled with investors out of court for $217 million and paid a fine. In the case of Sunbeam, Andersen settled with Sunbeam shareholders for $110 million in April 2001.

These cases can be interpreted as isolated incidents, driven by individual mistakes, or as warnings of a severe erosion of Andersen's culture and processes. Cultures die by a thousand cuts. Arthur Andersen's reaction to Waste Management, BFA, and Sunbeam continued to chip away at the foundation of the company's culture. Still hurting from the ugly divorce from its consulting unit and hampered by ineffective leadership structures, Arthur Andersen failed to act.

The rest is history. A few months after the collapse of Enron and news reports of massive document shredding at Andersen's Houston office, the U.S. Department of Justice indicted the firm for obstruction of justice. Clients had already started to leave the firm; they now abandoned Andersen in droves. With its global network disintegrating, the firm effectively ceased to operate. The subsequent trial was largely a formality. In mid-June the jury delivered a guilty verdict, and Andersen initiated an appeal of the conviction.

Although the Supreme Court unanimously overturned the conviction a few years later, in May 2005, the damage to the company's reputation had been irreparable. From a high of 28,000 employees in the United States and 85,000 employees worldwide, the company had been reduced to about 200 people, mostly in Chicago, dedicated to handling numerous outstanding lawsuits.[38] The fall of the House of Andersen was complete.

THINGS TO REMEMBER

Even the best reputation management system has to be implemented by people. They need to assess the situation, evaluate its risk, and then make the appropriate decision. Getting this right requires not only a strategic mindset but values and a culture that can provide guidance to individuals. We cannot expect each employee of a company to assess the reputational risk of an issue correctly, but we can expect him to raise a red flag when something does not "look right."

CEOs often refer to this behavior as "doing the right thing" or "personal integrity." Having a staff with high integrity is a tremendous asset to any company, but it is a misunderstanding to assume that these personal qualities are immutable. Getting the "right people" is only the first step; creating a culture in which they are encouraged and expected to "do the right thing" is just as important.

However, cultures are fragile; they need to be reinforced and nurtured constantly. Otherwise, they wither away. How leaders respond to crises, misconduct, or lack of integrity can have a tremendous impact on a company's culture. It is during these moments that employees are paying attention and inferring what the real values of the company are. Sweeping things under the rug or going back to business as usual is to miss a teachable moment, and when it happens, employees start to view a company's value statement with a good deal of cynicism. It is in these opportunities that leaders can reinforce a company's culture. They should not be wasted.

THE EXPERT TRAP

Reputation, People, and the Need for Strategic Thinking

When I am getting ready to reason with a man, I spend one-third of my time thinking about myself and what I am going to say and two-thirds about him and what he is going to say.

—Abraham Lincoln[1]

We began our investigation of corporate reputation with a reference to the CEO's agenda. Reputation, we found, and people were the two items that matter most to CEOs. And so, it appears, the arc comes to a close. To manage reputation effectively, the people and the reputation management process need to be inextricably linked. Building and maintaining reputational equity requires people to make the right decisions in their day-to-day responsibilities. Reputation management is not the domain of specialists or experts. Successful companies will instead insist that their people think and act as stewards of the company's most important asset. But like any other management skill, corporate stewardship needs to be developed.

Acting as corporate steward does not mean only doing right by customers, employees, and suppliers. It requires the ability to *think strategically*. This implies, on the one hand, viewing reputational decisions not solely as PR issues, but as tightly connected to the company's strategy, its core competencies and values, and its distinctive position in the marketplace. On the other hand, it requires the ability to view even a familiar business decision from the point of view of people who are not specialists, but still may have strong opinions on an issue. More often than not, these opinions are not just driven by cool reason, but involve powerful emotions and passionate views of what is right or wrong behavior.

We have identified the key factors that will drive these attitudes, and executives must be aware of them even if they do not agree. This is far from easy, especially in the presence of hostile media coverage and pressure from activists and public officials. It requires a high degree of emotional fortitude and the ability to analyze a situation clinically in an emotionally charged environment. The Trust Radar proves its value in these situations. Simply being aware of the four factors of trust can prevent a defensive and reactive attitude.

A strategic mindset also requires *situational awareness*. Reputation is essentially public. It is driven by third parties who have their own agenda. Understanding and anticipating the motivations and capabilities of these actors is essential for situational awareness. The Reputational Terrain provides such an orientation, whether we need to manage an ongoing issue or we want to assess the reputational risk associated with an important business decision. But reputational challenges are not simply the consequence of wrong decisions, accidents, or bad luck; they frequently are created by activists, interest groups, and public actors with the goal of forcing changes in business practices through "private politics." Activists are competitors for the company's reputation. They need to be treated as seriously as competitors in the marketplace.

The last component of a strategic mindset is to avoid the *expert trap*. Becoming an expert means learning to see the world in a particular way. This process is usually long and arduous, but at the end, experts are able to retrieve complex configurations from memory quickly and apply them reliably to new situations.[2] A doctor learns to identify symptoms and decide on a diagnosis, a poker player learns to identify "tells" of opponents that provide critical information on the strength of their hand, and a music enthusiast can pick a pianist from dozens of recordings of the same piece. Acquiring and using expertise in a coordinated fashion is, of course, tremendously valuable and is at the root of the efficient organization of business processes. But in the context of reputational challenges, it can lead us astray.

Do you remember Elián Gonzalez? Elián Gonzalez was a young boy from Cuba who made headlines in the winter of 1999 when he was miraculously rescued from the open sea by fishermen when a vessel that contained refugees from Cuba, including his mother, sank off the coast of Miami. Elián was brought to relatives in Miami, members of the city's large Cuban exile community. The situation became a major controversy when Elián's Miami relatives insisted that the boy should remain in the United States, while his father urged his return to Cuba. (Elián's mother had left Cuba without his father's knowledge or permission.) The U.S. government took the position that the boy had to return to his father in Cuba, and, after various asylum petitions were dismissed by the courts, ordered Elián's Miami relatives to send the boy back. Things took a dramatic turn when the family refused. After a standoff that lasted for days, a SWAT team of immigration agents entered the family residence and seized the boy. Elián was later returned to his father's custody in Cuba, where he still lives today.[3]

You may now remember this story. If you do, what comes to mind? Most likely you will recall the Pulitzer Prize–winning photo taken by an Associated Press journalist who was present in the house during the raid. It shows a member of the SWAT team pointing a gun at the boy, who is hiding in a closet.[4] Whenever I show this picture to a typical class of executives, there is a tangible emotional tension in the auditorium; people react immediately and viscerally. But things are very different when I teach a class of experts, such as security managers, many of whom have an FBI or a Secret Service background. Invariably a hand will go up and someone will point out that the boy was perfectly safe. After all, the agent's finger was not on the trigger! And indeed, on close inspection, we can all see that the agent had his index finger stretched out next to the trigger, a perfect example of how to perform expertly under such difficult circumstances.

I cannot think of a better example of the expert trap. While laypeople will be emotionally affected by the terror of a young boy, the expert will nod approvingly at the skill and composure of the agent. Most observers will react to this expert assessment with bewilderment. How can the expert not be affected by this terrifying image? Of course, this ability to focus on a particular, well-defined aspect of the situation is exactly what makes the expert an expert. The expert simply sees the world differently. Yet, in the context of reputation management, this expertise can become a trap. A supervisor who talks about a "job well done" may look monstrous and callous. The critical skill consists of the ability to set aside one's expertise and see the situation from the point of view of laypeople in a heightened emotional state.

This may seem easy in an industry (here, law enforcement) that most of us will not be familiar with, but we all are experts at something. When a company collapses as a result of an earnings restatement, a trained accountant may focus on the fact that no accounting rules were violated, while everybody else will be affected by images of crying employees leaving their office for the last time. A safety engineer will point to his company's industry-leading safety standards and may be bewildered when the media focus on one specific victim. A loan officer may view missed mortgage payments as lost revenue, while the borrower may experience them as the fear of losing the family home.

Reputation management is not a corporate function, but a capability. It requires the right mindset integrated with the company's strategy, guided by its culture and values, and supported by carefully designed governance and intelligence processes. Developing this capability is as demanding and as challenging as developing customer focus or the ability to execute. I hope this book has helped you to take a first step toward accomplishing this goal.

NOTES

PREFACE

1 Volcker's statement was widely covered in the press. Here is the original source: http://www.forbes.com/2009/02/20/volcker-banks-regulations-intelligent-investing_volcker.html (accessed January 24, 2011).

2 As examples, consider "Concerns about Risks Confronting Boards: First Annual Board of Directors Survey," Eisner LLP, May 2010, http://www.eisnerllp.com/Nep/Press Releases.aspx?id=5045 (accessed January 24, 2011); "Risk Reputation Report," *The Economist* (Economist Intelligence Unit, December 2005); Matteo Tonnelo, "Reputation Risk: A Corporate Governance Perspective," The Conference Board Research Report No. R-1412-07-WG, December 2007; and Deloitte, "Risk Intelligent Governance: A Practical Guide for Boards," Risk Intelligence Series Issue No. 16, http://www.deloitte.com/assets/Dcom-Global/Local%20Assets/Documents/dtt_riskintelligentgovernance.pdf (accessed January 24, 2011).

3 Unless otherwise noted, all stock prices in this book are from Yahoo! Finance, http://finance.yahoo.com/ (accessed January 24, 2011).

4 Company valuations are drawn from http://www.hoovers.com (accessed January 24, 2011).

5 The Harris Interactive surveys are available at http://www.harrisinteractive.com/vault/Harris-Interactive-Poll-Research-Industry-Regulation-2009-12.pdf (accessed January 24, 2011).

6 An early book on the increased importance of transparency is Don Tapscott and David Ticoll, *The Naked Corporation: How the Age of Transparency Will Revolutionize Business* (New York: Simon & Schuster, 2003).

7 The term is a reference to Thomas Friedman, *The World Is Flat: A Brief History of the Twenty-First Century* (New York: Farrar, Straus & Giroux, 2005).

8 For details on the Shell and Nike campaigns, see John Hendry, Kate Mellor, Zain Hak, Funmi Ade-Ajayi, Waldir Vieira, and Yuan Zou, "Shell in Nigeria," Cambridge Judge Business School Case 300-070-1, 2000; Ike Okonta and Oronto Douglas, *Where Vultures Feast: Shell, Human Rights, and Oil* (San Francisco: Sierra Club Books, 2003); Debora L. Spar and Jennifer Burns, "Hitting the Wall: Nike and International Labor Practices," Harvard Business School Case 700047-PDF-ENG, 2000; and Richard M. Locke, "The Promise and Perils of Globalization: The Case of Nike," MIT-IPC-02-007 (working paper, Massachusetts Institute of Technology, 2002).

9 The original papers introducing the concept of private politics are David P. Baron, "Private Politics," *Journal of Economics & Management Strategy* 12, no. 1 (2003): 31–66; David P. Baron and Daniel Diermeier, "Strategic Activism and Non-market Strategy," *Journal of Economics & Management Strategy* 16, no. 3 (2007): 599–634. For an overview see Daniel Diermeier, "Private Politics: A Research Agenda," *Political Economist* 14, no. 2 (2007): 1–9.

10 There is extensive literature on the consequences of shifting values, especially among younger generations. For example, see Lynn Sharp Paine, *Value Shift: Why Companies Must Merge Social and Financial Imperatives to Achieve Superior Performance* (New York: McGraw-Hill, 2003); and Dov Seidman, *How: Why How We Do Anything Means Everything . . . in Business (and in Life)* (Hoboken, N.J.: John Wiley & Sons, 2007). For a more skeptical perspective, see David Vogel, *The Market for Virtue: The Potential and Limits of Corporate Social Responsibility* (Washington, D.C.: The Brookings Institution, 2006).

11 The following are good introductions to the concept of customer focus: Ranjay Gulati and James B. Oldroyd, "The Quest for Customer Focus," *Harvard Business Review* 83, no. 4 (2005): 92–101; and Alice M. Tybout and Tim Calkins, ed., *Kellogg on Branding* (Hoboken, N.J.: John Wiley & Sons, 2005). For overviews on Starbucks's approach to customer focus, see Richard Honack and Sachin Waikar, "Growing Big while Staying Small: Starbucks Harvests International Growth," Harvard Business School Case KEL447-PDF-ENG, 2009; and Youngme Moon and John A. Quelch, "Starbucks: Delivering Customer Service," Harvard Business School Case 504016-PDF-ENG, 2003. For details on Caterpillar, see Thomas Knecht, Ralf Leszinski, and Felix A. Weber, "Making Profits after the Sale," *McKinsey Quarterly* 4 (1993): 79–86.

12 For some of the psychological factors shaping customer trust, see Devon Johnson and Kent Grayson, "Cognitive and Affective Trust in Service Relationships," *Journal of Business Research* 58, no. 4 (2005): 500–507; Robert M. Morgan and Shelby D. Hunt, "The Commitment-Trust Theory of Relationship Marketing," *Journal of Marketing* 58, no. 3 (1994): 20–38; and Elena Delgado-Ballester and Jose Luis Munuera-Aleman, "Brand Trust in the Context of Consumer Loyalty," *European Journal of Marketing* 35, no. 11-12 (2001): 1238–1258. For a study of customer trust in online environments, see Sherrie Xiao Komiak and Izak Benbasat, "Understanding Customer Trust in Agent-Mediated Electronic Commerce, Web-Mediated Electronic Commerce, and Traditional Commerce," *International Technology and Management* 5, no. 1-2 (2004): 181–207.

13 For details on the Edelman Trust Barometer, see http://www.edelman.com/trust/2010, especially page 6 of the Executive Summary (accessed January 24, 2011).

INTRODUCTION

1 John Maynard Keynes, *The General Theory of Employment, Interest, and Money* (London: Macmillan, 2007 [1936]).

2 Jim Collins, *Good to Great: Why Some Companies Make the Leap . . . and Others Don't* (New York: HarperCollins, 2001); and Larry Bossidy, Ram Charan, and Charles Burck, *Execution: The Discipline of Getting Things Done* (New York: Crown Business, 2002).

3 There is extensive literature in economics and game theory that treats reputation as a bilateral relationship. The classic example is a chain of stores that is protecting its markets against an entrant to obtain a reputation for toughness. See, for example, George

J. Mailath and Larry Samuelson, *Repeated Games and Reputations: Long-Run Relation-ships* (New York: Oxford University Press, 2006). Our approach here is quite different and critically involves public perception. For a pioneering work in this direction, see Charles J. Fombrun, *Reputation: Realizing Value from the Corporate Image* (Watertown, Mass.: Harvard Business School Press, 1996).

4 The company has used the name "Walmart" since 2008 instead of the original "Wal-Mart." We use "Wal-Mart" to ensure consistency with quotes and references.

5 For an example, see the recent study on the history of the Food and Drug Administra-tion (FDA): Daniel Carpenter, *Reputation and Power: Organizational Image and Pharma-ceutical Regulation at the FDA* (Princeton, N.J.: Princeton University Press, 2010).

CHAPTER 1

1 Lloyd Blankfein's quote is taken from an interview in Shaji Vikraman and Santosh Nair, "India Is a Very Good Investment: Lloyd Blankfein, CEO, Goldman Sachs," *Economic Times*, May 21, 2010.

2 "RC2 Corp. Recalls Various Thomas & Friends Wooden Railway Toys Due to Lead Poisoning Hazard," RC2 Corporation press release, June 13, 2007, http://www.rc2. com/Press/2007/Release_TWR_recall_07.pdf (accessed January 24, 2011).

3 For details on the dangers of lead contamination and the regulatory context, see the U.S. Environmental Protection Agency, http://www.epa.gov/lead/pubs/leadinfo.htm (accessed January 24, 2011).

4 For details on the Thomas the Tank Engine case, see Angel Jennings, "Thomas the Tank Engine Toys Recalled Because of Lead Paint," *New York Times*, June 15, 2007; David Barboza and Louise Story, "RC2's Train Wreck," *New York Times*, June 19, 2007; and RC2 Corporation press release, February 18, 2010, "RC2 Reports 2009 Fourth Quar-ter and Full Year Results and Provides Preliminary Outlook for 2010," http://www. rc2.com/investor/financial/2009/Q4_2009_Earnings_Release_Final.pdf (accessed January 25, 2011).

5 RC2 was not alone in its toy recalls. In 2007, the Consumer Product Safety Commis-sion issued 276 toy recalls, up from 152 the previous year. Other companies affected included Mattel, which had been an industry pioneer for over 50 years as one of the first toy companies to produce its products in Asia. In contrast to RC2 and most other toy companies, Mattel owned the factories in China where its products were made. In the summer of 2007, Mattel issued three separate recalls in just four weeks. In all, the company recalled more than 20 million toys because of lead-based paint or design flaws that made them potentially dangerous for children. The majority of the recalls (95 percent) involved toys manufactured in China, and many (52 percent) were related specifically to the presence of high concentrations of lead in paint. This rash of recalls ultimately led to the passage of new federal legislation, the Consumer Product Safety Improvement Act of 2008. The act dropped the tolerance level for surface lead (as in paint) from 600 parts per million to under 90 parts per million by August 2009. For details, see Seth M. Freedman, Melissa Schettini Kearney, and Mara Lederman, "Prod-uct Recalls, Imperfect Information, and Spillover Effects: Lessons from the Consumer Response to the 2007 Toy Recalls," NBER Working Paper No. 15183, 2009. On the Mattel recall, see David Baron, "Mattel: Crisis Management or Management Crisis,"

Stanford Business School Case P-59, 2008; and Jiangyong Lu, Tao Zhigang, Yu LinHui, and Grace Loo, "Mattel's Strategy after Its Recall of Products Made in China," Harvard Business School Case HKU810-PDF-ENG, 2009.

6   For details on the Tylenol case, see Stephen A. Greyser, "Johnson & Johnson: The Tylenol Tragedy," Harvard Business School Case 583043-PDF-ENG, 1982. More than 28 years later the Tylenol case remains unsolved.

7   As an example, consider the following definition from a typical crisis management textbook: "A crisis is an event or activity with the potential to negatively affect the reputation or credibility of a business." Jeffrey Caponigro, *The Crisis Counselor: A Step-by-Step Guide to Managing a Business Crisis* (New York: McGraw-Hill, 2000). See also Eric Dezenhall and John Weber, *Damage Control: Why Everything You Thought You Knew about Crisis Management Is Wrong* (New York: Portfolio Trade, 2007).

8   According to Merriam-Webster's Online Dictionary, the original meaning of the word *crisis* came from Latin, which in turn took it from the Greek *krisis,* which literally translates to "decision" from *krinein,* meaning "to decide." Definitions of crisis include: "1 a: the turning point for better or worse in an acute disease or fever; b: a paroxysmal attack of pain, distress, or disordered function; c: an emotionally significant event or radical change of status in a person's life <a midlife *crisis*>; 2: the decisive moment (as in a literary plot); 3 a: an unstable or crucial time or state of affairs in which a decisive change is impending; *especially* one with the distinct possibility of a highly undesirable outcome <a financial *crisis*>; b: a situation that has reached a critical phase <the environmental *crisis*>," http://www.merriam-webster.com (accessed January 25, 2011).

9   Johnson & Johnson has ranked in the top ten in *Fortune*'s annual most admired company ranking in each of the last five years, including fourth place in 2010, http://money.cnn.com/magazines/fortune/mostadmired/2010/ (accessed January 25, 2011).

10 The details on over-the-counter medications are from Michael Johnsen, "Top OTC Brands Ranked by 2003 Sales Dollars," *Drug Store News,* May 17, 2004, http://findarticles.com/p/articles/mi_m3374/is_7_26/ai_n6041136/ (accessed January 25, 2011).

11 For details on the over-the-counter sleep aid market, see "Sleep Aid Products in the U.S. Market: Non-Prescription OTC, Natural and Alternative Remedies," *Packaged Facts,* December 2008.

12 Steven Tenn and John M. Yun, "The Success of Divestitures in Merger Enforcement: Evidence from the J&J–Pfizer Transaction," FTC Working Paper No. 296, April 2009.

13 To convince yourself of the critical importance of whether an issue is capturing broad attention, compare the tampering case with ongoing concerns about Tylenol overdoses. Every year, there are approximately 56,000 emergency-room visits related to an overdose of acetaminophen, the active ingredient in Tylenol, leading to over 400 annual fatalities on average. See http://www.fda.gov/downloads/AdvisoryCommittees/CommitteesMeetingMaterials/Drugs/DrugSafetyandRiskManagementAdvisoryCommittee/UCM164897.pdf (accessed January 25, 2011).

14 For details on the psychology of brand perception, see, for example, Gerald Zaltman, *How Customers Think: Essential Insights into the Mind of the Market* (Cambridge, Mass: Harvard Business Press, 2003). For a popular overview, see Malcolm Gladwell, *Blink: The Power of Thinking without Thinking* (Boston, Mass.: Back Bay Books, 2007).

15 For details on the *Exxon Valdez* oil spill, see Samuel K. Skinner and William K. Reilly, "The *Exxon Valdez* Oil Spill: A Report to the President," National Response Team, May 1989; and "Oil Spill Case Histories: 1967–1991," National Oceanic and Atmospheric Administration's Hazardous Materials Response and Assessment Division Report No. HMRAD 92-11, September 1992.

16 Exxon CEO Lawrence Rawls's communication strategy has received a great deal of criticism. For details, see Stephen Greyser and Nancy Langford, "Exxon: Communications after Valdez," Harvard Business School Case 593014-PDF-ENG, 1992; Armin Töpfer, *Plötzliche Unternehmenskrisen. Gefahr oder Chance?* [in German] (Neuwied, Germany: Luchterhand, 1999); and Lawrence Susskind and Patrick Field, *Dealing with an Angry Public: The Mutual Gains Approach to Resolving Disputes* (New York: Free Press, 1996).

17 The size and scope of the disaster resulted in the passing of the Oil Pollution Act of 1990, which, among other provisions, increased liability limits and penalties.

18 For details on the court proceedings, see *Exxon v. Baker*, No. 07-219 (Supreme Court of the United States of America 2008-06-25), http://www.supremecourt.gov/opinions/07pdf/07-219.pdf (accessed January 25, 2011); and David G. Savage, "Justices Slash *Exxon Valdez* Verdict," *Los Angeles Times*, June 26, 2008. The cleanup effort itself was estimated to cost approximately $3.8 billion, with an additional $5.2 billion from various lawsuits claiming compensatory and punitive damages. After 15 years of appeals, the $5 billion in punitive damages was reduced to $507 million, bringing the total cost of the spill for Exxon roughly $4.3 billion.

19 Jad Mouawad, "For BP, a History of Spills and Safety Lapses," *New York Times*, May 8, 2010.

20 For details on Exxon's safety record after the *Exxon Valdez* accident, see Exxon Mobil Corporation, "Archive of Selected Awards in Corporate Citizenship," http://www.exxonmobil.com/corporate/community_ccr_awards_archive.aspx (accessed January 25, 2011); and Mouawad, "For BP, a History of Spills."

21 For details on the Stanford protests, see Julie Sevrens Lyons, "Stanford Poised to Buck Exxon," *San Jose Mercury News*, May 22, 2007.

22 See Michael Erman, "Exxon Mobil CEO: Climate Policy Would Be Prudent," Reuters, February 13, 2007.

23 For detailed accounts on BP and the Deepwater Horizon catastrophe see the National Commission on the BP Deepwater Horizon Oil Spill and Offshore Drilling, *Deep Water: The Gulf Oil Disaster and the Future of Offshore Drilling—Final Report*, January 11, 2011, http://www.oilspillcommission.gov/ (accessed January 29, 2011); David Barstow, David Rohde, Stephanie Saul, "Deepwater Horizon's Final Hours," *New York Times*, December 25, 2010; Peter Elkind and David Whitford with Doris Burke, "BP: 'An Accident Waiting to Happen,'" *Fortune*, January 24, 2011; Loren C. Steffy, *Drowning in Oil: BP and the Reckless Pursuit of Profit* (New York: McGraw-Hill, 2010); Stanley Reed and Alison Fitzgerald, *In Too Deep: BP and the Drilling Race That Took It Down* (Hoboken, N.J.: Bloomberg Press, 2011); and William Freudenburg and Robert Gramling, *Blowout in the Gulf: The BP Oil Spill Disaster and the Future of Energy in America* (Cambridge, Mass.: MIT Press, 2010). For an assessment of the company's communication approach, see Jad Mouawad and Clifford Krauss, "Another Torrent

BP Works to Stem: Its C.E.O.," *New York Times*, June 3, 2010. BP's internal report can be found at BP, "Deepwater Horizon Accident Investigation Report," September 8, 2010, http://www.bp.com/liveassets/bp_internet/globalbp/globalbp_uk_english/incident_response/STAGING/local_assets/downloads_pdfs/Deepwater_Horizon_Accident_Investigation_Report.pdf (accessed January 30, 2011).

24 For an overview on Johnson & Johnson's *annus horribilis*, see Mina Kimes, "Why J&J's Headache Won't Go Away," *Fortune*, August 19, 2010; and Natasha Singer and Reed Abelson, "Can Johnson & Johnson Get Its Act Together?" *New York Times*, January 15, 2011.

25 For details on the Pentium crisis, see Stephen A. Greyser and Norman Klein, "Intel's Pentium: When the Chips Are Down (A)," Harvard Business School Case 595058-PDF-ENG, 1994; V. G. Narayanan and James A. Evans, "Intel Pentium Chip Controversy (A)," Harvard Business School Case 196091-PDF-ENG, 1995; Thomas R. Nicely, "Pentium FDIV Flaw FAQ," http://www.trnicely.net/pentbug/pentbug.html (accessed January 25, 2011); "Intel Adopts Upon-Request Replacement Policy on Pentium Processors with Floating Point Flaw, Will Take Q4 Charge against Earnings," *Business Wire*, December 20, 1994; Cindy Williams, "Intel's Pentium Chip Crisis: An Ethical Analysis," *IEEE Transactions on Professional Communication* 40, no. 1 (1997); Mukul Pandya, Robbie Shell, Susan Warner, Sandeep Junnarkar, and Jeffrey Brown, "Best of the Best: Inside Andy Grove's Leadership at Intel," in *Nightly Business Report Presents Lasting Leadership: What You Can Learn From the Top 25 Business People of Our Times* (Upper Saddle River, N.J.: Pearson Prentice Hall, 2006); and "Intel Inside Program: Anatomy of a Brand Campaign," Intel Corporation, http://www.intel.com/pressroom/intel_inside.htm (accessed January 25, 2011).

26 Nicely, "Pentium FDIV Flaw FAQ."

27 John Markoff, "Company News: Flaw Undermines Accuracy of Pentium Chips," *New York Times*, November 24, 1994.

28 John Markoff, "The Chip on Intel's Shoulder," *New York Times*, December 18, 1994.

29 Leslie Helm, "Intel to Offer Replacements for Flawed Chip," *Los Angeles Times*, December 21, 1994.

30 Trust, defined as a willingness to rely on an exchange partner in whom one has confidence, reflects the vulnerability and uncertainty that trustors are willing to accept with the expectation of future behavior (e.g., cooperation, reciprocation) or reliability (e.g., predictability). Factors that typically influence trust include previous experience and predictability of future behavior, emotions with both positive or negative valence, perceived honesty or truthfulness, goal congruence, the ability to interpret others' true intentions, as well as cues of genetic relatedness such as facial resemblance. See Christine Moorman, Rohit Deshpande, and Gerald Zaltman, "Factors Affecting Trust in Market Research Relationships," *Journal of Marketing* 57, no. 1 (1993): 81–101; Lisa M. DeBruine, "Facial Resemblance Enhances Trust," *Proceedings of the Royal Society* 269 (2002): 1307–1312; Jennifer R. Dunn and Maurice E. Schweitzer, "Feeling and Believing: The Influence of Emotion on Trust," *Journal of Social and Personality Psychology* 88, no. 5 (2005): 736–748; and Spiros P. Gounaris, "Trust and Commitment Influences on Customer Retention: Insights from Business-to-Business Services," *Journal of Business Research* 58, no. 2 (2005): 126–140. For research in the area of risk perception, see

Richard G. Peters, Vincent T. Covello, and David B. McCallum, "The Determinants of Trust and Credibility in Environmental Risk Communication: An Empirical Study," *Risk Analysis* 17, no. 1 (1997): 43–54.

31 Sometimes there is also doubt about companies' competence. Examples include the performance of some of the major banks during the 2008–2009 financial crisis and BP's efforts to contain the May 2010 oil spill. Ironically, while BP got low marks on expertise and commitment (especially in its efforts to shift responsibility to its contractor Transocean), it did better on transparency, especially through the use of social media and Internet resources. See, for example, Christopher Beam, "Oil Slick: How BP Is Handling Its P.R. Disaster," Slate.com, May 5, 2010, http://www.slate.com/id/2253099/ (accessed January 25, 2011).

32 For evidence, see Jennifer Aaker, Kathleen D. Vohs, and Cassie Mogilner, "Nonprofits Are Seen as Warm and For-Profits as Competent: Firm Stereotypes Matter," *Journal of Consumer Research* 37, no. 2 (2010): 224–237.

33 For details on the criticism of the Red Cross after Katrina, see Shaila Dewan and Stephanie Strom, "Red Cross Faces Criticism over Aid Program for Hurricane Victims," *New York Times*, August 10, 2007.

34 For details on Sir Richard Branson's response see "It Is a Very Sad Day—Branson," BBC News, February 24, 2007.

35 For details on the Toyota recalls, see the press releases from Toyota USA at http://pressroom.toyota.com/pr/tms/toyota/toyota-consumer-safety-advisory-102572.aspx (accessed January 25, 2011). For an assessment see Hiroko Tabuchi and Bill Vlasic, "Toyota's Top Executive under Rising Pressure," *New York Times*, February 5, 2010. To investigate the unintended acceleration problem, the National Highway Traffic Safety Administration (NHTSA) enlisted the National Aeronautics and Space Administration (NASA) to conduct a 10-month study of potential electronics-based causes for unintended acceleration in Toyota vehicles. NASA engineers found no electronic flaws in Toyota vehicles capable of causing high-speed unintended acceleration incidents. According to the study, released on February 8, 2011, the two mechanical safety defects identified a year earlier ("sticking" accelerator pedals and entrapment of accelerator pedals by floor mats) remain the only known causes for unintended acceleration incidents. The study can be found at http://www.nhtsa.gov/UA (accessed February 15, 2011).

36 Empathy is thought to be very informative of future prosocial behaviors, in part because it is involuntary and difficult to fake. See Robert H. Frank, *Passions within Reason: The Strategic Role of the Emotions* (New York: W.W. Norton, 1988); C. Daniel Batson, "Altruism and Prosocial Behavior," in *Handbook of Social Psychology*, 4th ed., vol. 2, ed. Daniel T. Gilbert, Susan T. Fiske, and Gardner Lindzey (New York: McGraw Hill, 1998), 282–315; Nancy Eisenberg, "Empathy and Sympathy," in *Handbook of Emotions*, 2nd ed., ed. Michael Lewis and Jeannette M. Haviland-Jones (New York: Guilford Press, 2000), 677–693; and Jonathan Haidt, "The Emotional Dog and Its Rational Tail: A Social Intuitionist Approach to Moral Judgment," *Psychological Review* 108, no. 4 (2001): 814–834.

37 See Toyota's press release "Toyota Announces Comprehensive Plan to Fix Accelerator Pedals on Recalled Vehicles and Ensure Customer Safety," February 1, 2010, at http://

pressroom.toyota.com/pr/tms/toyota/toyota-announces-comprehensive-153311.aspx (accessed January 25, 2011).

38 See Nick Bunkley, "In Detroit, Toyota Vows to Earn Trust," *New York Times*, January 10, 2011.

39 For details on the Goldman Sachs case, see U.S. Securities and Exchange Commission, "SEC Charges Goldman Sachs with Fraud in Structuring and Marketing of CDO Tied to Subprime Mortgages," 2010-59, April 16, 2010, http://www.sec.gov/news/press/2010/2010-59.htm (accessed January 25, 2011); Christine Harper, Lorraine Woellert, and Ryan J. Donmoyer, "Goldman Sachs's Tourre 'Categorically' Denies SEC's Claims," Bloomberg.com, April 27, 2010; "Senate Turns Up Heat on Goldman Sachs Executives," CBS News, April 27, 2010; and Jacob Goldstein, "Blankfein Says He Was 'Humbled' by Senate Hearing," *NPR*, April 29, 2010, http://www.npr.org/blogs/money/2010/04/blankfein_says_he_was_humbled.html (accessed January 25, 2011).

40 Goldstein, "Blankfein Says He Was 'Humbled.'"

41 For more details on the settlement and Goldman Sachs's response, see U.S. Securities and Exchange Commission, "Goldman Sachs to Pay Record $550 Million to Settle SEC Charges Related to Subprime Mortgage CDO," 2010-123, July 15, 2010, http://www.sec.gov/news/press/2010/2010-123.htm (accessed January 25, 2011); Justin Baer and Francesco Guerrera, "Goldman Plans to Overhaul Practices," *Financial Times*, May 2, 2010; Francesco Guerrera, Henny Sender, and Justin Baer, "Goldman Sachs Settles with SEC," *Financial Times*, July 15, 2010; Nelson D. Schwartz, "Earnings and Revenue Decline at Goldman Sachs, Reflecting a Tough Stretch," *New York Times*, July 21, 2010; Jennifer Cummings, "Goldman Shares Jump on SEC Deal," *Wall Street Journal*, July 16, 2010; and Colin Barr, "Fear Trade Turns against Goldman," *Fortune*, July 20, 2010.

42 For details on the Goldman Sachs report, see Susanne Craig, "Goldman Sachs to Fine-Tune Its Practices," *New York Times*, January 10, 2011; Liz Rappaport, "Goldman Opens Up to Mollify Its Critics," *Wall Street Journal*, January 11, 2011; and Francesco Guerrera and Justin Baer, "Goldman Tries to Answer Its Critic," *Financial Times*, January 11, 2011.

43 Michael Powell, "In 9/11 Chaos, Giuliani Forged a Lasting Image," *New York Times*, September 21, 2007.

44 For additional details, see "Rudolph Giuliani: America's Mayor," *The Economist*, July 28, 2005; and Fred Siegel, *The Prince of the City: Giuliani, New York and the Genius of American Life* (San Francisco: Encounter Books, 2005).

45 President Bush's initial reaction to 9/11 has also been criticized, most polemically in Michael Moore's movie *Fahrenheit 9/11*.

46 Spencer S. Hsu and Susan B. Glasser, "FEMA Director Singled Out by Response Critics," *Washington Post*, September 6, 2005. For other assessments of the Katrina response, see Joe Allbaugh, "'Can I Quit Now?' FEMA Chief Wrote as Katrina Raged," CNN.com, November 4, 2005.

47 Bruce Alpert, "Bush Photo after Katrina Big Mistake, Ex-aide Says," *Times-Picayune*, May 29, 2008.

48 For details, see Eric L. Uhlmann, George Newman, Victoria L. Brescoll, Adam Galinsky, and Daniel Diermeier, "The Sounds of Silence: Corporate Crisis Communication and Its Effects on Consumers" (working paper, Kellogg School of Management, 2010).

49 For details on the Katrina emergency response, see Eric Lipton, Eric Schmitt, and Thom Shanker, "Political Issues Snarled Plans for Troop Aid," *New York Times*, September 9, 2005; Scott Shane and Thom Shanker, "When Storm Hit, National Guard Was Deluged Too," *New York Times*, September 28, 2005; and Manuel Roig-Franzia and Spencer Hsu, "Many Evacuated, but Thousands Still Waiting," *Washington Post*, September 4, 2005.

50 For more details, including quotes, see Daniel Diermeier and Justin Heinze, "Southwest Airlines Flight 1248 (A, B, C)," Kellogg School of Management Case 5-107-001(A, B, C); and National Transportation Safety Board Accident Report, "Runway Overrun and Collision, Southwest Airlines Flight 1248, Boeing 737-7H4," October 2, 2007, http://www.ntsb.gov/publictn/2007/AAR0706.pdf (accessed January 25, 2011).

51 On Southwest's financial performance, see Andy Serwer, "Southwest Airlines: The Hottest Thing in the Sky through Change at the Top, through 9/11, in a Lousy Industry, It Keeps Winning Most Admired Kudos. How?" *Fortune*, March 8, 2004.

52 John Schmeltzer, "Southwest Response Called Swift, Caring," *Chicago Tribune*, December 10, 2005.

53 "Southwest Airlines Reports December Traffic," Southwest Airlines press release, January 5, 2007, http://www.swamedia.com/releases/Southwest-Airlines-Reports-December-Traffic-6 (accessed January 25, 2011).

54 National Transportation Safety Board Accident Report, "Runway Overrun and Collision Southwest Airlines."

55 "BP CEO Takes Questions under Fire for Safety," *Good Morning America*, ABC News, May 3, 2010.

56 For more details, see Jim Efstathiou, Jr., "BP, Halliburton, Transocean Blame Each Other in Gulf Oil Spill," *Bloomberg Businessweek*, May 10, 2010; and Caren Bohan and Steve Gorman, "Obama Slams Oil Companies for Spill Blame Game," Reuters, May 14, 2010.

57 Tiger Woods's main sponsors lost 2 to 3 percent of their market value. His core sponsors (Nike, Pepsi Co. [Gatorade], and Electronic Arts) lost more than 4 percent. For details, see Christopher R. Knittel and Victor Stango, "Celebrity Endorsements, Firm Value and Reputation Risk: Evidence from the Tiger Woods Scandal" (working paper, University of California at Davis, August 25, 2010).

58 International Paper topped *Fortune*'s 2008 list of Corporate Social Responsibility. See "Most Admired Companies," *Fortune*, March 17, 2008. For a list of third-party environmental certifications, see "Third Party Certification—EMEA," International Paper, 2010, http://www.internationalpaper.com/POLAND/EN/Company/Sustainability/Certifications.html (accessed January 25, 2011).

59 For details on front-page coverage, see Michelle Wolfe, Amber E. Boydstun, and Frank R. Baumgartner, "Comparing the Topics of Front-Page and Full-Paper Stories in the *New York Times*," paper presented at the Midwest Political Science Association, Chicago, April 2–5, 2009.

60 The distribution of media coverage decays rapidly. If we double the window size to 16 hours, the total percentage increases only from 20 percent to 25 percent. See Jure Leskovec, Lars Backstrom, and Jon Kleinberg, "Meme-Tracking and the Dynamics of

the News Cycle," ACM SIGKDD International Conference on Knowledge Discovery and Data Mining, Paris, June 28–July 1, 2009.

61 Lack of awareness, however, does not preclude attitude formation. See Daniel M. Wegner and John A. Bargh, "Control and Automaticity in Social Life," in *Handbook of Social Psychology*, ed. Daniel T. Gilbert, Susan T. Fiske, and Gardner Lindzey (New York: McGraw-Hill, 1998), 446–496.

62 For an example of applying political strategies to corporate crises, see Eric Dezenhall and John Weber, *Damage Control: Why Everything You Know about Crisis Management Is Wrong* (New York: Portfolio Trade, 2007).

63 The former German Chancellor Helmut Kohl created a special term for waiting things out: *aussitzen*, literally, "to sit through" a potential crisis.

64 For more detail on Abu Ghraib, see Karen J. Greenberg and Joshua L. Dratel, ed., *The Torture Papers: The Road to Abu Ghraib* (Cambridge, U.K.: Cambridge University Press, 2005); and Seymour M. Hersh, *Chain of Command: The Road from 9/11 to Abu Ghraib* (New York: HarperCollins, 2004).

65 The company agreed in January 2005 to pay $850 million and to change its bid practices in a civil settlement with then New York Attorney General Elliot Spitzer. In the immediate aftermath of the crisis in October 2004, Marsh's stock price fell from $52 to $24. More than six years later it hovers around $26. In January 2011, the New York Attorney General's office dropped the last two criminal cases tied to the 2004 bid-rigging scandal after failing to win convictions of the remaining eight insurance executives indicted. See Michael Gormley, "Spitzer: Insurance Scheme Rigged Bids for Payoffs to Brokers," Associated Press Newswires, October 14, 2004; Rupal Parekh, "Bid-Rigging, Finite Re Probes Lead Insurers to Settlement Table: States Turn Attention to Sales of Annuities and Personal Lines," *Business Insurance*, January 1, 2007; and Jonathan Stempel, "NY Drops Last Marsh Bid-Rigging Criminal Cases," Reuters, January 14, 2011.

66 For details, see Philip E. Tetlock, Orie V. Kristel, S. Beth Elson, Melanie C. Green, and Jennifer S. Lerner, "The Psychology of the Unthinkable: Taboo Trade-Offs, Forbidden Base Rates and Heretical Counterfactuals," *Journal of Personality and Social Psychology* 78, no. 5 (2000): 853–870.

67 Among the widely quoted comments were "I think the environmental disaster is likely to have been very, very modest" (*Sky News*, May 18), and "The Gulf of Mexico is a very big ocean. The amount of volume of oil and dispersant we are putting into it is tiny in relation to the total water volume" (*The Guardian*, May 14). See also Jad Mouawad and Clifford Krauss, "Another Torrent BP Works to Stem: Its C.E.O.," *New York Times*, June 3, 2010.

68 For trust in various professions, see Lydia Saad, "Nurses Shine, Bankers Slump in Ethics Ratings," *Gallup News*, 2008, http://www.gallup.com/poll/112264/nurses-shine-while-bankers-slump-ethics-ratings.aspx (accessed January 25, 2011).

69 Research from social psychology has shown that individuals frequently overestimate themselves. One notable bias called illusory superiority (sometimes called the "better-than-average effect") describes the tendency for individuals to view themselves as better than average on various dimensions. For our discussion, the most important aspect is the tendency to overestimate one's popularity and likability. For more

details, see Mark D. Alicke, "Global Self-Evaluation as Determined by the Desirability and Controllability of Trait Adjectives," *Journal of Personality and Social Psychology* 49, no. 6 (1985): 1621–1630; Jonathon D. Brown, "Evaluations of Self and Others: Self-Enhancement Biases in Social Judgments," *Social Cognition* 4 (1986): 353–376; Ezra W. Zuckerman and John T. Jost, "What Makes You Think You're So Popular? Self Evaluation Maintenance and the Subjective Side of the 'Friendship Paradox,'" *Social Psychology Quarterly* 64, no. 3 (2001): 207–223; and Mark D. Alicke and Olesya Govorun, "The Better-Than-Average Effect," in *The Self in Social Judgment: Studies in Self and Identity*, ed. Mark D. Alicke, David A. Dunning, and Joachim I. Krueger (New York: Psychology Press, 2005), 85–106. For research on negativity bias, see Roy F. Baumeister, Ellen Bratslavsky, Catrin Finkenauer, and Kathleen D. Vohs, "Bad Is Stronger Than Good," *Review of General Psychology* 5, no. 4 (2001): 323–370; and Paul Rozin and Edward B. Royzman, "Negativity Bias, Negativity Dominance, and Contagion," *Personality and Social Psychology Review* 5, no. 4 (2001): 296–320.

70 The polling results are discussed in Karlyn Bowman, "Taking Stock of Business," *AEI Public Opinion Studies*, May 2010, http://www.aei.org/docLib/20100422-Business.pdf (accessed January 25, 2011).

71 Anxiety is one such stress factor. See Andrew Mathews and Bundy Mackintosh, "A Cognitive Model of Selective Processing in Anxiety," *Cognitive Therapy and Research* 22, no. 6 (1998): 539–560. Another example is sleep deprivation. See Yvonne Harrison and James A. Horne, "The Impact of Sleep Deprivation on Decision Making: A Review," *Journal of Experimental Psychology: Applied* 6, no. 3 (2000): 236–249.

72 On team performance during times of stress, see Janice R. Kelly and Timothy J. Loving, "Time Pressure and Group Performance: Exploring Underlying Processes in the Attentional Focus Model," *Journal of Experimental Social Psychology* 40, no. 2 (2004): 185–198.

73 For a criticism of the widespread belief that apologies increase liability, see Ameeta Patel and Lamar Reinsch, "Companies Can Apologize: Corporate Apologies and Legal Liability," *Business Communication Quarterly* 66, no. 1 (2003): 9–25.

74 For the literature on medical malpractice, see Jeffrey Allen and Alice Burkin, "How Plaintiffs' Lawyers Pick Their Targets," *Medical Economics* 77, no. 18 (2000): 103–104; Wendy Levinson, Debra L. Roter, John P. Mullooly, Valerie T. Dull, Richard M. Frankel, "Physician-Patient Communication: The Relationship with Malpractice Claims among Primary Care Physicians and Surgeons," *Journal of the American Medical Association* 277, no. 7 (1997): 553–559; and Rachel Gotbaum, "Practice of Hospital Apologies Is Gaining Ground," NPR, October 6, 2007.

75 The company released information indicating that approximately 12,000 Toad vehicles were to be recalled and estimated that 2,000 of those were sent to June recall participants. For additional details, see RC2 recalls page, http://recalls.rc2.com/recalls_Wood_0607.html (accessed January 25, 2011). For assessments, see David Leonhardt, "Lessons Even Thomas Could Learn," *New York Times*, October 24, 2007; and Michael Watkins, "Engine of Destruction: Lessons from the Thomas the Tank Engine Debacle," *Harvard Business Review*, June 22, 2007, http://blogs.hbr.org/watkins/2007/06/engine_of_destruction_lessons_1.html (accessed January 25, 2011).

76 According to RC2's Web site, the Multi-Check Safety System includes the following: "Increased scope and frequency of testing both incoming materials and finished products, including testing of finished products from every production run, a tougher certification program for contract manufacturers and paint suppliers, including evidence that toy safety standards and quality control procedures are in place and operate effectively. Mandatory paint control procedures for contract manufacturers, including certified independent lab test results of every batch of wet paint before the paint is released for production, and increased random inspections and audits of both manufacturers and their suppliers, including semi-annual audits and quarterly random inspections for key suppliers. Zero tolerance for compromise on RC2 specifications reinforced by mandatory vendor compliance seminars and signed agreements." http://recalls.rc2. com/recalls_Wood_0907_multiStep.html (accessed January 25, 2011).

77 For details on the license, see Lorene Yue, "Licensing Deal Threatens RC2's Thomas Sales," *Chicago Business*, January 5, 2009; and Miriam Gottfried, "Mattel, Like Barbie, Is Getting a Makeover," *Barron's*, May 27, 2010.

CHAPTER 2

1 The introductory quote is from "The Late Show with David Letterman," CBS Television, May 5, 2010.

2 The case of the A-Class is comprehensively documented and analyzed in Armin Töpfer, *Die A-Klasse* [in German] (Neuwied, Germany: Luchterhand, 1999). See also Daniel Diermeier and Astrid Marechal, "Mercedes and the Moose Test (A) (B)," Harvard Business School Cases KEL048-PDF-ENG and KEL049-PDF-ENG. All quotes of Mercedes executives are from these sources. The translations from the original German are my own.

3 There is some ambiguity over the exact name of the test. The German term is *Elch* Test, but this is what language teachers call a "false friend," as the German word *Elch* does not refer to what Americans call elk. In short, what Americans call moose are *Alces alces*, identified by their rounded palmate antlers and bulbous noses. *Alces alces* are indigenous to Canada and the United States, and also to northern Europe (Sweden and Norway) and Russia. Europeans, however, call these animals elk, or *Elch* in German. What Americans refer to as elk are *Cervus canadensis*; they have more pointed antlers than moose and are generally smaller. This species does not exist in Europe, but a commonly used term is *wapiti*. In addition, red deer (*Rotwild* in German) can be found in large numbers across Europe. These look quite similar to American elk, but are a different species (*Cervus elaphus*).

4 Moose accidents are a serious traffic hazard in the northern United States, Canada, and Scandinavia. The Alaska Moose Federation reported an average of 142 moose accidents each year over a ten-year span, with an average cost of $8,355 per collision. In the northern U.S. state of Maine, moose accidents make up 15 percent of animal crashes, but account for 47 percent of the economic damage from animal-vehicle collisions. Swedish officials report roughly 4,500 moose-related accidents each year, with 10 to 15 fatalities. A male moose weighs, on average, 900 to 1,600 pounds and a female 600 to 800, and both are roughly six feet high from the ground to the shoulder. This means that the animal's abdomen is usually above a typical car hood, making moose

accidents particularly dangerous. Their dark coats do not reflect car lights, and their eyes are typically too high to catch light. For more details, see "Moose Kills 2006," Alaska Moose Federation, http://www.growmoremoose.org/10yearmoosekillstats.asp (accessed January 26, 2011); "The Maine Department of Transportation's Large Animal Brochure," Maine Department of Transportation, http://www.maine.gov/mdot/safety/documents/pdf/MaineDOTLgAnimalBroch2010.pdf (accessed January 26, 2011); Andreas Seiler, "Predicting Locations of Moose-Vehicle Collisions in Sweden," *Journal of Applied Ecology* 42, no. 2 (2005): 371–382; and Theresa E. Rattey and Neil E. Turner, "Vehicle-Moose Accidents in Newfoundland," *Journal of Bone and Joint Surgery* 73, no. 10 (1991): 1487–1491.

5   The media have widely reported studies alleging a potential link between French fries and a variety of cancers. For details, see Karin B. Michels, Bernard A. Rosner, Wm. Cameron Chumlea, Graham A. Colditz, and Walter C. Willett, "Preschool Diet and Adult Risk of Breast Cancer," *International Journal of Cancer* 118, no. 3 (2006): 749–754; Christine Gorman, "Do French Fries Cause Cancer?" *Time*, May 6, 2002; and "California Wants Cancer Warnings on French Fries and Chips," *Medical News*, August 29, 2005.

6   For a study on peer-to-peer influence, see Shyam Gopinath, Jacquelyn Thomas, and Lakshman Krishnamurthi, "When Talk Matters—A Study of Online Word of Mouth and Firm Performance," (working paper, Kellogg School of Management, 2009).

7   David P. Baron, *Business and Its Environment*, 6th ed. (Upper Saddle River, N.J.: Prentice Hall, 2009).

8   In 2010, *The Economist* had 822,695 North American subscribers and 1,443,083 subscribers worldwide. The average personal income for North American subscribers was $172,000, average household income was $243,000, and average household net worth was $1.69 million. See "Worldwide Circulation," *The Economist*, http://ads.economist.com/the-economist/circulation/worldwide-circulation/ (accessed January 25, 2011).

9   *60 Minutes* has been recognized with numerous awards including a Lifetime Achievement Emmy. During the 2008–2009 season, the program was the most watched television news program in the United States, and the thirteenth most watched program overall. See "About Us: 60 Minutes," CBS News, 2009, http://www.cbsnews.com/stories/1998/07/08/60minutes/main13503.shtml (accessed January 25, 2011); and Chris Ariens, "*60 Minutes* Up Double Digits, Finishes as 13th Most-Watched Show, Best in Nine Years," Mediabistro.com, May 28, 2009.

10 For details, see Marcia Vickers, "The Fallen Financier," *BusinessWeek*, December 9, 2002.

11 In February 2007, passersby noticed a dozen or more rats on the floor of a New York City Taco Bell/KFC. A video of the rats scurrying along the floor and countertops circulated through the Internet and television talk shows, including NBC, CBS, CNN, and Fox. Yum! Brands, the parent company, temporarily closed the restaurants pending health inspections and blamed basement construction. For details, see Caleb Silver, Chris Kokenes, Mythili Rao, and Katy Byron, "Taco Bell Rats Are Stars for a Day," *CNNMoney.com*, February 23, 2007; and Associated Press, "N.Y.C. Admits Taco Bell Rat Infestation Ignored," April 10, 2007.

12 For more information on bariatric surgery, see the National Institutes of Health Weight-Control Information Network at http://win.niddk.nih.gov/publications/ gastric.htm#issurgfor (accessed January 25, 2011). For a general overview, see "The Second Annual HealthGrades Bariatric Surgery Trends in American Hospitals Study," *Health Grades*, July 2007.

13 See Henry Buchwald, "Bariatric Surgery for Morbid Obesity: Health Implications for Patients, Health Professionals, and Third-Party Payers," *Journal of the American College of Surgeons* 200, no. 4 (2005): 593-604; and Henry Buchwald, Yoav Avidor, Eugene Braun-wald, Michael D. Jensen, Walter Pories, Kyle Fahrbach, and Karen Schoelles, "Bariatric Surgery: A Systematic Review and Meta-Analysis," *Journal of the American Medical Asso-ciation* 292, no. 14 (2004): 1724-1737. Some studies report much higher mortality rates. For the case of Medicare patients, see, for example, David R. Flum, Leon Salem, Jo Ann Broeckel Elrod, E. Patchen Dellinger, Allen Cheadle, Leighton Chan, "Early Mortality among Medicare Beneficiaries Undergoing Bariatric Surgical Procedures," *Journal of the American Medical Association* 294, no. 15 (2005): 1903-1908. To assess the net health benefit for bariatric surgery, some studies compare mortality rates after surgery with mortality rates of an untreated population. See Ted D. Adams, Richard E. Gress, Sher-man C. Smith, R. Chad Halverson, Steven C. Simper, Wayne D. Rosamond, Michael J. LaMonte, Antoinette M. Stroup, and Steven C. Hunt, "Long-Term Mortality after Gastric Bypass Surgery," *New England Journal of Medicine* 357 (2007): 753–761.

14 "Bariatric Surgery Statistics," Bariatric Surgery.info, http://www.bariatric-surgery. info/statistics.htm (accessed January 26, 2011).

15 Michelle Tauber, "100 and Counting," *People*, November 18, 2002.

16 For details, see "Extremely Perfect: Bypass Mania," *48 Hours*, CBS, March 5, 2004.

17 Phil Galewitz, "Insurer Drops Gastric Bypass," *Palm Beach Post*, February 13, 2004.

18 For details, see Tania Branigan, "Chinese Figures Show Fivefold Rise in Babies Sick from Contaminated Milk," *Guardian*, December 2, 2008; David Barboza, "Death Sen-tences in Chinese Milk Case," *New York Times*, January 22, 2009; and Richard Spencer, "Starbucks and KFC Are Drawn into China's Tainted Milk Scandal," *Daily Telegraph*, September 19, 2008.

19 Frank Ahrens, "U.S. Outlaws Internet Gambling," *Washington Post*, October 14, 2006; and Matt Richtel, "Companies Aiding Internet Gambling Feel U.S. Pressure," *New York Times*, March 15, 2004.

20 Cassell Bryan-Low and Sven Grundberg, "Hackers Rise for WikiLeaks: Cyber Attack-ers Seek Revenge against Organizations That Have Tangled with Document-Leaking Site," *Wall Street Journal*, December 8, 2010.

21 David M. Herszenhorn, "Bill Passed in Senate Broadly Expands Oversight of Wall Street," *New York Times*, May 20, 2010.

22 Frank Rich, "Fight On, Goldman Sachs!" *New York Times*, April 24, 2010.

23 Terry Flew, *New Media: An Introduction*, 3rd ed. (South Melbourne, Australia: Oxford University Press, 2007); and Dennis Baron, *A Better Pencil: Readers, Writers, and the Digi-tal Revolution* (New York: Oxford University Press, 2009).

24 The consequences of making an event public are not always positive and can be subtle. The mass media, for example, can lead investors to coordinate beliefs that overvalue a

stock. The subtlety here is the nature of public, rather than private, information. If an event is public, not only do I know it, but so do you, and I know that you know and so forth. Such "common knowledge" events can have intriguing strategic consequences. See Robert J. Aumann, "Agreeing to Disagree," *Annals of Statistics* 4, no. 6 (1976): 1236–1239; and Stephen Morris and Hyun Song Shin, "The CNBC Effect: Welfare Effects of Public Information," Cowles Foundation Discussion Paper No. 1312, Yale University, 2001.

25 Chris Ayers, "Revenge Is Best Served Cold on YouTube," *The Times*, July 22, 2009.

26 Jure Leskovec, Lars Backstrom, and Jon Kleinberg, "Meme-Tracking and the Dynamics of the News Cycle," ACM SIGKDD International Conference on Knowledge Discovery and Data Mining (KDD), Paris, June 28–July 1, 2009.

27 Like the antilock braking system (ABS), which also had made its world premiere in a Mercedes, the ESP, developed by Mercedes supplier Bosch, was a safety milestone. The system helps to stabilize a car even in extreme driving situations. The ESP's secret is an intelligent on-board computer that constantly receives information about driving conditions through sensors. Whenever the danger of instability is detected, the system reacts by selectively braking the front and rear wheels and reducing or increasing engine torque, thus helping the car to stay on course.

28 The ads later received various awards from German advertising councils.

29 In his book on the A-Class, Armin Töpfer, a German management professor, analyzed the impact of the Moose Test and Mercedes's response on media sentiment about the brand and the key decision makers. The image profile of the A-Class in the media was quite high before the crisis, thanks to Mercedes's successful introduction strategy and the excellent reception of the car in the automotive press. After the failed Moose Test, the image of the car dropped suddenly into a negative region. In the following weeks, the situation worsened, with very negative coverage in the media. Once Mercedes announced the recall, the image of the A-Class went back to a neutral position. The positive results of the tests in Spain brought the A-Class image back into the positive region. This positive trend continued in early 1998 with the relaunch in February. The image dynamics of the Mercedes brand overall broadly paralleled those of the A-Class, with a similar decline after the Swedish Moose Test and recovery after the relaunch. At the personal level, the evaluation of CEO Jürgen E. Schrempp in the media fell from very positive to very negative after the announcement of the failed test. He was particularly criticized for his complete absence from the public eye during the initial days of the crisis. However, after the public announcement of the recall, his image quickly improved and reached a neutral level. Perceptions that he had taken charge and proved himself a strong leader helped Schrempp's image recover faster than that of the A-Class or the Mercedes brand as a whole. In contrast, the media image of Jürgen Hubbert, head of the car division, never fully recovered. The decision to suspend deliveries was perceived as being Schrempp's decision, not Hubbert's. For details, see Töpfer, *Die A-Klasse*.

30 In the original German, the phrase "*Wir werden aus der A-Klasse wieder eine JA-Klasse machen*" involves a play of words based on the German word *Ja*, meaning "yes."

31 The Moose Test also set the standard for Mercedes's competitors. A few years later Audi introduced a uniquely designed sports car, the Audi TT, into the German market. Soon after its launch, concerns were raised that the car would flip over at high speeds. While management believed that there was nothing wrong, it offered customers the option of adding the ESP and a spoiler to the TT. "20,000 Audi TT werden nachgerüstet" [in German], *Manager Magazin*, February 2, 2000.

CHAPTER 3

1 Paula Owen and Tony Rice, *Decommissioning the Brent Spar* (New York: Spon Press, 1999).

2 The account of the Brent Spar case is based on Daniel Diermeier, "Shell, Greenpeace, and Brent Spar," Harvard Business School Case P19-PDF-ENG. Reprinted in David Baron, *Management and Its Environment*, 6th ed. (Upper Saddle River, N.J.: Prentice Hall, 2009). Unless otherwise noted all quotes are taken from this source. The translations from the original German are my own. For additional details, see Owen and Rice, *Decommissioning the Brent Spar*; and Grant Jordan, *Shell, Greenpeace and Brent Spar* (New York: Palgrave MacMillan, 2001). For Shell's version, see "Brent Spar Dossier," Shell, http://www-static.shell.com/static/gbr/downloads/e_and_p/brent_spar_dos sier.pdf (accessed January 26, 2011). For Greenpeace's account, see "The Brent Spar," http://www.greenpeace.org/international/about/history/the-brent-spar/ (accessed January 26, 2011).

3 The reports can be found at "Brent Spar Abandonment Impact Hypothesis," Greenpeace, December 1994, http://archive.greenpeace.org/comms/brent/bshyp.html; and "Brent Spar Abandonment BPEO," Greenpeace, December 1994, http://archive.greenpeace.org/comms/brent/Bpe-0.html (accessed January 26, 2011).

4 "Post Note 65: Oil 'Rig' Disposal," Parliament Office of Science and Technology (United Kingdom), July 1995, http://www.parliament.uk/documents/post/pn065.pdf (accessed January 27, 2011).

5 "Greenpeace 1995 Annual Report," Greenpeace, 1995, http://www.greenpeace.org/international/Global/international/planet-2/report/2006/11/greenpeace-inter national-annua.pdf (accessed January 27, 2011).

6 Richard Miniter, "Are the Greens Losing Their Grip?" *Insight*, December 27, 1993.

7 Jon Entine, "Shell, Greenpeace and Brent Spar: The Politics of Dialogue," in *Case Studies in Business Ethics*, ed. Chris Megone and Simon J. Robinson (London: Routledge, 2002): 59–95; and Marlise Simons, "For Greenpeace Guerrillas, Environmentalism Is Again a Growth Industry," *New York Times*, July 8, 1995.

8 Euan G. Nisbet and C. Mary R. Fowler, "Is Metal Disposal Toxic to Deep Oceans?" *Nature* 375 (1995): 715.

9 Entine, "Shell, Greenpeace and Brent Spar," 74.

10 Bhushan Bahree, Kyle Pope, and Allanna Sullivan, "Giant Outsmarted: How Greenpeace Sank Shell's Plan to Dump Big Oil Rig in Atlantic," *Wall Street Journal*, July 7, 1995.

11 Terry Brighton, *Patton, Montgomery, Rommel: Masters of War* (New York: Crown Publishers, 2009).

12 For an overview on war gaming, see Thomas B. Allen, *War Games* (New York: Berkley Publishing Group, 1989).

13 For more on Greenpeace's self-image, see Greenpeace, http://www.greenpeace.org/international/en/about/ (accessed January 26, 2011).

14 Ibid.

15 For various examples of punitive boycotts, see Monroe Friedman, *Consumer Boycotts: Effecting Change through the Marketplace and the Media* (New York: Routledge, 1999).

16 Article 2.1(a) of the OSPAR Commission, The OSPAR Convention, 2010, http://www.ospar.org/content/content.asp?menu=00340108070000_000000_000000 (accessed January 27, 2011). For a discussion, see Jordan, *Shell, Greenpeace and Brent Spar.*

17 David Lascelles, Ronald Van de Krol, and Judy Dempsey, "Brent Spar Dents Oil Giant's Pride Rather Than Its Profit," *Financial Times*, June 20, 1995.

18 For further information on the Nike antisweatshop campaign, see the "Nike Chronology," Center for Communication and Civic Engagement, http://depts.washington.edu/ccce/polcommcampaigns/NikeChronology.htm#1989 (accessed January 27, 2011); Debora L. Spar and Jennifer Burns, "Hitting the Wall: Nike and International Labor Practices," Harvard Business School Case 700047-PDF-ENG, 2000; and Richard M. Locke, "The Promise and Perils of Globalization: The Case of Nike," MIT-IPC-02-007 (working paper, Massachusetts Institute of Technology, 2002).

19 For more information on the October 2000 BBC feature, see Paul Kenyon and Fiona Campbell, "Gap and Nike: No Sweat?" BBC, October 2000; or its follow-up, "Gap and Nike: No Sweat?" BBC, May 2001, http://news.bbc.co.uk/2/hi/programmes/panorama/970385.stm (accessed January 27, 2011).

20 Nike has worked with foreign governments to increase the monitoring and standards of its affiliate factories through the Fair Labor Association (FLA). For more information, see http://www.fairlabor.org/ (accessed January 27, 2011). Nike continues to evolve its monitoring protocol; see "Profile: Factories, Monitoring and Workers," Nike, Inc., http://www.nikebiz.com/crreport/content/workers-and-factories/3-2-2-factory-monitoring-and-results.php?cat=profiles (accessed January 27, 2011). However, as recently as 2008, an Australian news program reported poor working conditions in a Malaysian factory. A video clip of the news footage can be found at "Nike Contractor in Malaysia Using Force," http://www.youtube.com/watch?v=9Qzm7MCusGM&fmt=18 (accessed January 27, 2011).

21 Randy Shaw, *The Activist's Handbook: A Primer for the 1990s and Beyond* (Berkeley: University of California Press, 1996), 155.

22 Associated Press, "Putnam Paying $110 Million in Fines," April 8, 2004; "Putnam Gets Subpoena in Trading Inquiry," *New York Times*, October 31, 2003; and Marcia Vickers, "The Secret World of Marsh Mac," *BusinessWeek*, November 1, 2004.

23 Nike had broken new ground by effectively making Jordan the face of the company, spending all of the $500,000 that it had allocated for endorsement deals on Jordan (then a record-breaking amount) before he had played a single game in the NBA. The gamble paid off, and the "Air Jordan" line of shoes and apparel has been one of Nike's biggest sellers since the relationship began in 1984. The brand exploded as Jordan's career accelerated and eventually became a separate Nike subsidiary, grossing $800 million in 2007. See Darren Rovell, "CNBC Special Report: Swoosh! Inside Nike,"

CNBC, February 12, 2008, http://www.cnbc.com/id/22492149/ (accessed January 28, 2011). Jordan's responses during the campaign initially tried to deflect the issue: "I don't know the complete situation. Why should I? I'm trying to do my job. Hopefully, Nike will do the right thing." He later followed up with pledges to see the conditions for himself. See Bob Herbert, "In America, Nike's Pyramid Scheme," *New York Times*, June 10, 1996.

24 Bahree, Pope, and Sullivan, "Giant Outsmarted."

25 Paul A. Argenti, "Collaborating with Activists: How Starbucks Works with NGOs," *California Management Review* 47, no. 1 (2004): 91–116.

26 For more information, see Lane T. La Mure and Debora L. Spar, "The Burma Pipeline," Harvard Business School Case 798078-PDF-ENG, 2000; and Debora L. Spar and Lane T. La Mure, "The Power of Activism: Assessing the Impact of NGOs on Global Business," *California Management Review* 45, no. 3 (2003).

27 For details, see Mark D. Kielsgard, "Unocal and the Demise of Corporate Neutrality," *California Western International Law Journal* 36, no. 1 (2005): 185–215.

28 John Vidal, *McLibel: Burger Culture on Trial* (London: Macmillan, 1997).

29 Heather Timmons, "Britain Faulted over McDonald's Libel Case," *New York Times,* February 16, 2005.

30 For a discussion of the market for socially beneficial credence goods, see Timothy J. Feddersen and Thomas W. Gilligan, "Saints and Markets: Activists and the Supply of Credence Goods," *Journal of Economics and Management Strategy* 10, no. 1 (2001): 149–171.

31 For some evidence on this, see Roger E. Kasperson and Jeanne X. Kasperson, "The Social Amplification and Attenuation of Risk," *Annals of the American Academy of Political and Social Science* 545, no.1 (1996): 95–105; Richard G. Peters, Vincent T. Covello, and David B. McCallum, "The Determinants of Trust and Credibility in Environmental Risk Communication: An Empirical Study," *Risk Analysis* 17, no. 1 (1997): 43–54; and Justin Heinze, Eric Luis Uhlmann, and Daniel Diermeier, "Private Politics—Public Image," (working paper, Kellogg School of Management, 2010). For some recent global survey data, see the Edelman Trust Barometer, http://www.edelman.com/trust/2010/ (accessed January 27, 2011).

32 Heinze, Uhlmann, and Diermeier, "Private Politics—Public Image."

33 For details on McDonald's work with third parties, see its corporate responsibility report, "Values in Practice," McDonald's, http://www.aboutmcdonalds.com/mcd/csr/report.html (accessed January 27, 2011).

34 Michael Specter, "The Extremist: The Woman behind the Most Successful Radical Group in America," *The New Yorker*, April 14, 2003; and PETA, "The History of McDonald's Cruelty," McCruelty: I'm Hatin' It, http://www.mccruelty.com/why.aspx (accessed January 27, 2011).

35 Mike Hughlett, "PETA Targets McDonald's over Slaughter of Chickens," *Chicago Tribune*, February 16, 2009.

36 David P. Baron, *Business and Its Environment*, 6th ed. (Upper Saddle River, N.J.: Prentice Hall, 2009).

37 Activists sometimes target an entire industry at the same time (e.g., the tobacco industry). For an analysis of sequential versus simultaneous targeting, see Daniel Diermeier

and Mathieu Trepanier, "Value-Chain Targeting and Vertical Integration" (working paper, Kellogg School of Management, 2010).

38 For a general discussion, see Jonathan GS Koppell, *World Rule: Accountability, Legitimacy, and the Design of Global Governance* (Chicago: University of Chicago Press, 2010).

39 Elisabeth Kübler-Ross, *On Death and Dying* (New York: Scribner's, 1997).

40 The Wal-Mart example is based on Daniel Diermeier, "Wal-Mart and Katrina," Kellogg School of Management Case 7-406-750, 2011; and "Wal-Mart: The Store Wars," Kellogg School of Management Case 7-406-751, 2011. Both cases were written in collaboration with Rob Crawford. See also David P. Baron, "Wal-Mart: Nonmarket Pressure and Reputation Risk (A) (B)," Stanford University Graduate School of Business Cases P52A and P52B, 2006.

41 "Wal-Mart Annual Report," 2005, 8.

42 Misha Petrovic and Gary G. Hamilton, "Making Global Markets: Wal-Mart and Its Suppliers" in *Wal-Mart: The Face of Twenty-First Century Capitalism*, ed. Nelson Lichtenstein (New York: New Press, 2006), 133.

43 Baron, "Wal-Mart: Nonmarket Pressure and Reputation Risk (A)."

44 Liza Featherstone, "Wal-Mart's P.R. War," *Salon.com*, August 2, 2005.

45 Jon Ortiz, "Local Grocery Industry Keeps Eye on Tense Talks Down South," *Sacramento Bee*, April 16, 2006.

46 N. Craig Smith and Robert J. Crawford, "The Wal-Mart Supply Chain Controversy," London Business School Case 706-043-1, 2006.

47 Charles Fishman, *The Wal-Mart Effect* (New York: Penguin Press, 2006), 176–181.

48 Michael Barbaro, "A New Weapon for Wal-Mart: A War Room," *New York Times*, November 1, 2005.

49 Paul Ingram, Hayagreeva Rao, and Lori Yue, "Trouble in Store: Probes, Protests and Store Openings by Wal-Mart, 1998–2007," *American Journal of Sociology* 116, no. 1 (2010): 53–92.

50 Robert Slater, *The Wal-Mart Triumph* (New York: Portfolio, 2004), 202.

51 Barbaro, "A New Weapon for Wal-Mart."

52 Robert Berner, "Can Wal-Mart Wear a White Hat?" *BusinessWeek*, September 22, 2005.

53 Pia Sarkar, "Wal-Mart's World View: Giant Retailer Says It's Ready to Tackle Hot-Button Issues," *San Francisco Chronicle*, October 26, 2005.

54 Ylan Q. Mui and Dale Russakoff, "Wal-Mart, Union Join Forces on Healthcare; Alliance's Goal Is to Improve Coverage," *Washington Post,* February 8, 2007.

55 Stephanie Rosenbloom, "At Wal-Mart, Labeling to Reflect Green Intent," *New York Times*, July 15, 2009.

56 Ibid.

57 "Wal-Mart Launches Exclusive Sam's Choice Line of Organic, Rainforest Alliance and Fair Trade Certified Coffees," Wal-Mart Stores press release, April 1, 2008, http://walmartstores.com/pressroom/news/8162.aspx (accessed January 27, 2011).

58 "Wal-Mart Adds a New Facet to Its Fine Jewelry Lines: Traceability," Corporate Social Responsibility Newswire, July 15, 2008.

59 "Environmental Defense Will Add Staff Position in Bentonville, Arkansas," Environmental Defense Fund press release, July 12, 2006, http://www.edf.org/pressrelease.cfm?contentID=5322 (accessed January 27, 2011).

60 Renee Montagne, "Wal-Mart CEO Stepping Down after 9 Years," NPR, January 30, 2009.

CHAPTER 4

1 As cited in David Owen, "The Pay Problem. What Can Be Done about C.E.O. Compensation?" *The New Yorker*, October 12, 2009.

2 Brian Ross and Joseph Rhee, "Big Three CEOs Flew Private Jets to Plead for Public Funds," ABC News, November 19, 2008.

3 See Jonathan Spicer, "AIG Getting Fresh Billions from Fed, Defends Event," Reuters, October 8, 2008; and Peter Whoriskey, "AIG Spa Trip Fuels Fury on Hill," *Washington Post*, October 8, 2008.

4 David Cutler, "Timeline: AIG Developments since US Rescue," Reuters, April 17, 2009; and Edmund L. Andrews and Peter Baker, "Bonus Money at Troubled A.I.G. Draws Heavy Criticism," *New York Times*, March 15, 2009.

5 Associated Press, "Obama Speaks on AIG: How Do They Justify This Outrage?" April 12, 2009.

6 Charlie Gasparino, "John Thain's $87,000 Rug," CNBC, January 22, 2009.

7 See Owen, "The Pay Problem."

8 The CEO salary number is the average over experimental conditions in Victoria L. Brescoll and Eric Luis Uhlmann, "Can Angry Women Get Ahead? Status Conferral, Gender, and Workplace Emotion Expression," *Psychological Science* 19 (2008): 268–275.

9 The issue is not only how the prophet was depicted, but the fact that the prophet Mohammed was depicted at all, violating an Islamic prohibition that dates back to the very birth of the religion in seventh-century Arabia. For more details on the incident and its consequences, see Eric Weiner, "Why Cartoons of the Prophet Insult Muslims," NPR, February 8, 2006; "Muslim Cartoon Row Timeline," BBC News, February 19, 2006; and David Rising, "Muslim Boycotts Hurt Danish Firms," Associated Press, February 16, 2006.

10 See Jonathan Haidt, "The Moral Emotions," in *Handbook of Affective Sciences*, ed. Richard J. Davidson, Klaus R. Scherer, and H. Hill Goldsmith (New York: Oxford University Press, 2002), 852–870; and Paul Rozin, Jonathan Haidt, and Clark McCauley, "Disgust," in *Handbook of Emotions*, ed. Michael Lewis and Jeannette Haviland (New York: Guilford Press, 1993), 575–594.

11 Jolie Solomon, "Texaco's Troubles: A Scandal over Racial Slurs Forces the Oil Giant to Rethink—and Remake—Its Corporate Identity," *Newsweek*, November 25, 1996.

12 David Tannenbaum, Eric Luis Uhlmann, and Daniel Diermeier, "Moral Signals, Public Outrage, and Immaterial Harms" (working paper, Kellogg School of Management, 2010).

13 For details, see Peter C. Wason, "Reasoning," in *New Horizons in Psychology*, ed. Brian M. Foss (Harmondsworth, U.K.: Penguin, 1966); and Leda Cosmides and John Tooby, "Cognitive Adaptations for Social Exchange," in *The Adapted Mind: Evolutionary Psychology and the Generation of Culture*, ed. Jerome H. Barkow, Leda Cosmides, and John Tooby (New York: Oxford University Press, 1992).

14 The original example comes from British philosopher Philippa Foot, "The Problem of Abortion and the Doctrine of the Double Effect," in *Virtues and Vices* (Oxford, U.K.:

Basil Blackwell, 1978). For the variant with the heavy man, see Judith Jarvis Thomson, "Killing, Letting Die, and the Trolley Problem," *The Monist* 59 (1976): 204–217; and Judith Jarvis Thomson, "The Trolley Problem," *Yale Law Journal* 94 (1985): 1395–1415. The cited version is from Joshua Greene and Jonathan Haidt, "How (and Where) Does Moral Judgment Work?" *Trends in Cognitive Sciences* 6, no. 12 (2002): 519. See also Joshua D. Greene, R. Brian Sommerville, Leigh E. Nystrom, John M. Darley, and Jonathan D. Cohen, "An fMRI Investigation of Emotional Engagement in Moral Judgment," *Science* 293, no 5573 (2001): 2105–2108.

15 In one such experiment, infants are presented with puppets where in one case one puppet is helping another puppet to climb up a hill, while in the other it is hindering the climber. When presented with these puppet performances, 10-month-old infants will tend to reach for the helping puppet rather than the hinderer. See J. Kiley Hamlin, Karen Wynn, and Paul Bloom, "Social Evaluation by Preverbal Infants," *Nature* 450 (2007): 557–559.

16 Brain imaging and experimental research suggest that moral judgments may be based on two separate processes: one underlies rapid intuitive judgments and is correlated with increased brain activity typically associated with emotional processing, and the other is correlated with working memory, indicative of deliberative processes. See Greene and Haidt, "How (and Where) Does Moral Judgment Work?"; and Greene et al., "An fMRI Investigation of Emotional Engagement." See also Jonathan Haidt and Selin Kesebir, "Morality," in *Handbook of Social Psychology*, 5th ed., ed. Daniel T. Gilbert, Susan T. Fiske, and Gardner Lindzey (Hoboken, N.J.: John Wiley & Sons, 2010).

17 Philip E. Tetlock, Orie V. Kristel, S. Beth Elson, Melanie C. Green, and Jennifer S. Lerner, "The Psychology of the Unthinkable: Taboo Trade-Offs, Forbidden Base Rates, and Heretical Counterfactuals," *Journal of Personality and Social Psychology* 78 (2000): 853–870.

18 For evidence, see Jonathan Baron and Ilana Ritov, "Intuitions about Penalties and Compensation in the Context of Tort Law," *Journal of Risk and Uncertainty* 7, no. 1 (1993): 17–33; Kevin M. Carlsmith, John M. Darley, and Paul H. Robinson, "Why Do We Punish? Deterrence and Just Deserts as Motives for Punishment," *Journal of Personality and Social Psychology* 83 (2002): 284–299; Philip E. Tetlock, Penny S. Visser, Ramadhar Singh, Mark Polifroni, Amanda Scott, Sara Beth Elson, Philip Mazzocco, Phillip Rescober, "People as Intuitive Prosecutors: The Impact of Social-Control Goals on Attributions of Responsibility," *Journal of Experimental Social Psychology* 43 (2007): 195-209; Cass R. Sunstein, "Moral Heuristics," *Behavioral and Brain Sciences* 28 (2005): 531–573; Ernst Fehr and Simon Gächter, "Cooperation and Punishment in Public Goods Experiments," *American Economic Review* 90, no. 4 (2000): 980-994; and Armin Falk, Ernst Fehr, and Urs Fischbacher, "Driving Forces behind Informal Sanctions," *Econometrica* 73, no. 6 (2005): 2017-2030.

19 For example, the Aztecs force-fed captured Spanish conquistadors molten gold to symbolize the punishment for the Spaniards' greed. See also the depictions of punishments in the *Inferno* in Dante Alighieri, *The Divine Comedy, Volume 1: Inferno*, ed. Mark Musa (Bloomington: Indiana University Press, 2002). The hazardous waste example comes from Jonathan Baron, Rajeev Gowda, and Howard Kunreuther, "Attitudes toward

Managing Hazardous Waste: What Should Be Cleaned Up and Who Should Pay for It?" *Risk Analysis* 13, no. 2 (1993): 183–192.

20 See Jonathan J. Koehler and Andrew D. Gershoff, "Betrayal Aversion: When Agents of Protection Become Agents of Harm," *Organizational Behavior and Human Decision Processes* 90, no. 2 (2003): 244–261; Jonathan Haidt and Jonathan Baron, "Social Roles and the Moral Judgment of Acts and Omissions," *European Journal of Social Psychology* 26, no. 2 (1996): 201–218; and Maurice E. Schweitzer, John C. Hershey, and Eric T. Bradlow, "Promises and Lies: Restoring Violated Trust," *Organizational Behavior and Human Decision Processes* 101, no. 1 (2006): 1–19.

21 See Jennifer Aaker, Kathleen D. Vohs, and Cassie Mogilner, "Nonprofits Are Seen as Warm and For-Profits as Competent: Firm Stereotypes Matter," *Journal of Consumer Research* 37, no. 2 (2010): 224-237.

22 Karen W. Arenson, "Ex-United Way Leader Gets 7 Years for Embezzlement," *New York Times*, June 23, 1995; and Charles E. Shepard, "United Way Head Resigns over Spending Habits," *Washington Post*, February 28, 1992.

23 Eric Luis Uhlmann, David Tannenbaum, Justin Heinze, Malavika Srinivasan, Victoria L. Brescoll, George Newman, and Daniel Diermeier, "The Role of Trust in Reputation Management" (working paper, Kellogg School of Management, 2010).

24 For details, see Nicholas Allen and Sarah Birch, "Political Conduct and Misconduct: Probing Public Opinion," *Parliamentary Affairs* 64, no. 1 (2011): 61–81; Daniel Diermeier, Michael Keane, and Antonio Merlo, "A Political Economy Model of Congressional Careers," *American Economic Review* 95, no. 1 (2005): 347–373; and D. Roderick Kiewiet and Langche Zeng, "An Analysis of Congressional Career Decisions, 1947–1986," *American Political Science Review* 87, no. 4 (1993): 928–941.

25 See "MP's Expenses Scandal: A Timeline," *Daily Telegraph*, November 4, 2009; Nick Allen, "MP's Expenses: Sir Peter Viggers Claimed for £1,600 Floating Duck Island," *Daily Telegraph*, May 21, 2009; and Sam Coates, "Husband's Porn Bill Pushes Jacqui Smith to Brink over Expenses," *Sunday Times,* March 30, 2009.

26 For details, see Uri Gneezy and Aldo Rustichini, "A Fine Is a Price," *Journal of Legal Studies* 29, no. 1 (2000): 1–17.

27 Werner Güth, Rolff Schmittberger, and Bernd Schwarze, "An Experimental Analysis of Ultimatum Bargaining," *Journal of Economic Behavior and Organization* 3, no. 4 (1982): 367–388.

28 For an overview, see Colin F. Camerer, *Behavioral Game Theory* (Princeton, N.J.: Princeton University Press, 2003).

29 Much like in the case of moral outrage, receiving (and rejecting) unfair offers stimulates the emotional regions of the brain. See Michael Koenigs and Daniel Tranel, "Irrational Economic Decision-Making after Ventromedial Prefrontal Damage: Evidence from the Ultimatum Game," *Journal of Neuroscience* 27, no. 4 (2007): 951–956; and Alan G. Sanfey, James K. Rilling, Jessica A. Aronson, Leigh E. Nystrom, and Jonathan D. Cohen, "The Neural Basis of Economic Decision-Making in the Ultimatum Game," *Science* 300, no. 5626 (2003): 1755–1758. For third-party punishment, see Ernst Fehr and Urs Fischbacher, "Third-Party Punishment and Social Norms," *Evolution and Human Behavior* 25 (2004): 63–87. On the other hand, providing subjects with the hormone oxytocin, which has been hypothesized to increase empathy, leads to more generous offers. For

details, see Paul J. Zak, Angela A. Stanton, and Sheila A. Ahmadi, "Oxytocin Increases Generosity in Humans," *PLoS ONE* 2, no. 11 (2007): e1128.

30 The threshold amount can vary substantially between cultures. The Machiguenga farmers in Peru offered only about 25 percent of the total pie, but had these offers routinely accepted. Yet other cultures, such as the Ache headhunters of Paraguay, offered more than half the amount. Subsequent anthropological research has pointed out that these variations correlate with other cultural characteristics, such as social isolation for the Machiguenga (there are no proper names for other Machiguengas outside the immediate family) or the existence of oversharing in a collective hunt or competitive gift-giving ("potlatch") traditions for the Ache. For details, see Joseph Henrich, Robert Boyd, Samuel Bowles, Colin Camerer, Ernst Fehr, Herbert Gintis, Richard McElreath, Michael Alvard, Abigail Barr, Jean Ensminger, Kim Hill, Francisco Gil-White, Michael Gurven, Frank Marlowe, John Q. Patton, Natalie Smith Henrich, and David Tracer, "'Economic Man' in Cross-Cultural Perspective: Ethnography and Experiments from 15 Small-Scale Societies," *Behavioral and Brain Sciences* 28, no. 6 (2005): 795–815; and Alvin E. Roth, Vesna Prasnikar, Masahiro Okuno-Fujiwara, and Shmuel Zamir, "Bargaining and Market Behavior in Jerusalem, Ljubljana, Pittsburgh, and Tokyo: An Experimental Study," *American Economic Review* 81, no. 5 (1991): 1068–1095.

31 For a sample of the policy debate, see "Fannie Mae, NAACP in Pact to Provide More Mortgage Financing," Dow Jones News Service, January 21, 1999; Glenn B. Canner, and Wayne Passmore, "The Role of Specialized Lenders in Extending Mortgages to Lower-Income and Minority Homebuyers," *Federal Reserve Bulletin*, November 1999; Kenneth Temkin, Jennifer E. H. Johnson, Diane Levy, and the Urban Institute, "Subprime Markets, the Role of GSEs, and Risk-Based Pricing," U.S. Department of Housing and Urban Development, March 2002; "HUD's Regulation of the Federal National Mortgage Association (Fannie Mae) and the Federal Home Loan Mortgage Corporation (Freddie Mac)," *Federal Register* 65, no. 211 (2000); and U.S. Department of Housing and Urban Development, "HUD's Affordable Lending Goals for Fannie Mae and Freddie Mac," Issue Brief No. 5, Office of Policy Development and Research, 2001.

32 Connie Bruck, "Angelo's Ashes," *The New Yorker*, June 29, 2009; and Kathleen Day, "Fannie Mae Vows More Minority Lending," *Washington Post*, March 16, 2000.

33 See Charles W. Calomiris, "What to Do, and What Not to Do, about 'Predatory Lending,'" statement before the Senate Banking Committee, June 26, 2001.

34 Edward Wyatt, "Countrywide Settles Fee Complaint," *New York Times*, June 7, 2010.

35 "Bank of America Announces Nationwide Homeownership Retention Program for Countrywide Customers," Bank of America Corporation press release, October 6, 2008; and Gretchen Morgenson, "Countrywide to Set Aside $8.4 Billion in Loan Aid," *New York Times*, October 5, 2008.

36 Alex Dobuzinskis and Dan Levine, "Mozilo Settles Countrywide Fraud Case at $67.5 Million," Reuters, October 15, 2010.

37 "FTC Charges One of Nation's Largest Subprime Lenders with Abusive Lending Practices," Federal Trade Commission, March 6, 2001, http://www.ftc.gov/opa/2001/03/associates.shtm (accessed January 27, 2011).

38　"Citigroup Settles FTC Charges against The Associates: Record-Setting $215 Million for Subprime Lending Victims," Federal Trade Commission, September 19, 2002, http://www.ftc.gov/opa/2002/09/associates.shtm (accessed January 27, 2011).

39　For details on the AIDS epidemic, ARV drugs, and challenges for the pharmaceutical industry, see, for example, Charles R. Kennedy, Frederick H. deB. Harris, and Michael Lord, "Integrating Public Policy and Public Affairs in a Pharmaceutical Marketing Program: The AIDS Pandemic," *Journal of Public Policy and Marketing* 23, no. 2 (2004): 128–139; David P. Baron, Deborah Liu, and Soon Jin Lim, "GlaxoSmithKline and AIDS Drug Policy," Harvard Business School Case P39-PDF-ENG, 2003; and William W. Fisher III and Cyrill P. Rigamonti, "The South Africa AIDS Controversy: A Case Study in Patent Law and Policy," Harvard Law School case study, 2005.

40　Nevin M. Gewertz and Rivka Amado, "Intellectual Property and the Pharmaceutical Industry: A Moral Crossroads between Health and Property," *Journal of Business Ethics* 55, no. 3 (2004): 295–308; and Melody Petersen, "Lifting the Curtain on the Real Costs of Making AIDS Drugs," *New York Times*, April 24, 2001.

41　Baron, Liu, and Lim, "GlaxoSmithKline and AIDS Drug Policy"; and Fisher and Rigamonti, "The South Africa AIDS Controversy."

42　Rachel L. Swarns, "Drug Makers Drop South Africa Suit over AIDS Medicine," *New York Times*, April 20, 2001.

43　Karen DeYoung and Bill Brubaker, "Another Firm Cuts HIV Drug Prices; Sub-Saharan Africa Is the Focus of Bristol-Myers Move," *Washington Post*, May 15, 2001; and Baron, Liu, and Lim, "GlaxoSmithKline and AIDS Drug Policy."

44　Monali J. Bhosle and Rajesh Balkrishnan, "Drug Reimportation Practices in the United States," *Journal of Therapeutics and Clinical Risk Management* 3, no. 1 (2007): 41–46.

45　"Recapturing the Vision: Restoring Trust in the Pharmaceutical Industry by Translating Expectations into Actions," PricewaterhouseCoopers, 2007, http://www.pwc.com/gx/en/pharma-life-sciences/recapturing-vision-restoring-trust-pharmaceutical-translating-expectations-actions.jhtml (accessed January 27, 2011).

46　Bhosle and Balkrishnan, "Drug Reimportation Practices in the United States."

47　Paul H. Rubin, "Folk Economics," *Southern Economic Journal* 70, no. 1 (2003): 157–171.

48　See Robert J. Blendon, John M. Benson, Mollyann Brodie, Richard Morin, Drew E. Altman, Daniel Gitterman, Mario Brossard, and Matt James, "Bridging the Gap between the Public's and Economists' Views of the Economy," *Journal of Economic Perspectives* 11, no. 3 (1997): 105–118; and Bryan Caplan, "Systematically Biased Beliefs about Economics: Robust Evidence of Judgmental Anomalies from the Survey of Americans and Economists on the Economy," *Economic Journal* 112, no. 479 (2002): 433–458.

49　This intuition goes back to Aristotle. The idea is that if we see an action, we ask ourselves whether a responsible person would behave that way. For an overview, see G. E. M. Anscombe, "Modern Moral Philosophy," *Philosophy* 33, no. 124 (1958): 1–19. For psychological approaches, see, for example, Glenn D. Reeder and Marilynn Brewer, "A Schematic Model of Dispositional Attribution in Interpersonal Perception," *Psychological Review* 86, no. 1 (1979): 61–79; and Glenn D. Reeder, "Mindreading: Judgments about Intentionality and Motives in Dispositional Inference," *Psychological Inquiry* 20, no. 1 (2009): 1–18. For a discussion in the context of crisis management, see Eric Luis Uhlmann, David Tannenbaum, and Daniel Diermeier, "When Actions Speak Volumes" (working paper, Kellogg School of Management, 2010).

50 See Susan Fiske, Amy Cuddy, and Peter Glick, "Universal Dimensions of Social Cognition: Warmth and Competence," *Trends in Cognitive Sciences* 11, no. 2 (2007): 77–83; Hamlin, Wynn, and Bloom, "Social Evaluation by Preverbal Infants"; Janine Willis and Alexander Todorov, "First Impressions: Making Up Your Mind after a 100-ms Exposure to a Face," *Psychological Science* 17 (2006): 592–598; Robert H. Frank, *Passions within Reason: The Strategic Role of Emotions* (New York: Norton, 1988); and Jonathan Haidt, "The Emotional Dog and Its Rational Tail: A Social Intuitionist Approach to Moral Judgment," *Psychological Review* 108 (2001): 814–834.

51 James B. Stewart, "Spend! Spend! Spend!" *The New Yorker*, February 17, 2003. For more details on Dennis Kozlowski, see also "Top 10 Crooked CEOs," *Time*, June 9, 2009, http://www.time.com/time/specials/packages/article/0,28804,1903155_1903156_1903152,00.html (accessed January 27, 2011).

52 The examples and results are from Tannenbaum, Uhlmann, and Diermeier, "Moral Signals, Public Outrage, and Immaterial Harms."

53 Owen, "The Pay Problem."

CHAPTER 5

1 Devin Leonard, "The Only Lifeline Was the Wal-Mart," *Fortune*, October 3, 2005.

2 Jason Jackson issued this statement before the Homeland Security and Governmental Affairs Committee of the U.S. Senate on November 16, 2005, during a hearing entitled "Hurricane Katrina: What Can Government Learn from the Private Sector's Response?" http://hsgac.senate.gov/public/index.cfm?FuseAction=Files.View& FileStore_id=de5d874c-b0ea-4342-9aaf-d9809b9cc236 (accessed January 30, 2011).

3 Michael E. Porter and Mark R. Kramer, "Strategy and Society: The Link between Competitive Advantage and Corporate Social Responsibility," *Harvard Business Review* (December 2006): 78–92. See also Archie B. Carroll, "Corporate Social Responsibility—Evolution of a Definitional Construct," *Business & Society* 38, no. 3 (1999): 268–295.

4 The discussion of corporate social responsibility is based on Daniel Diermeier, "From Corporate Social Responsibility to Values-Based Management," in *Global Corporate Citizenship*, ed. Anuradha Dayal-Gulati and Mark Finn (Evanston, Ill.: Northwestern University Press, 2007), 1–24; and Daniel Diermeier, "A Strategic Perspective on Corporate Social Responsibility," in *Responsible Leadership*, ed. Nicola M. Pless and Thomas Maak (London: Routledge, 2006), 155–169.

5 The question of the social responsibility of companies has concerned companies and commentators since the birth of the modern corporation. Much of the debate is normative in nature, centering on the questions of what socially beneficial actions companies should engage in and under what conditions. We focus instead on the question of under what conditions and how philanthropic and other socially beneficial acts can improve a company's reputation. There is extensive literature on this topic. The following contributions are good places to start: Michael. E. Porter and Claas van der Linde, "Green and Competitive: Ending the Stalemate," *Harvard Business Review* (1995):

120–134; Porter and Kramer, "Strategy and Society"; Clive Crook, "The Good Company," *The Economist*, January 22, 2005; Milton Friedman, "The Social Responsibility of Business Is to Increase Its Profits," *New York Times Magazine*, September 13, 1970; Aneel Karnani, "The Case against Corporate Social Responsibility," *Wall Street Journal*, August 23, 2010; David Vogel, *The Market for Virtue* (Washington, D.C.: Brookings Institution Press, 2005); Glen Dowell, Stuart Hart, and Bernard Yeung, "Do Corporate Global Environmental Standards Create or Destroy Market Value?" *Management Science* 46 (2000): 1059–1074; Ray Fisman, Geoffrey Heal, and Vinay Nair, "Corporate Social Responsibility: Doing Well by Doing Good" (working paper, Columbia University, 2006); and Geoffrey Heal, "Corporate Social Responsibility: An Economic and Financial Framework," *Geneva Papers on Risk and Insurance—Issues and Practice* 30, no. 3 (2005): 387-409.

6   Ian Davis and Elizabeth Stephenson, "Ten Trends to Watch in 2006," *McKinsey Quarterly Web Edition*, January 10, 2006, http://www.mckinseyquarterly.com/Strategy/Globalization/Ten_trends_to_watch_in_2006_1734 (accessed January 29, 2011). See also Sheila M. J. Bonini, Lenny T. Mendonca, and Jeremy M. Oppenheim, "When Social Issues Become Strategic," *McKinsey Quarterly*, no. 2 (2006): 20–32.

7   The following contributions provide some overviews on this debate: Dowell, Hart, and Yeung, "Do Corporate Global Environmental Standards Create or Destroy Market Value?"; and Joshua D. Margolis and James P. Walsh, "Misery Loves Companies: Rethinking Social Initiatives by Business," *Administrative Science Quarterly* 48 (2003): 268–305; and Vogel, *The Market for Virtue*.

8   Forest Reinhardt, "Global Climate Change and BP Amoco," Harvard Business School Case 9-700-106, 2000.

9   See the extensive literature on equilibria in nonprice competition, for example, Jean Tirole, *The Theory of Industrial Organization* (Cambridge, Mass.: MIT Press, 2002).

10   "Socially Responsible Investing Facts," Social Investment Forum, http://www.social invest.org/resources/sriguide/srifacts.cfm (accessed January 28, 2011).

11   Indeed, some researchers have argued that SRI should yield a lower average return. A recent paper by Hong and Kacperczyk has provided some compelling evidence for this claim in the context of "sin stocks," or publicly traded companies with involvement in the alcohol, tobacco, or gambling industries. Of course, to the extent that individual investors in SRI funds are willing to make such trade-offs between financial and social goals, this finding is not entirely problematic. SRI funds and their investors need to satisfy potentially conflicting goals. To put it differently, since socially responsible investors value both financial *and* social goals, it is a mistake to measure only financial performance. Harrison Hong and Marcin Kacperczyk, "The Price of Sin: The Effects of Social Norms on Markets," *Journal of Financial Economics* 93, no. 1 (2009): 15–36. For an overview and analysis of socially responsible investing, see also Christopher C. Geczy, Robert F. Stambaugh, and David Levin, "Investing in Socially Responsible Mutual Funds" (working paper, University of Pennsylvania—The Wharton School, 2005); and Heal, "Corporate Social Responsibility."

12   For some empirical evidence, see Dowell, Hart, and Yeung, "Do Corporate Global Environmental Standards Create or Destroy Market Value?"; James T. Hamilton, "Pollution as News: Media and Stock Market Reactions to the Toxic Release Inventory

NOTES **279**

Data," *Journal of Environmental Economics and Management* 28, no. 1 (1995): 98–113; and
Heal, "Corporate Social Responsibility."

13 For some evidence, see Dylan B. Minor, "Corporate Social Responsibility as Reputation Insurance: Theory & Evidence" (working paper, Haas School of Business, 2010).

14 This Wal-Mart example is based on Daniel Diermeier, "Wal-Mart and Katrina," Kellogg School of Management Case 7-406-750, 2010. The case was written in collaboration with Rob Crawford. It is based on public sources, especially Devin Leonard,
"The Only Lifeline Was the Wal-Mart." For more details and the quotes by Wal-Mart's
director of business continuity and global security, Jason Jackson, see also the "Hurricane Katrina: What Can Government Learn from the Private Sector's Response?"
hearing transcript of the U.S. Senate's Homeland Security and Governmental Affairs
Committee on November 16, 2005. Unless otherwise noted, all quotations are from
these sources.

15 Michael Barbaro and Justin Gillis, "Wal-Mart at Forefront of Hurricane Relief," *Washington Post*, September 6, 2005.

16 Parija Bhatnagar, "Wal-Mart Redeems Itself, but What's Next," CNN/Money, September 9, 2005.

17 The research discussed in this section is based on Jennifer M. Jordan, Daniel Diermeier,
and Adam D. Galinsky, "The Corporate Samaritan: The Promise and Perils of Corporate Responses to External Crises" (working paper, Kellogg School of Management,
2009). For the distinction between communal and exchange orientation, see Marga-
ret S. Clark and Judson Mills, "Interpersonal Attraction in Exchange and Communal
Relationships," *Journal of Personality and Social Psychology* 37, no. 1 (1979): 12–24; and
Susan T. Fiske, Amy J. C. Cuddy, and Peter Glick, "Universal Dimensions of Social Cognition: Warmth and Competence," *Trends in Cognitive Sciences* 11, no. 2 (2007): 77–83.

18 See Bogdan Wojciszke, Rosa Bazinska, and Marcin Jaworski, "On the Dominance of
Moral Categories in Impression Formation," *Personality and Social Psychology Bulletin*
24, no. 12 (1998): 1251–1263.

19 Jordan, Diermeier, and Galinsky, "The Corporate Samaritan."

20 Dan Harris, "Corporate Goodwill or Tainted Money? Philip Morris' Charitable Con-
tributions, Ad Campaign Seen as Smokescreen," ABC News, February 8, 2001; and
Kenneth E. Warner, "What's a Cigarette Company to Do?" *American Journal of Public
Health* 92, no. 6 (2002): 897–900.

21 For experimental evidence, see Eric Luis Uhlmann, George Newman, Victoria L.
Brescoll, and Daniel Diermeier, "Expecting Empathy: The Role of Moral Intuitions
in a Reputational Crisis" (working paper, Kellogg School of Management, 2010); and
Eric Luis Uhlmann, David Tannenbaum, Justin Heinze, Malavika Srinivasan, Victoria L.
Brescoll, George Newman, "The Role of Trust in Reputation Management" (working
paper, Kellogg School of Management, 2010).

CHAPTER 6

1 The quote by Dr. Virginia Walbot, a biological sciences professor at Stanford University,
can be found in Kurt Eichenwald, Gina Kolata, and Melody Petersen, "Biotechnology
Food: From the Lab to a Debacle," *New York Times*, January 25, 2001. Less well known is
the fact that Edison also filmed a movie of an elephant being electrocuted by alternat-

ing current to scare people away from Tesla's competing technology. Tony Long, "Jan. 4, 1903: Edison Fries an Elephant to Prove His Point," *Wired*, January 4, 2008.

2 There is extensive literature on risk perception. A good overview is provided in two books by Paul Slovic, one of the pioneers of this research area: Paul Slovic, *The Perception of Risk* (Sterling, Va.: Earthscan, 2000); and Paul Slovic, *The Feeling of Risk: New Perspectives on Risk Perception* (Sterling, Va.: Earthscan, 2010). Classic studies include Amos Tversky and Daniel Kahneman, "Availability: A Heuristic for Judging Frequency and Probability," *Cognitive Psychology* 5 (1973): 207–232; Amos Tversky and Daniel Kahneman, "Judgment under Uncertainty: Heuristics and Biases," *Science* 185, no. 4157 (1974): 1124–1131; and Ellen J. Langer, "The Illusion of Control," *Journal of Personality and Social Psychology* 32, no. 2 (1975): 311–328. For a collection of cognitive fallacies, see Rüdiger F. Pohl, ed., *Cognitive Illusions: A Handbook on Fallacies and Biases in Thinking, Judgement and Memory* (Hove, U.K.: Psychology Press, 2004). Consequences for risk communications are discussed in Vincent T. Covello, David B. McCallum, and Maria T. Pavlova, ed., *Effective Risk Communication: The Role and Responsibility of Government and Nongovernment Organizations (Contemporary Issues in Risk Analysis)* (New York: Springer, 1989).

3 See Dan M. Kahan, Paul Slovic, Donald Braman, John Gastil, and Geoffrey L. Cohen, "Nanotechnology Risk Perceptions: The Influence of Affect and Values" (Cultural Cognition Project Working Paper No. 22, Yale Law School, 2007); and James N. Druckman and Toby Bolsen, "Framing, Motivated Reasoning, and Opinions about Emergent Technologies" (working paper, Northwestern University, 2009).

4 Felicia Mello, "Like Surf, Sand Can Kill, Says Doctor," *Boston Globe*, June 21, 2007.

5 For an example in the context of HIV/AIDS, see Julie R. Irwin, Lawrence E. Jones, and David Mundo, "Risk Perception and Victim Perception: The Judgment of HIV Cases," *Journal of Behavioral Decision Making* 9 (1996): 1–22. The cell phone tower case is discussed in Simon Chapman and Sonia Wutzke, "Not in Our Back Yard: Media Coverage of Community Opposition to Mobile Phone Towers—An Application of Sandman's Outrage Model of Risk Perception," *Australian and New Zealand Journal of Public Health* 21, no. 6 (1997): 614–620.

6 Cultural and ideological orientations influence risk perception. Views of new risks, such as nanotechnology, tend to fall along the same ideological lines as other risk-salient issues, such as global warming and nuclear power. See Kahan, Slovic, Braman, Gastil, and Cohen, "Nanotechnology Risk Perceptions"; Roger E. Kasperson, Ortwin Renn, Paul Slovic, Halina S. Brown, Jacque Emel, Robert Goble, Jeanne X. Kasperson, and Samuel Ratick, "The Social Amplification of Risk: A Conceptual Framework," *Risk Analysis* 8, no. 2 (1988): 177–187; Daniel Diermeier, "Managing Public Reputation," in *Kellogg on Advertising and the Media*, ed. Bobby Calder (Evanston, Ill.: Northwestern University Press, 2008), 178–195; and Slovic, *The Perception of Risk*.

7 The discussion of emerging technologies is based on Daniel Diermeier, "Gaining Public Acceptance for Emerging Technologies—The Case of Biotech" (working paper, Northwestern University, 2009); and Daniel Diermeier, "Public Acceptance and the Regulation of Emerging Technologies—The Role of Private Politics," in *The Nanotechnology Challenge*, ed. David Dana (Cambridge, U.K.: Cambridge University Press, forthcoming).

8 Monsanto's troubles have been well documented. References are drawn from Michael D. Watkins and Ann Leamon, "Robert Shapiro and Monsanto," Harvard Business School Case 801426-PDF-ENG, 2001; Baruch Fischhoff, Paul Slovic, Sarah Lichtenstein, Stephen Read, and Barbara Combs, "How Safe Is Safe Enough? A Psychometric Study of Attitudes Towards Technological Risks and Benefits," *Policy Studies* 9 (1978): 127–152; Lucia Savadori, Stefania Savio, Eraldo Nicotra, Rino Rumiati, Melissa Finucane, and Paul Slovic, "Expert and Public Perception of Risk from Biotechnology," *Risk Analysis* 24, no. 5 (2004): 1289–1299; Daniel Charles, *Lords of the Harvest: Biotech, Big Money, and the Future of Food* (New York: Perseus Books, 2002); Ulrich Steger, Mope Ogunsulire, Catherine A. Ramus, and Carina Hum, "Monsanto's Genetically Modified Organisms: The Battle for Hearts and Shopping Aisles," Harvard Business School Case IMD137-PDF-ENG, 2001; and Eichenwald, Kolata, and Petersen, "Biotechnology Food."

9 Diermeier, "Gaining Public Acceptance for Emerging Technologies"; "Monsanto Seed Brands," Monsanto Corporation, http://www.monsanto.com/products/brands.asp (accessed January 28, 2011); and Mark Parry, "Monsanto—The Launch of Roundup Ready Soybeans," Harvard Business School Case UV0-321, 2000; and Charles, *Lords of the Harvest.*

10 Charles, Prince of Wales, "The Seeds of Disaster," *Daily Telegraph,* June 7, 1998.

11 Research by Gaskell and colleagues that looked at risk perception in 17 European countries found that it was a perceived lack of benefits, rather than an intolerable amount of risk, that ultimately determined consumer opinions on GM foods. This was in contrast to the United States, where 69 percent of Americans acknowledged benefits associated with GM foods (compared with 46 percent in Europe). See George Gaskell, Nick Allum, Wolfgang Wagner, Nicole Kronberger, Helge Torgersen, Juergen Hampel, and Julie Bardes, "GM Foods and the Misperception of Risk Perception," *Risk Analysis* 24, no. 1 (2004): 185–194. See also Diermeier, "Gaining Public Acceptance for Emerging Technologies."

12 "Agent Orange: Background on Monsanto's Involvement," Monsanto Corporation, http://www.monsanto.com/newsviews/Pages/agent-orange-background-monsanto-involvement.aspx (accessed January 28, 2011).

13 John Losey, Linda Rayor, and Maureen Carter, "Transgenic Pollen Harms Monarch Larvae," *Nature* 399, no. 6733 (1999): 214.

14 For a detailed timeline on genetic use restriction technologies, see "Seeds," History Commons, http://www.historycommons.org/timeline.jsp?timeline=seeds_tmln&seeds_cases_studies-other=seeds (accessed January 28, 2011).

15 For an overview, see Sonia Y. Hunt, "Controversies in Treatment Approaches: Gene Therapy, IVF, Stem Cells, and Pharmacogenomics," *Nature Education* 1, no. 1 (2008).

16 Guangwen Tang, Jian Qin, Gregory Dolnikowski, Robert Russell, and Michael Grusak, "Golden Rice Is an Effective Source of Vitamin A," *American Journal of Clinical Nutrition* 89, no. 6 (2009): 1776–1783.

17 See Carlene Wilson, Greg Evans, Phil Leppard, and Julie Syrette, "Reactions to Genetically Modified Food Crops and How Perception of Risks and Benefits Influences Consumers' Information Gathering," *Risk Analysis* 24, no. 5 (2004): 1311–1321; and

Druckman and Bolsen, "Framing, Motivated Reasoning, and Opinions about Emergent Technologies."

18 For some evidence on this, see Roger E. Kasperson and Jeanne X. Kasperson, "The Social Amplification and Attenuation of Risk," *ANNALS of the American Academy of Political and Social Science* 545, no. 1 (1996): 95–105; and Justin Heinze, Eric Luis Uhlmann, and Daniel Diermeier, "Private Politics—Public Image" (working paper, Kellogg School of Management, 2010).

19 For details on Calgene and the Flavr Savr tomato, see Belinda Martineau, *First Fruit: The Creation of the Flavr Savr Tomato and the Birth of Biotech Food* (New York: McGraw-Hill, 2001); Ray A. Goldberg and John T. Gourville, "Calgene, Inc.," Harvard Business School Case 9-502-041, 2002; and David P. Baron, "Integrative Case: Calgene Inc. and Infrastructure Marketing," in *Business and Its Environment,* 3rd ed. (Upper Saddle River, N.J.: Prentice Hall, 1999), 119–126.

20 For a detailed study on the reputation of the FDA, see Daniel Carpenter, *Reputation and Power: Organizational Image and Pharmaceutical Regulation at the FDA* (Princeton, N.J.: Princeton University Press, 2010).

21 Although Calgene made history by successfully introducing the first genetically modified food to market, the Flavr Savr tomato was short-lived. By the time it was ultimately rolled out, Calgene was deeply in debt because of untenable research costs and growing production problems. Picking the ripe tomatoes in a cost-efficient way proved particularly challenging. The company ultimately was sold off to Monsanto in bits, mainly for its cotton and oil products.

22 For details on Monsanto and rBGH, see David P. Baron, *Business and Its Environment,* 3rd ed.

23 U.S. Food and Drug Administration, "Voluntary Labeling of Milk and Milk Products from Cows That Have Not Been Treated with Recombinant Bovine Somatotropin: Interim Guidance," 59 FR 6279, February 10, 1994, http://www.fda.gov/Food/GuidanceComplianceRegulatoryInformation/GuidanceDocuments/FoodLabelingNutrition/ucm059036.htm (accessed January 29, 2011).

24 Ben & Jerry's was one of the first companies to begin labeling its products "rBGH-free." This led to a long battle regarding labeling restrictions. For examples, see Lisa Rathke, "Ben & Jerry's in Fight over Labeling," Associated Press, February 5, 2008; and April Fulton, "Court OKs Hormone-Free Label on Dairy Products in Ohio," NPR, October 1, 2010. Many other companies have since declared that they would use only rBGH-free milk as well. See http://www.foodandwaterwatch.org/take-action/consumer-tools/the-milk-tip/rbgh-free-guide/ (accessed January 29, 2011).

25 See "2010 Edelman Trust Barometer," Edelman Public Relations, http://www.edelman.com/trust/2010/ (accessed January 28, 2011).

26 Alexander H. Arnall, "Future Technologies, Today's Choices: Nanotechnology, Artificial Intelligence and Robotics; A Technical, Political and Institutional Map of Emerging Technologies," Greenpeace Environmental Trust, 2003.

27 For research on the perception of nanotechnology, see Kahan, Slovic, Braman, Gastil, and Cohen, "Nanotechnology Risk Perceptions"; and Peter D. Hart Research Associates, Inc., "Report Findings," Nanotech Project, September 19, 2006, http://www.nanotechproject.org/file_download/files/HartReport.pdf (accessed January 29, 2011).

28 For details, see "Sizing Up Nanotechnology: How Nanosized Particles May Affect Skin Care Products," American Academy of Dermatology, http://www.aad.org/media/background/news/Releases/Sizing_Up_Nanotechnology_How_Nanosized_Particles_M/ (accessed January 29, 2011); and Jonathan Hale Zippin and Adam Friedman, "Nanotechnology in Cosmetics and Sunscreens: An Update," *Journal of Drugs in Dermatology* 8, no. 10 (2009): 955–958.

29 See Baron, *Business and Its Environment,* 3rd ed., 85.

30 Throughout its short history, Facebook has been the source of many concerns regarding its privacy policies. See, for example, Jessica E. Vascellaro, "Facebook Grapples with Privacy Issues," *Wall Street Journal,* May 19, 2010.

31 Orange County's treasurer, Robert Citron, had invested much of the county's funds in highly leveraged derivates, which were affected by changes in federal interest rates. As federal interest rates rose, the funds sustained losses of around $2 billion. John Greenwald, Bernard Baumohl, Patrick E. Cole, and Bill Walsh, "The California Wipeout," *Time,* December 19, 1994.

32 Launched in May 2007, Google Street View is a feature that allows people to explore streets, including individual houses, based on photos taken by roving cameras. In August 2010, Google announced plans to provide Street View in 20 of Germany's largest cities by the end of the year, which led to protests based on privacy concerns. In response, Google introduced the option for residents to request that their homes be obscured. Although Google has permitted residents of other countries to request this after the mapping service was launched, Germany is the first country to have the option ahead of time. For more information, see Christopher Lawton, "Google Hears German Calls to Blur Maps," *Wall Street Journal,* October 21, 2010; and "Thousands of Germans Opt Out of Google Street View," BBC News, October 21, 2010. A host of additional concerns were raised when it was discovered that Google's Street View mapping cars were gathering private information from unsecured wireless networks. The company was subsequently charged with illegal data collection. For more information, see Eric Pfanner, "British Agency Says Google Violated Privacy Law," *New York Times,* November 3, 2010.

CHAPTER 7

1 Jenny Anderson, "Wall Street Pursues Profit in Bundles of Life Insurance," *New York Times,* September 5, 2009.

2 Thomas W. Gilligan, "Living Benefits," in David Baron, *Business and Its Environment,* 4th ed., (Upper Saddle River, N.J.: Prentice Hall/Pearson Education, 2003), 709–710.

3 This terminology is derived from the Latin term *viaticum,* referring to a travel allowance for a journey [*Collins English Dictionary—Complete & Unabridged,* 10th ed. (London: William Collins Sons & Co. Ltd., 2009)]. *Merriam-Webster's Medical Dictionary* defines a *viator* as "a person with a catastrophic or life-threatening illness who has a life insurance policy and sells or intends to sell it in a viatical settlement" [*Merriam-Webster's Medical Dictionary* (Springfield, Mass.: Merriam-Webster, Inc., 2007)].

4 "The History and Future of Life Settlements," RTG Consultants, LLC, http://www.rtgconsultants.com/history.html (accessed January 29, 2011).

5 The Prudential example is based on Kirk O. Hanson, Penelope Rowlands, and David Bollier, "The Prudential Insurance Company of America (A) (B) (C)," Business Enterprise Trust cases 92-011 (A), 92-012 (B), and 92-013 (C), 1992. Unless otherwise noted, all quotes are from these sources.

6 "Prudential Financial, Inc.," Hoovers, http://www.hoovers.com/company/Pruden tial_Financial_Inc/cfykki-1.html (accessed January 29, 2011).

7 See, for example, "Life Insurance Market Report," *Highbeam Business*, http://business. highbeam.com/industry-reports/finance/life-insurance (accessed January 29, 2011).

8 Similar concepts have been developed in the area of issue management and nonmarket strategy. See, for example, David Baron, *Business and Its Environment*, 6th ed. (Upper Saddle River, N.J.: Prentice Hall, 2010); and Deborah D. Anderson, "Key Concepts in Anticipatory Issues Management," *Corporate Environmental Strategy* 5, no. 1 (1997): 6–17.

9 Nick Bunkley, "In Detroit, Toyota Vows to Earn Trust," *New York Times*, January 10, 2011.

10 Michel Crouhy, Dan Galai, and Robert Mark, *The Essentials of Risk Management* (New York: McGraw-Hill, 2006).

11 For details, see, for example, "Cooling Off Rules," Better Business Bureau, July 2009, http://www.la.bbb.org/GIReport.aspx?DocumentID=72 (accessed January 29, 2011).

12 The collaboration with advocacy groups brought advantages in the regulatory and political arena as well. According to the IRS, accelerated benefits and viatical settlements were taxable to terminally ill patients. This changed with the passage of the Health Insurance Portability and Accountability Act ("HIPAA") of 1996, which contained a provision that exempted terminally ill patients from paying federal taxes on the proceeds of a viatical settlement. This political success was a direct consequence of heavy lobbying by a coalition of advocacy groups, viatical settlement companies, and the insurance industry. The relevant section can be found in Section 331 at http:// www.gpo.gov/fdsys/pkg/PLAW-104publ191/pdf/PLAW-104publ191.pdf (accessed January 29, 2011).

13 See, for example, "The Viatical Process," Viatical Web, http://www.viatical-web.org/ process.htm (accessed January 29, 2011).

14 Francis Flaherty, "Death Benefits Become Living Benefits," *New York Times*, October 16, 1993.

15 Arthur M. Louis, "S.F. Investment Company Sells 'Death Notes,'" *San Francisco Chronicle*, March 4, 1995.

16 David Dunlap, "AIDS Drugs Alter an Industry's Math: Recalculating Death-Benefit Deals," *New York Times,* July 30, 1996; and Naomi Freundlich, "AIDS: Hope Where the Money Is," *BusinessWeek,* July 22, 1996.

17 "Point West Capital Corporation Announces Resolution with Noteholders of Dignity Partners Funding Corp. I," Business Wire, April 12, 2000; and "Point West Capital Corp. Announces Common Stock Delisted from the Nasdaq Stock Market," Reuters, April 11, 2001. For Point West Capital Corp's bankruptcy filing on September 24, 2004, see http://esignal.brand.edgar-online.com/fetchFilingFrameset. aspx?FilingID=3192329&Type=HTML (accessed January 30, 2011)

18 For details on the securitization of life settlements and all quotes used in this section, unless otherwise noted, see Anderson, "Wall Street Pursues Profit in Bundles of Life Insurance."

19 Liam Pleven and Rachel Emma Silverman, "Cashing In: An Insurance Man Builds a Lively Business in Death," *Wall Street Journal*, November 26, 2007; and Anita Huslin, "Wealthy Engage in Controversial Re-selling of Life Insurance Policies," *Washington Post*, November 27, 2007.

20 The growth of life insurance settlements had become a growing concern for life insurance companies, as their pricing model for term insurance is based on the assumption that policyholders will often let their life insurance lapse before they die as the need for life insurance lessens with age. But if a policy is purchased and packaged into a security, investors will keep paying the premiums. Consequently, more payouts will occur over time than are assumed by existing models.

21 James R. Hagerty and Jonathan Karp, "Countrywide Tells Workers, 'Protect Our House,'" *Wall Street Journal*, October 3, 2007.

CHAPTER 8

1 The National Commission on Terrorist Attacks upon the United States, *The 9/11 Commission Report: Final Report of the National Commission on Terrorist Attacks upon the United States* (New York: W.W. Norton, 2004), 339.

2 Ben Dobbin, "Bausch & Lomb Stock Plunges as Lens Solution Is Suspect in Fungus Outbreak," Associated Press, April 12, 2006.

3 "Warburg Pincus to Buy Bausch & Lomb," Reuters, May 16, 2007.

4 Claudia H. Deutsch, "Reaction Time of Bausch Is Questioned," *New York Times*, April 15, 2006.

5 "Concerns about Risks Confronting Boards: First Annual Board of Directors Survey," Eisner LLP, May 2010, http://www.eisnerllp.com/Nep/PressReleases.aspx?id=5045 (accessed January 29, 2011).

6 For an example and discussion, see David Besanko, David Dranove, and Mark Shanley, *Economics of Strategy* (New York: John Wiley & Sons, 1996), 558.

7 Larry Bossidy, Ram Charan, and Charles Burck, *Execution: The Discipline of Getting Things Done* (New York: Crown Business, 2002), 167.

8 "Financial and Operating Information 2005–2009," BP Global, http://www.bp.com/assets/bp_internet/globalbp/STAGING/global_assets/downloads/F/FOI_2005_2009_full_book.pdf (accessed January 29, 2011); and Anna Fifield, "Deepwater Horizon: Frills and Spills," *Financial Times*, June 12, 2010.

9 For a detailed discussion of the use of intelligence in business applications, see Leonard Fuld, *The Secret Language of Competitive Intelligence* (New York: Crown Business, 2006).

10 For a nice discussion of this difference, see Malcolm Gladwell, "Open Secrets," *The New Yorker*, January 8, 2007.

11 Donald H. Rumsfeld, "Department of Defense News Briefing," U.S. Department of Defense, February 12, 2002, http://www.defense.gov/Transcripts/Transcript.aspx?TranscriptID=2636 (accessed January 29, 2011).

12 "'Foot in Mouth' Prize for Rumsfeld," Reuters, December 1, 2003.

13 For details on Wilson's disease, see the information provided by the National Institutes of Health: "NINDS Wilson's Disease Information Page," National Institutes of Health, http://www.ninds.nih.gov/disorders/wilsons/wilsons.htm (accessed January 29, 2011).

14 The concept originates from a common expression used to describe an impossibility, the assertion that swans must be white because all the swans that had been observed were white. The irony of this example is that after hundreds of years of confirmatory evidence from observations in Europe, black swans were discovered in western Australia in the seventeenth century. The notion of a "black swan event" is closely related to the work of the philosopher of science Sir Karl Popper, himself following in the footsteps of philosopher David Hume, who had used it to illustrate the principal limits of scientific knowledge. For more details, see Nassim Taleb, *The Black Swan: The Impact of the Highly Improbable* (New York: Random House, 2007); Sir Karl Popper, *The Logic of Scientific Discovery* (London: Routledge, 2002 [first published in German as *Logik der Forschung*, Berlin: Springer, 1934]); and David Hume, *A Treatise of Human Nature*, (Mineola, N.Y.: Dover, 2003 [first published in 1739–1740]).

15 The National Commission on Terrorist Attacks upon the United States, *The 9/11 Commission Report*, 339.

16 I wish to thank my colleague Eitan Zemel for pointing out this insight to me.

17 For the critical role of innovation and imagination in counterinsurgency and intelligence and the role of organization and culture, see John A. Nagl, *Learning to Eat Soup with a Knife: Counterinsurgency Lessons from Malaya and Vietnam* (Chicago: University of Chicago Press, 2005).

18 Jim Lovell and Jeffrey Kluger, *Apollo 13* (New York: Houghton Mifflin, 2000).

19 Innovation companies such as IDEO operate in a similar fashion. See Tom Kelley and Jonathan Littman, *The Art of Innovation: Lessons in Creativity from IDEO, America's Leading Design Firm* (New York: Crown Business, 2001).

20 Deborah D. Anderson, "Key Concepts in Anticipatory Issues Management," *Corporate Environmental Strategy* 5, no. 1 (1997): 6–17.

21 For details, see Jure Leskovec, Lars Backstrom, and Jon Kleinberg, "Meme-Tracking and the Dynamics of the News Cycle," ACM SIGKDD International Conference on Knowledge Discovery and Data Mining (ACM KDD), Paris, June 28–July 1, 2009.

22 For further information, see Scott Spangler and Jeffrey Kreulen, *Mining the Talk: Unlocking the Business Value in Unstructured Information* (New York: IBM Press, 2007); and Christopher D. Manning and Hinrich Schuetze, *Foundations of Statistical Natural Language Processing* (Cambridge, Mass.: MIT Press, 1999).

23 For an overview of these approaches, see Bo Pang and Lillian Lee, "Opinion Mining and Sentiment Analysis," *Foundations and Trends in Information Retrieval* 2, no. 1–2 (2008): 1–135. For applications in reputation management, see Daniel Diermeier and Mathieu Trepanier, "Reputation Metrics" (working paper, Kellogg School of Management, 2008).

24 There is consistent evidence for this negativity bias. While the 5-to-1 ratio has been established in some contexts, the relative impact of negative to positive messages is likely to vary across issues. See Roy F. Baumeister, Ellen Bratslavsky, Catrin Finkenauer,

and Kathleen D. Vohs, "Bad Is Stronger Than Good," *Review of General Psychology* 5, no. 4 (2001): 323–370; and Paul Rozin and Edward B. Royzman, "Negativity Bias, Negativity Dominance, and Contagion," *Personality and Social Psychology Review* 5, no. 4 (2001): 296–320.

CHAPTER 9

1 Flynn McRoberts, "A Final Accounting: Civil War Splits Andersen," *Chicago Tribune*, September 2, 2002.

2 The Waste Management and Arthur Andersen examples are based on the following cases: Daniel Diermeier, "Arthur Andersen (A), (B), (C)," Kellogg School of Management Case 5-205-253 (A)(B)(C), 2006. The cases were jointly developed with Rob Crawford. For additional information, see Susan E. Squires, Cynthia J. Smith, Lorna McDougall, and William R. Yeack, *Inside Arthur Andersen: Shifting Values, Unexpected Consequences* (Upper Saddle River, N.J.: FT Press, 2003); and Barbara Ley Toffler and Jennifer Reingold, *Final Accounting: Ambition, Greed and the Fall of Arthur Andersen* (New York: Broadway Books, 2003). Unless otherwise noted, all information and quotations are drawn from these three sources.

3 *U.S. Securities and Exchange Commission v. Dean L. Buntrock, Phillip B. Rooney, James E. Koenig, Thomas C. Hau, Herbert A. Getz, and Bruce D. Tobecksen*, Civil Action No. 02C 2180, Release no. LR-17435, March 26, 2002.

4 U.S. Securities and Exchange Commission, "In the Matter of Arthur Andersen, LLP," Release No. 34-44444, June 19, 2001.

5 McRoberts, "A Final Accounting."

6 U.S. Securities and Exchange Commission, "In the Matter of Arthur Andersen, LLP."

7 *U.S. Securities and Exchange Commission v. Arthur Andersen LLP, et al.*, no. 1:01CV01348 (JR) (D.D.C.), Release No. LR-17039, June 19, 2001. In addition to paying the fine of $7 million to the SEC, Andersen faced a series of lawsuits by Waste Management stockholders; eventually, both firms settled with the plaintiffs for a total of $228 million. Waste Management was acquired by a competitor, giving its name to the new entity.

8 Mike Brewster, *Unaccountable: How the Accounting Profession Forfeited a Public Trust* (Hoboken, N.J.: John Wiley & Sons, 2003).

9 McRoberts, "A Final Accounting."

10 See Arthur Levitt and Paula Dwyer, *Take On the Street: What Wall Street and Corporate America Don't Want You to Know* (New York: Pantheon, 2002).

11 Brewster, *Unaccountable*.

12 Kurt Eichenwald, *Conspiracy of Fools: A True Story* (New York: Broadway Books, 2005).

13 U.S. Securities and Exchange Commission, "Final Rule: Revision of the Commission's Auditor Independence Requirements," 17 CFR Parts 210 and 240, RIN 3235-AH91.

14 For an influential model of corporate cultures as equilibria, see David M. Kreps, "Corporate Culture and Economic Theory," in *Perspectives on Positive Political Economy*, ed. James E. Alt and Kenneth A. Shepsle (New York: Cambridge University Press, 1990), 90–143.

15 The quote is from Jean-Jacques Rousseau, *A Discourse on a Subject Proposed by the Academy of Dijon: What Is the Origin of Inequality among Men, and Is It Authorized by Natural*

Law (1754), trans. G. D. H. Cole, *A Discourse on Inequality* (Whitefish, Mont.: Kessinger, 2004), 43. Similar ideas on social contracts have been expressed in David Hume, *A Treatise of Human Nature*. (Mineola, N.Y.: Dover, 2003 [first published 1739–1740]). For example, "Two men who pull at the oars of a boat, do it by an agreement or convention, tho' they have never given promises to each other" (page 348) and "Two neighbors may agree to drain a meadow, which they possess in common; because 'tis easy for them to know each others mind, and each may perceive that the immediate consequence of failing in his part is the abandoning of the whole project" (page 383). For a detailed discussion of these ideas, see Brian Skyrms, *The Stag Hunt and the Evolution of Social Structure* (Cambridge, U.K.: Cambridge University Press, 2003).

16 For game-theoretic models of this issue with applications to finance and macroeconomics, see Stephen Morris and Hyun Song Shin, "The Social Value of Public Information," *American Economic Review* 92 (2002): 1521–1534; Stephen Morris and Hyun Song Shin, "Global Games: Theory and Applications," in *Advances in Economics and Econometrics: Theory and Applications, Eighth World Congress, Vol. 1*, ed. Mathias Dewatripont, Lars Hansen, and Stephen Turnovsky (Cambridge, U.K.: Cambridge University Press, 2003), 56–114; Stephen Morris and Hyun Song Shin, "Coordination Risk and the Price of Debt," *European Economic Review* 48 (2004): 133–153; and Stephen Morris and Hyun Song Shin, "Heterogeneity and Uniqueness in Interaction Games," *The Economy as an Evolving Complex System III*, ed. Lawrence Blume and Steven Durlauf (New York: Oxford University Press, 2005), 207–224.

17 Philip. G. Zimbardo, "Pathology of Imprisonment," *Society* 9, no. 6 (1972).

18 Stanley Milgram, "Behavioral Study of Obedience," *Journal of Abnormal and Social Psychology* 67 (1963): 371–378.

19 In addition to reinforcing the company's culture, crises also provide learning opportunities on processes. During a crisis, the company's processes and capabilities are tested thoroughly. A postcrisis audit can assess where there are gaps. After the Moose Test crisis in 1997, Mercedes conducted an audit and concluded that its preparation strategy was underdeveloped. In particular, the company did not have a recall strategy ready. This may come as a surprise, but then we should remember that the company had never had a recall in previous years. In Mercedes's assessment, this lack of a plan led to improvised decision making with insufficient strategy depth. As a result, the company introduced scenario planning for all new model launches using the Red Team–Blue Team approach discussed in Chapter 3.

20 General information regarding Siemens's size and financial performance are gathered from "Siemens' New Boss," *BusinessWeek*, January 24, 2005.

21 For details on the Siemens case, see Siri Schubert and T. Christian Miller, "At Siemens, Bribery Was Just a Line Item," *New York Times*, December 21, 2008. See also David P. Baron, "Siemens: Anatomy of Bribery," in *Business and its Environment*, 6th ed. (Upper Saddle River, N.J.: Prentice Hall, 2009). Unless otherwise noted, all quotations are from these two sources.

22 The U.S. Foreign Corrupt Practices Act of 1977 was "enacted for the purpose of making it unlawful for certain classes of persons and entities to make payments to foreign government officials to assist in obtaining or retaining business. Specifically, the anti-

bribery provisions of the FCPA prohibit the willful use of the mails or any means of instrumentality of interstate commerce corruptly in furtherance of any offer, payment, promise to pay, or authorization of the payment of money or anything of value to any person, while knowing that all or a portion of such money or thing of value will be offered, given or promised, directly or indirectly, to a foreign official to influence the foreign official in his or her official capacity, induce the foreign official to do or omit to do an act in violation of his or her lawful duty, or to secure any improper advantage in order to assist in obtaining or retaining business for or with, or directing business to, any person." "Foreign Corrupt Practices Act," U.S. Department of Justice, http://www.justice.gov/criminal/fraud/fcpa/ (accessed January 30, 2011).

23 Mark Landler, "Hoping to Calm the Waters, Chairman of Siemens, Heinrich von Pierer, Resigns," *New York Times*, April 20, 2007.

24 Interview with Siemens CEO Peter Löscher, "The Management Culture Failed," *Spiegel Online*, December 12, 2007, http://www.spiegel.de/international/business/0,1518,522790-2,00.html (accessed January 30, 2011).

25 See Archibald Preuschat and Matthias Karpstein, "Siemens Settles with Former CEOs," *Wall Street Journal*, December 2, 2009.

26 Greg Hills, Leigh Fiske, and Adeeb Mahmud, "Anti-Corruption as Strategic CSR: A Call to Action for Corporations," FSG Social Impact Advisors, May 2009, http://www.ethics.org/files/u5/Anti-corruptionFINAL.pdf (accessed January 26, 2011).

27 Jack Welch and John Byrne, *Jack: Straight from the Gut* (New York: Warner Books, 2001), 294.

28 Additional information on the GE fraud case can be found in Frank Collins, "Through Soundproof Glass: Israel Refuses Direct Questioning," *Washington Report on Middle East Affairs*, December/January 1992/1993: 9; Louis M. Seagull, "Whistleblowing and Corruption Control: The GE Case," *Crime, Law & Social Change* 22, no. 4 (1995): 381–390; and Brian H. Rowe and Martin Ducheny, *The Power to Fly: An Engineer's Life* (Reston, Va.: American Institute of Aeronautics and Astronautics, Inc., 2005).

29 The False Claims Act allows private persons to file a *qui tam*, or whistle-blower suit, on behalf of the government. If the government is successful in resolving or litigating its claims, the whistle-blower may receive a share of the recovery. See also United States Department of Justice ,"False Claims Act Cases: Government Intervention in Qui Tam (Whistleblower) Suits," http://www.justice.gov/usao/pae/Documents/fcaprocess2.pdf (accessed January 30, 2011).

30 Welch and Byrne, *Jack*, 280.

31 Rowe and Ducheny, *The Power to Fly*, 116.

32 Welch and Byrne, *Jack*, 281.

33 After testifying before a congressional committee, GE pleaded guilty on July 22, 1992, and was fined $69 million in criminal fines and civil penalties. A company statement was released: "Today's settlement fulfills G.E.'s pledge of full investigation, full cooperation and full restitution that it made to the Government 18 months ago when it first learned of the Dotan affair." See Richard W. Stevenson, "Company News; GE Guilty Plea in US Aid to Israel," *New York Times*, July 23, 1992.

34 Welch and Byrne, *Jack*, 282.

35 Rowe and Ducheny, *The Power to Fly*, 116.

36 "The Management Culture Failed."

37 McRoberts, "A Final Accounting."

38 While Andersen had in effect ceased to exist, overturning the conviction could protect the personal assets of Andersen partners from at least certain lawsuits, and also unfreeze certain assets for distribution to former Andersen partners; it would also reopen the possibility that the shareholders of failed Andersen clients might receive some financial compensation from their insurers. Linda Greenhouse, "Justices Reject Auditor Verdict in Enron Scandal," *New York Times*, June 1, 2005.

CONCLUSION

1 In their application of game theory to corporate strategy, Adam Brandenburger and Barry Nalebuff use this quote by Lincoln to illustrate the concept of "allocentrism": the ability to view a strategic situation from someone else's point of view. See Adam M. Brandenburger and Barry J. Nalebuff, *Co-Opetition* (New York: Doubleday, 1996), 61. Their reference to the quote is James Charlton, ed., *The Executive's Quotation Book* (New York: St. Martin's Press, 1983).

2 For a classic investigation of expertise in the context of master chess players, see Herbert A. Simon and William G. Chase, "Skill in Chess," *American Scientist* 61, no. 4 (1973): 394–403. On differences in representations between experts and novices, see Michelene T. H. Chi, Paul J. Feltovich, and Robert Glaser, "Categorization and Representation of Physics Problems by Experts and Novices," *Cognitive Science* 5, no. 2 (1981): 121–152. For an overview, see K. Anders Ericsson, Neil Charness, Paul J. Feltovich, and Robert B. Hoffman, *The Cambridge Handbook of Expertise and Expert Performance* (Cambridge, U.K.: Cambridge University Press, 2006). For an informal discussion of expert judgment and related phenomena, see Malcolm Gladwell, *Blink: The Power of Thinking without Thinking* (Boston, Mass.: Back Bay Books, 2007).

3 Karen DeYoung, "7 Months Later, Elián Goes Home to Cuba," *Washington Post*, June 29, 2000.

4 Associated Press photographer Alan Diaz took the picture on April 22, 2000, and went on to win the 2001 Pulitzer Prize for Breaking News Photography. The photograph can be found at http://www.pulitzer.org/works/2001-Breaking-News-Photography (accessed January 31, 2011).

INDEX

ABOUT THE AUTHOR

Daniel Diermeier, Ph.D., is the IBM Professor of Regulation and Competitive Practice and director of the Ford Motor Company Center for Global Citizenship at the Kellogg School of Management, Northwestern University. He has served as an advisor to leading companies, including Accenture, Cargill, Johnson & Johnson, Kraft, McDonald's, and Shell. He is also a senior advisor to the FBI. In 2007, Dr. Diermeier won the Faculty Pioneer Award from the Aspen Institute, named the "Oscar of Business Schools" by the *Financial Times*. He is also the recipient of the 2011 Chookaszian Prize in Risk Management. Dr. Diermeier lives with his family in Evanston, IL.